Witches, Goddesses, and Angry Spirits

*À ma mère,
qui a toujours été
une source d'inspiration
dans ma vie*

Witches, Goddesses, and Angry Spirits

The Politics of Spiritual Liberation in
African Diaspora Women's Fiction

MAHA MAROUAN

 THE OHIO STATE UNIVERSITY PRESS / COLUMBUS

Copyright © 2013 by The Ohio State University.
All rights reserved.

Library of Congress Cataloging-in-Publication Data
Marouan, Maha, 1975–
Witches, goddesses, and angry spirits : the politics of spiritual liberation in African diaspora women's fiction / Maha Marouan.
p. cm.
Includes bibliographical references and index.
ISBN-13: 978-0-8142-1219-6 (cloth : alk. paper)
ISBN-10: 0-8142-1219-0 (cloth : alk. paper)
ISBN-13: 978-0-8142-9320-1 (cd)
1. American fiction—African American authors—History and criticism. 2. American fiction—Women authors—History and criticism. 3. African American women in literature. 4. African diaspora in literature. 5. African American women authors. 6. Danticat, Edwidge, 1969– Breath, eyes, memory. 7. Morrison, Toni. Paradise. 8. Condé, Maryse. Moi, Tituba, sorcière. I. Title.
PS374.N4M35 2013
813'.5409928708996—dc23
2012039927
Paper (ISBN: 978-0-8142-5663-3)
Cover design by Janna Thompson-Chordas
Text design by Juliet Williams
Type set in Adobe Sabon and ITC Novarese

Contents

List of Illustrations vii

Acknowledgments ix

Chapter 1 Introduction: A Theoretical and Thematic Framework 1

Chapter 2 In the Spirit of Erzulie: Vodou and the Reimagining of Haitian Womanhood in Edwidge Danticat's *Breath, Eyes, Memory* 37

Chapter 3 "Thunder, Perfect Mind": Candomblé, Gnosticism, and the Utopian Impulse in Toni Morrison's *Paradise* 71

Chapter 4 Conjuring History: The Meaning of Witchcraft in Maryse Condé's *I, Tituba, Black Witch of Salem* 103

Chapter 5 Conclusion: The Return of Witches, Goddesses, and Angry Spirits 153

Bibliography 159

Index 167

Illustrations

Figure 1. The front cover of the first French edition by Mercure de France (1986) — 132

Figure 2. The front cover of the 1988 edition published by Mercure de France in the Folio series — 135

Figure 3. The (alternative) front cover of the 1988 edition published by Mercure de France in the Folio series — 136

Figure 4. The front cover of the English-language edition by Ballantine Books (1992) — 144

Figure 5. The front cover of the English-language edition by Caraf Books (1992) — 146

Acknowledgments

WHILE the rough seed of this book started during my Ph.D. years at the University of Nottingham, this project did not take shape until few years later at the University of Alabama. I have been lucky to have had people along the way who supported and inspired me, but most of all, offered me the most precious gift a researcher could ask for, patience.

Of all those at the University of Nottingham, I would like to thank my advisors Judith Newman and Sharon Monteith, who were there at the beginning, as well as Susan Billingham and Marie Condé, who were generous with their comments and suggestions. I would also like to express my appreciation to the School of American and Canadian Studies and the International Office at The University of Nottingham, who provided me with the Ph.D. Research Scholarship that made this project possible.

My appointment at the University of Alabama put me in touch with a wonderful group of scholars. Of those, I am fully indebted to my friend and colleague Stacy Morgan. The revisions of the manuscript would not have been completed without his patience, insightfulness, and extensive feedback on the various drafts of this work. The University of Alabama Research Grant Committee, Capstone International Center, the Office for Academic Affairs Williams' Fund, and the Committee for the College Academy for Research, Scholarship and Creative Activity awarded me funding that allowed me to travel to various libraries and conferences around the country and abroad to develop this research. I also want to thank the Americanist Group at the University of Alabama for their valuable comments on my chapter examining Edwidge Danticat's *Breath, Eyes, Memory*. I was also lucky to have been offered a Visiting Scholarship at the Department of Modern Languages at Howard University in Summer 2008, which enabled me to complete important work on my second chapter. For that, I owe thanks to James Davis.

At The Ohio State University Press, I would like to thank my anonymous readers for their valuable comments and suggestions that have helped me sharpen this work, and my editor Sandy Crooms for her support and patience.

Finally, a big thanks and gratitude to my wonderful friends Erica Arthur, John Fagg, Celeste-Marie Bernier, Dave Deverick, Shilpa Venkatachalam, Ahmed Al Jarro, and Cornelius Carter, and to my wonderful family—although I don't get to see them as much as I would like to their spirit is always with me: Amina Agmir, Mohammad Marouan, Houda, Soufian and Hanae. Thank you for your love.

Introduction
A Theoretical and Thematic Framework

THIS STUDY inquires into the construction of African diaspora female spirituality as it features in representative fictions by three contemporary writers of the African Americas: *Breath, Eyes, Memory* (1994) by the Haitian American novelist Edwidge Danticat, *Paradise* (1998) by the African American Nobel laureate Toni Morrison, and *I, Tituba, Black Witch of Salem* (1992) by the Guadeloupean author Maryse Condé.[1] All three novels use African diaspora religious practices (Vodou, Candomblé, and "witchcraft") in order to create a space to refashion personal, cultural, and historical identities for women of the African diaspora. Further, these alternative religious frameworks provide the main avenues by which the novelists empower their female protagonists and celebrate African diaspora womanhood in a broad sense, all while encouraging readers to maintain a healthy skepticism toward identity essentialisms.

While these works engage with multiple geographic locations of the African Americas—Danticat (Haiti, United States), Morrison (United

---

1. *I, Tituba, Black Witch of Salem*, trans. Richard Philcox (Charlottesville: University of Virginia Press, 1992) is the English translation of Maryse Condé's novel *Moi, Tituba, sorcière . . . noire de Salem* (Paris: Gallimard, 1986). Chapter 4 will address both the French and the English texts in detail.

States, Brazil), Condé (Barbados, United States)—these authors conjure up symbolic diasporic connections beyond these geographic specificities. Danticat, Morrison, and Condé stage transnational and transcultural narratives that undermine any attempt to define their texts as national or regional literature. They evoke fictional worlds where history, fantasy, legend, folklore, and myth merge to create a multilayered vision of African diaspora identities.

This study reads Danticat's, Morrison's, and Condé's novels as narratives of revision. These authors stage radical interventions in the way they unsettle, modify, and undercut traditional historical, religious, and cultural discourses. They use oral histories, legend, and folklore to challenge traditional narratives of history and their claim to "truth" or "accuracy"; they protest the exclusion of women from a male Judeo-Christian discourse; and through a meditation on the symbol of the witch, they explore narratives of female violence and persecution. In their use of parody, irony, and allusion, these authors maintain healthy skepticism toward notions of diasporic authenticity. Their revisionist practices allow them to disturb the European literary canon and insert their own marginalized voices in its center. The structure of this study reflects the parameters within which these authors' works articulate their diasporic visions and relate to Africanist beliefs as validated in Danticat's *Breath, Eyes, Memory,* reinvented in Toni Morrison's *Paradise,* and commodified/critiqued in Maryse Condé's *I, Tituba.* This introductory chapter elaborates these and similar comparative threads of discussion in order to contextualize the selected novels of Danticat, Morrison, and Condé and in relation to the larger body of African diaspora literature. This study also attempts to establish the thematic terrain these authors share with their peers while also making a case for the qualities that make the three novels especially nuanced and significant in their conceptualization.

When Christopher the Maroon in Maryse Condé's *I, Tituba* asks Tituba if she is a witch, Tituba replies: "Everyone gives that word a different meaning. Everyone believes he can fashion a witch to his way of thinking so that she will satisfy his ambitions, dreams, and desires" (146). Tituba's words provide an insight into this study's central thread of inquiry. Like Tituba, who questions the appropriation of her spirituality, each author interrogates the way black female spirituality has been constructed in Western cultural and historical narratives. Yet, while Tituba laments the ways in which others attempt to "frame" her spirituality, she is also aware that this unfortunate rendering of her spirituality provides her with an ambiguous space from which she can fashion her own notion of witchcraft.

The texts discussed in this study operate in a similar manner. By playing on the category of religion, these authors secure for themselves a space from which they can fashion an empowering model of black female spirituality for their female protagonists, and rewrite them against historical and religious discourses that have silenced women's powers and constructed women as spiritually inferior. The symbol of the witch or the "deviant" woman recurs in all three narratives discussed in this study. The image of the witch in all her manifestations—as a Jezebel, a whore, a Marinet, a priestess, an angry spirit, a healer, and an Obeah woman—becomes a positive symbol of women's empowerment in these works, celebrating womanhood in all its aspects including its shortcomings, and thus, resisting any attempt to idealize it. The symbol of the witch allows these authors to reflect on a history of female violence and persecution and revalidate the metaphor of the witch to make it relevant to the reality of twentieth- and twenty-first-century women and their struggle against violence and oppression. Most importantly, these writers create new religious associations and new forms of creolizations in their construction of the witch as a symbol of womanhood. They blend Africanist with Western Christian symbols to create images of womanhood with a liberating potential, images that reenact the adaptive and transformative aspect of African diaspora religions, thus providing an alternative space where women can perform their spiritual roles against a male-centered Judeo-Christian discourse. Women become the main bearers of their societies' cultural legacy, as they are the ones responsible for preserving the link with the past and maintaining an African diaspora consciousness through their practices. Yet, these women are not always recognized in such roles by their respective communities. In fact, they all face persecution of various sorts, and even execution.

Thematic concerns

Breath, Eyes, Memory, Paradise, and *I, Tituba* share four central interlocking and related concerns that make these texts rich ground for comparative analysis: (1) the preservation of African diaspora consciousness, (2) the celebration of black female spirituality, (3) historical recovery and revision, (4) intertextuality, creolization, and transnational identities.

Preserving African diaspora consciousness

Danticat, Morrison, and Condé engage with African diaspora female identities through their female characters' religious practices and the effect of these practices on their respective communities. These religious beliefs include Haitian Vodou as practiced by the Caco women in *Breath, Eyes, Memory,* Afro-Brazilian Candomblé as practiced by the Convent women in *Paradise,* and Tituba's witchcraft in *I, Tituba* as derived from various religious traditions, African and European. It is not the intention of this study to collapse these belief systems in its reading of these texts, but to explore and demonstrate the way these female writers use these traditions to articulate a diasporic consciousness and vision. The works discussed here highlight the interconnectedness of diasporic cultures, while at the same time engaging with diaspora as a discourse of difference and discontinuity. I do not want to imply that these authors articulate the same diasporic experiences, as that is not the case, but that they use similar strategies of resistance.

A major aspect of African diaspora religious beliefs is the role they play in preserving a historical and cultural link with the African past. They are traditions that developed in secrecy in the New World, as they were often outlawed by the authorities. They emphasize the importance of healing, knowledge of plants, and a close relationship with all elements of nature, which are seen as endowed with levels of energy important to the maintenance and restoration of the adherents' physical and emotional balance. The worlds of humans and spirits are actively interconnected through rituals and ceremonies of possession. The spirits or the gods are, in many respects, a replica of human character. They are fallible; they have both virtues and shortcomings just like their devotees, and their actions reflect the drama of human life. African diaspora belief systems also preserve a strong link between the living and the dead, through communication with deceased ancestors who continue to be part of the reality of the living.

Danticat, Morrison, and Condé map African diaspora religions for their female protagonists as sites of liberation. The openness offered to women in African diaspora religious systems can be traced to West and Central African cultures that do not exclude women from the domain of priesthood and spiritual authority. In fact, a religion such as Afro-Brazilian Candomblé goes beyond providing the space for women as priestesses and attributes to women a spiritual status superior to men. Joseph Murphy reports that women in Candomblé "are seen as more suited for priesthood than men" because "men have 'hot blood.' They have neither the patience to submit to discipline of Candomblé, nor the control of their passions necessary to incarnate the spirits."[2] To this end, these authors do not just attempt to reclaim diaspora women's places in history, but to resituate them in this diasporic discourse as powerful models of spirituality with self-affirming agency. The female protagonists in these texts become the main carriers and transmitters of African diaspora spirituality.

However, diasporic traditions as validated, reinvented, and critiqued by these authors raise important questions about the nature and the processes of syncretism that characterize African diaspora religions. To what extent do these traditions articulate a "unique" diasporic experience? Is the cultural syncretism and blending—often celebrated in African diaspora religions as the harmonious mixing of cultures—an indication of their democratic and eclectic character? Or is this syncretism the result of forced conversions and equally forced appropriation of Christianity? Can African diaspora religions also leverage a broad social empowerment for women? Or does women's authority remain constrained within the walls of the temple?

Margarite Fernández Olmos and Lizabeth Paravisini-Gebert describe African diaspora religions of the Caribbean as "creolized belief systems" to communicate their complex processes of adaptation and transformation.[3] This study does not intend to construct African diaspora religions as coherent models of cultural hybridity, but to highlight the dynamic tension between continuity and rupture, and assimilation and resistance, that is emblematic of the nature of diasporic cultures.

Robert Voeks, who explores the violence that characterized the cultural encounter of the enslaved Africans with the Europeans, explains: "First, the actors [enslaved Africans] were unwilling participants in the migration, and second, cultural retention occurred both in spite and partly as a result of barriers to diffusion that were erected by European society."[4] Further, he argues that this syncretic process was an attempt by enslaved Africans to survive the pressure of the New World, which shows that the interaction and juxtaposition of European and African cultures was not a process of mutual exchange, but a one-sided attempt from the nonwhite underprivileged to preserve what they could of familiar religious traditions.[5]

---

2. Joseph Murphy, *Working the Spirit: Ceremonies of the African Diaspora*. Boston: Beacon Press, 1995), 53.
3. Margarite Fernández Olmos and Lizabeth Paravisini-Gebert, *Creole Religions of the Caribbean* (New York: New York University Press, 2003).
4. Robert A. Voeks, *Sacred Leaves of Candomblé: African Magic, Medicine, and Religion in Brazil* (Austin: University of Texas Press, 1997), 63.
5. Ibid.

In addition, while African diaspora religions indeed articulate a narrative of resistance to Western Christian hegemony, they can also be seen as the triumph of the Catholic Church in implementing Christian values. The Catholic Church historically showed a calculated tolerance toward "pagan" rituals in its conversion policies through a gradual acculturation into Christianity. This is quite apparent in most Africanist traditions of the new world, where adherents often also see themselves as good Christians. They attend both the Sunday Mass as well as Africanist ceremonies. In many Candomblé terrieros, for instance, "baptism into the Catholic faith is a pre-requisite of initiation into Candomblé."[6] Fernández Olmos and Paravisini-Gebert describe this syncretism as "the active transformation through renegotiation, reorganization, and redefinition of clashing belief systems."[7] They observe: "The flexibility, eclecticism, and malleability of African religions allowed practitioners to adapt to their new environments, drawing spiritual power from wherever it originated."[8]

Consequently, this study engages with African diaspora religions as sites of both continuity and rupture, resistance and assimilation. I do not subscribe to these belief systems merely as "countercultural" narratives, but as an integral part of what constitute the cultures of the Americas. I use the terms "syncretic," "hybrid," and "creole" interchangeably to communicate the cultural dynamism of African diaspora religions, which does not imply that these traditions are "nonlegitimate" or "less whole," since syncretism is a process that is a characteristic aspect of all religions.

The gender dynamics of African diaspora religions are equally contested. The authority that women have in their roles as priestesses does not necessarily apply to social realities. In *Secrets, Gossip, and Gods* Paul Christopher Johnson argues that the question of women's empowerment in Candomblé "is embedded in larger questions of local and private versus public and institutional forms of power." He concludes: "I have witnessed no sources of prestige at the public, institutional level, at least for Afro-Brazilian women, that would compensate for the local forms of social capital offered within the religious hierarchies of the terrieros."[9]

Again, while African diaspora religions may not be models of female liberation, nor examples of a fully democratic process of hybridity, Danti-

---

6. Ibid., 61.
7. Ibid, 7.
8. Fernández Olmos and Paravisini-Gebert, *Creole Religions*, 3.
9. Paul Christopher Johnson, *Secrets, Gossip, and Gods: The Transformation of Brazilian Candomblé* (Oxford: Oxford University Press, 2002), 48.

cat, Morrison, and Condé strategically construct them as such in order to inscribe black female spirituality into history and effectively address social injustices against women.

These authors also preserve a healthy skepticism of essentialist constructions of diasporic linkages and question the place of Africa in the formation of diaspora identities. When Sophie in *Breath, Eyes, Memory* meets Joseph, the African American jazz musician she ends up marrying, he tells her: "'I am not American . . . I am African-American.' 'What is the difference?' [asks Sophie.] 'The African. It means you and I, we are already part of each other'" (72). Sophie's relationship with Joseph, in this example, develops out of a diasporic awareness that goes beyond the present reality, and that is based on a shared past and legacy. Yet, while Sophie and Joseph are linked together by race and a diasporic notion of blackness, the Brazilian-born Consolata in *Paradise* is betrayed by the very people she felt this "authentic" diasporic connection with. Consolata is first struck by the strong sense of familiarity she feels when she sees the people of Ruby, as they instantly remind her of her people in Brazil: "And although they were living here in a hamlet, not in a loud city full of glittering black people, Consolata knew she knew them" (226). Paradoxically, these are the very people who end up raiding the Convent and killing her.

To address the issue of authenticity, Condé, for instance, uses parody to subvert stereotypical renderings of African diaspora identities as she challenges her own representation of Tituba, who despite all her powers cannot save herself from all the misfortunes that befall her. In an interview with Françoise Pfaff, Condé contends that her book is "a pastiche of the feminine heroic novel, a parody containing a lot of clichés about the grandmother, the sacrosanct grandmother, and about women and their relationship to the occult."[10] Condé here consciously undercuts simplistic notions of black female spirituality and challenges what Wilson Moses, in *Afrotopia,* refers to as "sentimental notions of Africanness" defined by "a predisposition to communalism, a harmony with nature, and a propensity for artistic expression and emotional experience."[11]

---

10. Françoise Pfaff, *Conversations with Maryse Condé* (Lincoln: University of Nebraska Press, 1991), 60.
11. Wilson Jeremiah Moses, *Afrotopia: The Roots of African American Popular History* (Cambridge: Cambridge University Press, 1998), 19.

Celebrating black female spirituality

The term *diaspora* is also used in this study as an analytical tool for investigating the place and the role women play in subverting set notions of identity. Their experiences are called diasporic, not just in the traditional sense of carrying a diasporic memory, but mainly in the way women—in a diasporic context—maneuver, shift, invent, and subvert existing cultural dynamics to create a space for healing themselves and their communities.

The emphasis on spiritual agency is a direct response to the reality of violence, since all female protagonists in these works are either implicitly or explicitly victims of male violence. The practice of spiritual healing and looking inward becomes necessary for the protagonists' self-recovery. In *Paradise*, when Consolata was asked if she was not afraid of living in the isolated Convent, Consolata laughed and replied: "Scary things not always outside. Most scary things inside" (39). Here, female spirituality is perceived as facing one's inner fears, with emphasis on psychological healing and inner growth.

By articulating women's experiences with violence, these authors demand a reconsideration of women's realities in their respective societies. The violence committed against women in patriarchal settings is closely connected to the reductive binary construction of women as virgins or whores. The fact that women have to live up to nonrealistic standards of womanhood as passive and desexualized beings makes them easy targets of violence when they fail to live up to these standards. The example of the Convent women in Morrison's *Paradise* is a case in point. The men of Ruby feel justified in their violence against these women because, to them, they are "bitches more like witches" (276). By critiquing patriarchal images of womanhood these authors want to restore social power to women as well as spiritual power, since the two are inextricably linked.

In their introduction to *Women and Religion in the African Diaspora*, Marie Griffith and Barbara Dianne Savage write: "Studying women in the African diaspora context enables us to return to time-honored questions about authority, leadership, and power and to conceive and perceive them in new ways."[12] This study indeed calls into question these categories. It argues that these female authors make a radical shift in the way they perceive women's authority, leadership, and power. Their fictional writ-

---

12. R. Marie Griffith and Barbara Dianne Savage, eds., *Women and Religion in the African Diaspora: Knowledge, Power, and Performance* (Baltimore: Johns Hopkins University Press, 2006), xiv.

ings respond to a male-centered Judeo-Christian discourse and challenge a colonial construction of African diaspora religions as dangerous and demonic, focusing on the liberating potential of these religious practices, but not because they are universally and inherently liberating. Rather, the empowering potential of these traditions lies in their political implications, as they provide an alternative space for African diaspora women to defy hegemonic constructs that confine them to very limited and limiting spaces of spiritual expression.

The criminalization of women's diasporic religious practices is clearly documented in the history of the new world. For instance, Rachel Harding's research on the history of Candomblé in Brazil relied mainly on police reports and trial records. She writes: "The documents indicate that authorities regularly conducted raids against black religio-cultural gatherings, often breaking or burning any ritual items they discovered and jailing participants or impressing them into military service."[13] African diaspora practices were associated with magic, harm, and spells. The knowledge of plants was seen as dangerous, because while plants are used to cure devotees, they also can be easily used to poison those in power. When Toni Morrison visited Brazil in the 1980s to learn about the religious practices of Candomblé, she heard a story (which turned out to be untrue) about a community of black nuns who were murdered by a group of men for practicing Candomblé. The story of the black nuns certainly resembles *Paradise*'s plot: that is, a female community with ambiguous religious beliefs massacred by a self-righteous Christian male community. And although the story was untrue, the violence it communicates certainly reflects the reality of Candomblé in Brazil.

In part because they provoked fear of poisoning and slave revolts, African diaspora religions were and still are deemed dangerous and barbaric, a result of a racist ideology inherent in a European discourse of enlightenment that associates blackness with evil. Condé's narrative, for instance, explores how Tituba's connection with magic in Puritan society is an expression of the way blackness has been associated with the concept of evil in the Puritans' imagination. She reports about her white mistress: "Susanna Endicott had already told me she was convinced my color was indicative of my close connections with Satan" (65). This fear of the other is also articulated by Reverend Parris, who tells Tituba and John Indian: "I know that the color of your skin is a sign of your damnation, but as long

---

13. Rachel E. Harding, *A Refuge in Thunder: Candomblé and Alternative Spaces of Blackness* (Bloomington: Indiana University Press, 2000), 64.

as you are under my roof you will behave as Christians!" (41). Here, Parris articulates the Puritans' division of the world into moral absolutes based on color symbolism. In his chapter "Freedom, Otherness, and Religion: Theologies Opaques," in *Significations: Signs, Symbols, and Images in the Interpretation of Religion* Charles Long talks about the semiotics of racism within Western religious and cultural discourses: "The nonwhite color symbolizes and its significations have been acted upon within the modern Western world as signs of defilement and uncleanliness.... Blacks, the colored races, caught up into this net of the imaginary and symbolic consciousness of the West, rendered mute through the words of military, economic, and intellectual power, assimilated as if by osmosis structures of this consciousness of oppression."[14]

Black women's spirituality is often contested based on preconceived notions about their sexuality. The history of slavery in the African Americas shows that the black female body has always been a site of contention. African diaspora religious and cultural ceremonies of drumming and dancing throughout the African Americas evoked extreme reactions from white authorities. They were seen as barbaric and lacking in decorum, reinforcing the stereotype of the morally corrupt and sexually deviant black woman. In his article "Batuque: African Drumming and Dance between Repression and Concession: Bahia, 1808–1855," João Jose Reis describes the reaction of one of the militia captains to these ceremonies: "He detected so much physical energy lost to labor, exhibited in those seminaked, dancing black bodies, adorned with golden trinkets—nakedness and dance which suggested excessive sensuality, always unsettling for the white man in an environment where African women are scarce."[15]

This vilification of the black female body has also excluded African diaspora women from a Christian discourse that confines womanhood to the reductive stereotype of the virgin/whore and virgin/witch dichotomy, expressing a deep fear of female sexuality. Condé's exploration of the witch craze of Salem in Tituba's trial refers to a long history of women's persecution that started with Christianity's rise to power. Christian law condemned sorcery and was responsible for the introduction of the concept of the demonic alliance between witches and the devil. This was fed by Christian theology, which perceived women as seducers and tempt-

---

14. Charles H. Long, *Significations: Signs, Symbols, and Images in the Interpretation of Religion* (Philadelphia: Fortress Press, 1986), 189–90.

15. João Jose Reis, "Batuque: African Drumming and Dance between Repression and Concession: Bahia, 1808–1855," in *Diasporic Africa: A Reader*, ed. Michael Gomez (New York: New York University Press, 2006), 48.

resses, supported by the dualistic opposition of spirit/body and good/evil that associated women with body and evil.[16]

These images are still embedded in today's world. The exclusion of women from the priesthood in many Christian denominations is still justified through body politics, as women's bodies are still seen as deterrents to spirituality. In the case of black women, this reality is even more intensified as it evokes historically based negative perceptions of their bodies and sexuality. Wallace Best, who explores the relationship between the Black Church and the black female body, argues that defending their sexual respectability remains a central aspect of black women's activities in the church today. He writes: "The stigma of sexual immorality that was attached to black women because of white men's long history of claiming access to their bodies intensified the objections, even antagonism, that black women who dared to operate in a public manner encountered."[17] Best argues: "Even when women are free from coercion and live within a predominantly black community, they navigate a terrain that remains shaped by black people's collective efforts to define themselves under circumstances in which the body is a highly charged site of freedom and identity."[18]

The authors discussed in this study understand the restriction put on black womanhood in a Judeo-Christian discourse and challenge it by strategically constructing African diaspora religions as mechanisms of female transformation. All three authors evoke female spiritual figures that are far removed from patriarchal and traditional Judeo-Christian standards of women's propriety and purity. They conjure up various representations of the witch as: archetypal goddess, Jezebel, angry spirit, and female warrior in order to challenge the image of the desexualized and passive woman in the Christian Mariology. To further destabilize this unrealistic image of womanhood, these authors highlight women's sexuality as inextricably connected to their spirituality. Morrison evokes ancient African goddesses, such as the Egyptian goddess Isis, who represents an ambiguous model of spirituality: "I am the honored one and the scorned one. I am the whore and the holy one. I am the wife and the virgin."[19] This is the

16. Jeffrey B. Russell, *A History of Witchcraft: Sorcerers, Heretics, and Pagans* (London: Thames and Hudson, 1980), 28.

17. Wallace Best, "The Spirit of the Holy Ghost Is a Male Spirit: African American Preaching Women and the Paradox of Gender," in Griffith and Savage, *Women and Religion in the African Diaspora*, 108.

18. Ibid., 103.

19. *"The Thunder: Perfect Mind,"* trans. Anne McGuire, in *Diotima: Material for the Study of Women and Gender in the Ancient World* (CG VI.2: 13,121,32), http://www.stoa.org/diotima/anthology/thunder.shtml.

voice—attributed to Isis—from "The Thunder: Perfect Mind," the Gnostic poem that Morrison chooses parts of as the epigraph for her novel.

Danticat, Morrison, and Condé seek alternative narratives of female spirituality for their protagonists. Sophie in *Breath, Eyes, Memory*, who suffers from what her therapist terms a "Madonna complex" in relation to the way she perceives her mother, eventually liberates herself from a passive and desexualized image of womanhood, and chooses to see her mother as the aggressive Erzulie/Jezebel who in the text emerges as an empowering image of female sexuality. To celebrate this new image of her mother, Sophie dresses her in bright red for her burial: "I picked out the most crimson of all my mother's clothes, a bright red, two-piece suit that she was too afraid to wear to Pentecostal services" (227). The dismayed priest tells her when he sees her mother dressed in red: "Saint Peter won't allow your mother into Heaven in that," to which Sophie replies: "She is going to Guinea" (228). Vodou here provides a necessary space for Sophie's empowerment: she is able to celebrate her mother only when she lets go of the idealized image of the Virgin Mary.

Sophie's conversation with the priest also highlights the theological aspect of this historical tension between Christianity and African diaspora religions in the New World. The criminalization of Africanist religions stems from the belief that Christianity holds the ultimate truth. The history of Vodou in Haiti, Candomblé in Brazil, and Obeah in other parts of the Caribbean reveals an attempt to suppress these religious traditions, not simply for the political reasons mentioned earlier (fear of poisoning and of slave rebellions), but also because these beliefs were and still are seen as "pagan." The Catholic Church, indeed, played a major role in suppressing African diaspora beliefs in many parts of the New World. Again, whether the process of religious syncretism was forced or spontaneous, African diaspora religions in the texts discussed provide strategic models of openness that are historically lacking in traditional Judeo-Christian tradition.

In *Paradise*, Morrison reenacts the dynamics between Christianity and African traditional religions in the relationship between Ruby and the Convent. The men of Ruby, uncomfortable with the Convent women's ambiguous model of spirituality, accuse them of perversion and satanic practices. They are "obviously not nuns, real or even pretend, but members, it was thought, of some other cult. Nobody knew" (11). The men thus feel justified in their violent retribution against a perceived threat emanating from female sexuality and alternative religious practices, both of which have been dangerously intertwined in their imagination. The massacre of the Convent women is clearly reminiscent of the witch hunts of early European and American history, where women were executed under the pretext of sexual deviancy and practices of dark magic. After the shooting, however, the bodies of the Convent women mysteriously disappear in the surrealist manner of a witch tale, only to reappear in another realm, as strong and triumphant spirits.

Yet, what is most impressive about the texts of Danticat, Morrison, and Condé is that they create new models of female spirituality. They do not simply highlight the limitations imposed on women's spiritual authority by Western hegemony; they go a step further, creating new cultural associations and new forms of religious creolization, generating new possibilities for African diaspora women's spirituality. In *Breath, Eyes, Memory,* Danticat replaces the binary image of Erzulie/Mary with Erzulie/Jezebel, turning the figure of Jezebel into an empowering symbol of women's sexuality. Through the emerging image of Erzulie/Jezebel Sophie fashions a new identity for her mother, liberating her from a passive and desexualized image of womanhood.

For her part, Morrison evokes religious traditions such as Candomblé and Gnosticism and constructs them as belief systems that have granted more significant roles for women than mainstream Judeo-Christian traditions. Through Gnosticism and Candomblé Morrison creates a female community that exemplifies the power of the feminine principle in its spirituality, tolerance, and regeneration. Morrison ends her novel with her vision of paradise where Consolata is sitting on Isis's lap, blurring them into one another and reincorporating them against the image of a supreme male God in mainstream Judeo-Christianity.

Condé skillfully blurs the boundaries between European and Africanist models of witchcraft. While the reader expects Tituba to exhibit an African-derived form of witchcraft, Condé cunningly uses books on European witchcraft from the seventeenth century to construct Tituba's practices. Condé reveals in an interview: "I don't have any knowledge of witchcraft. . . . The recipes that I give in the novel are merely recipes that I found in seventeenth-century books: how to cure people with certain plants, what kind of prayers to say in certain circumstances, and so on. I found that in books printed and published in America or in England."[20]

---

20. See Ann Armstrong Scarboro, "An Interview with Maryse Condé," afterword to *I, Tituba, Black Witch of Salem,* 206.

Through this process of borrowing, Condé challenges the association of witchcraft with blackness and creates new connotations that defy any attempt to see European and Africanist traditions of the New World in isolation from one another.

These processes of religious creolization fashioned by these authors, while reflecting the symbiosis between Africanist and Christian symbols characteristic of African diaspora traditions, also allow these authors to communicate the complexities of African diaspora cultures. These authors fashion new realities for their female characters, communicating endless possibilities for African diaspora women to map their own models of spirituality. All three authors grant an afterlife to their female characters, who are all either implicitly or explicitly victims of male violence. The witch returns in these texts to avenge and instill terror in her oppressors beyond the limits of time and history, but also to watch over those who need her support. After her death, Danticat's Martine is transformed into a malevolent and defiant manifestation of Erzulie: the Marinet, the wild Vodou spirit of the night who eats her victims. Morrison's Convent women, Consolata, Mavis, Gigi, and Pallas, after being shot by the men of Ruby, return as goddess-like figures, accomplishing after death what they could not in their lives. In a similar vein, Condé's Tituba also returns victoriously after her execution, as a revolutionary spirit, inspiring her people's rebellion. What is crucial about these characters' return is the symbolic role they continue to play in the cultural memory of their communities.

The witch emerges in these revisionist narratives as a creolized construct highlighting the intersection of African cosmology with Catholic imagery. Through the symbol of the witch Danticat, Morrison, and Condé create narratives of continuity between the past and the present where the living and the dead are brought together in close proximity, articulating an African vision of the intimacy between the living and their deceased ancestors, as well as images of Christian demonology and the European Gothic where evil dead spirits return to haunt the living. As the boundaries between the real and the surreal become blurred, these authors posit their female characters in a liminal space between life and death, oppression and liberation, heroism and defeat, suggesting a model of spirituality that is imperfect and close to human reality. This ambivalence communicated through the symbol of the witch also speaks to the condition of diaspora, connoting fragmentation and rupture, but also seeking to imagine itself as whole.

Historical recovery and revision

As writers from the African Americas, these authors share a historiographic enterprise: the revision of their respective histories. Toward this end, they look beyond Western traditions and use African and African-derived beliefs, rituals, and folklore as the primary vehicle to reconstruct a diasporic historical and cultural memory. What makes them intellectually challenging is the fact that rather than fashion historical novels in the conventional sense, they instead open up the past to imaginative reinventions. In doing so, these authors use the past to reflect on contemporary concerns, and to reconnect with experiences that have been rendered invisible by Western historical narratives.

To reclaim black women's place in history, Danticat, Morrison, and Condé do not attempt to recover history, but to inscribe their female characters' subjectivity, denied to them by traditional historical discourses. Danticat uses the power of naming as a major tool to rewrite women into the history of Haiti. Caco, the name she attributes to her female characters, belongs to the famous Haitian peasant guerilla known for its resistance to Haitian corrupt regimes and foreign occupation. Sophie's grandfather, Charlemagne Caco, also brings to mind Charlemagne Peralte, one of the leaders of the Caco resistance who was brutally killed by U.S. Marines during the U.S. invasion of Haiti. Here, Danticat associates her female protagonists with the spirit of rebellion in Haiti and gives them a voice within Haiti's national heroic discourse, which typically does not acknowledge women's achievements in any substantial way.

In doing this, Danticat also conjures up the silenced memory of the 1920s U.S. occupation of Haiti that many in the United States saw as necessary interventionist policy. Even Zora Neale Hurston, who visited Haiti during the time of the U.S. occupation, portrays a violent Haiti, in much need of U.S. intervention. Hurston's description of the Caco does not differ much from that of the U.S. Marines' accounts, as she writes about the end of the occupation in *Tell My Horse:* "This was the last hour of the last day of the last year that ambitious and greedy demagogues could substitute bought Caco blades for voting power. It was the end of the revolution and the beginning of peace."[21]

Unlike Hurston, decades later, Danticat, a daughter of the Haitian

---

21. Zora Neale Hurston, *Tell My Horse: Voodoo and Life in Haiti and Jamaica* (New York: Harper and Row, 1990), 72.

peasantry, writes against the U.S. intervention, which caused major damage to the peasantry. The military's use of violence and forced labor completely destroyed the peasantry's way of life. Thus, by defeating the Caco, the U.S. military silenced the only voice of resistance that the peasantry had against corrupt and oppressive Haitian governments.[22] Being from the peasant class herself, Danticat here gives voice to a silenced episode of Haitian history, paying homage to the Caco, and boldly attributing the Caco genealogy to contemporary Haitian women, making them the primary carriers of the peasantry's spirit of resistance.

Similarly, fact and fiction merge in Morrison's construction of history, challenging official narratives of American history, and questioning the U.S. attitude toward its minorities. Morrison's engagement with the concept of utopias is inevitably an engagement with the politics of exclusion that constitute utopias as both religious and historical constructs. Morrison uses the concept of utopias to comment on American national discourse that has always been built around a utopian religious narrative that excluded others from it.

At the center of Morrison's meditation on American history are the silenced voices of women, especially within a mainstream Judeo-Christian discourse that still constructs women as spiritually inferior. The violence committed against the Convent women, who were believed to be immoral and practice non-Christian rituals, conjures a long history of persecution and violence against women. Against this narrative of female victimization, Morrison's novel rewrites women into history as powerful spiritual figures and demands that their roles as goddesses and spiritual figures be acknowledged. Consolata, for instance, emerges in the novel as an ancient goddess with supernatural qualities and the power of regeneration, or what Morrison describes as "stepping in" to resurrect the dead. In this way, Morrison ascribes to contemporary women the power of life and creation of ancient goddesses.

In the same vein, Condé's engagement with history is multifaceted. Following the format of a confessional narrative in her account of Tituba, Condé conveys the illusion of factuality to her readers. The novel is prefaced by Condé's words: "Tituba and I lived for a year in close intimacy. During our endless conversations she told me things she had confided to nobody else." Here Condé becomes Tituba's confidant and the only one who knows Tituba's "true" story, giving the reader a sense of assurance

---

22. Mary A. Renda, *Taking Haiti: Military Occupation and the Culture of U.S. Imperialism, 1915–1940* (Chapel Hill: University of North Carolina Press, 2001), 10.

about her intimate/factual knowledge of Tituba's life, and challenging the historical truth of Tituba's confession to Salem's judges. Tituba is also a forgotten historical figure, although her testimony was a key catalyst of the witch hunt of Salem—even as she was also one of its victims—Tituba has remained overlooked in the folds of history, despite the large quantity of literature produced on the witches of Salem. Perhaps, this also partly has to do with the complexity of her character.

Tituba is a complex historical figure. She was a Christianized Indian from Barbados who practiced white European magic she learned from her English mistress, and was gradually transformed in the American imagination to a black woman who practices "Voodoo." In a particularly influential (albeit wildly inaccurate) portrayal, Arthur Miller's *The Crucible* describes her as a deranged black woman who consorts with the devil and speaks jarring English. Condé directly contests imagery such as Miller's and undercuts America's racial and cultural narratives that contributed to Tituba's interesting transformation. Moreover, Condé's interrogation of seventeenth-century Puritans' discourse of othering is also an interrogation of America's contemporary racial and historical politics. Her own account of Tituba's testimony, then, is not an attempt to retrieve history in a precisely literal sense, but rather an attempt to give Tituba a voice denied to her by history.

Barbara Foley's "History, Fiction, and the Ground Between," which explores the use of documentary history in African American fiction, argues that texts that engage with history in this particular way "retell American history from an alternative perspective. Yet because they veil their references to actual persons and events and thus do not insist on exact historical correspondence, these texts secure for themselves at once the benefits of the illusion of factuality and the advantages of imaginative re-creation."[23] Foley's words express the way in which these authors are constantly blurring the boundaries between fact and fiction in order to destabilize traditional narratives of history and their claim to "truth" or "accuracy." Indeed, these female authors ambitiously highlight the systematic silencing and misrepresentation of minorities' histories in America.

African diaspora religious traditions remain central to the way these authors' female characters construct their histories for themselves and their communities. As powerful sites of memory, African diaspora religious traditions articulate in their cosmologies, ritual practices, music, and

---

23. Barbara Foley, "History, Fiction, and the Ground Between: The Uses of the Documentary Mode in Black Literature," *PMLA* 95 (1980): 399.

dance silenced histories of violence, rupture, and displacement. Through cultural discontinuities and survivals, as well as transformations and syncretism, they express a dynamic tension between forgetting and remembering. In *Cities of the Dead* Joseph Roach proposes a new way of reading traumatic histories, through an examination of performances as sites of memory, arguing that "performances carry with them the memory of forgotten substitutions," especially in relation to the genocidal histories of the African Americas.[24] Thus, Africa remains central to this articulation of African diaspora silenced histories. At her mother's funeral, Sophie tells the priest that her mother "is going to guinea." Significantly, Guinea/Genin in Vodou cosmology evokes Africa both as a physical and mythical place. This interpretation of Guinea allows the connection to Africa to take both a concrete and an imagined form: Guinea is also the place underwater where the ancestors and loa reside. The Caco women expect to go to Guinea after their death, a place where they will reunite with their ancestors. Here, Vodou becomes a vital cultural and spiritual link that connects the living to the dead, and the present with the past, as acutely articulated by Roach who argues that the politics of communicating with the dead refer not only to a history of forgetting, but also to a strategy of empowering the living.[25] The imagined Guinea highlights the historical rupture with Africa as an actual place but at the same time provides a sense of empowerment as an ancestral home and originary point to people of African descent in the Americas.

In a similar vein, Morrison's communication with the African past also assumes a mythical and symbolic form. Morrison starts her novel with an epigraph in the voice of the Egyptian goddess Isis and ends it with a vision of paradise where Consolata is resting on the beach with her head on Piedade's lap, "In ocean hush, a woman black as firewood is singing. Next to her is a younger woman whose head rests on the singing woman's lap" (318). Piedade also alludes to the Egyptian goddess Isis. This vision evokes the iconic image of the Pietà or Piety (Piedade in Portuguese), which displays Jesus in Mary's arms after his crucifixion. In Morrison's rendition, the mother and son image in the famous iconography is replaced by mother and daughter—Consolata in Piedade's arms. In short, Morrison creates an alternative iconography that has women at its center. By bringing Consolata and Isis together she is emphasizing continuity between the past and the present in a diasporic vision of black female spirituality.

---

24. Joseph Roach, *Cities of the Dead: Circum-Atlantic Performance* (New York: Columbia University Press, 1996), 6.
25. Ibid., 34–63.

Contrary to Morrison, Condé questions these ancestral linkages. Her tongue-in-cheek approach in *I, Tituba* accentuates Tituba's constant but futile communication with the dead African spirits of her ancestors, from whom she constantly seeks guidance and protection. Ironically, Tituba's ancestors hardly provide her with any advice. The symbolic voice of the ancestor, which often represents wisdom and guidance, becomes comical and ineffective in Condé's text, articulating a failure in establishing a narrative of meaning with the African past.

Intertextuality, creolization, and transnational identities

The term *creolization* is used in this study to refer to textual and linguistic strategies exhibited in these texts. While the term has often been used to describe Caribbean identities, languages, and literary aesthetic, it is used here to describe a cultural and literary phenomenon characteristic of the African Americas as a whole, and not just the Caribbean. Thus, this book employs creolization as a diasporic concept that encapsulates the process or the processes of cultural and linguistic fusion (smooth and violent) that characterize African diaspora histories. Through an analytical framework inspired by these authors' texts, this study will address the multiple intersecting axes that constitute African diaspora identities.

In "Créolité without the Creole Language?" Maryse Condé writes: "The differences between such theories as miscegenation, mistizaje, creolization, creolité are due to the ethnic and sociopolitical configurations of the colonized American world in which they were born and, consequently, to the languages in which they are articulated."[26] Through this approach this study intends to highlight a literary aesthetic shared by these three authors.

Creolization is defined by a blending of cultures. In his *Poétique de la relation,* Edward Glissant writes: "Creolization carries in itself the adventure of multilingualism along with the extraordinary explosion of cultures. But this explosion of cultures does not mean their scattering nor their mutual dilution. It is the violent manifestation of their assented, free sharing."[27] Here, Glissant refers to a linguistic and cultural phenomenon that describes the complex social, political, and economic conditions of

---

26. Maryse Condé, "Créolité without the Creole Language?" in *Caribbean Creolization: Reflections on the Cultural Dynamics of Language, Literature, and Identity,* ed. Kathleen M. Balutansky and Marie-Agnès Sourieu (Gainesville: University of Florida Press, 1998), 106.

27. Edward Glissant, *Poétique de la relation* (Paris: Gallimard, 1990), 46–47. Translated in Kathleen M. Balutansky and Marie-Agnès Sourieu, ed. *Caribbean Creolization,* 1.

people of the African Americas, but a process that was nevertheless "violent." In *The Black Atlantic,* Paul Gilroy addresses the difficulty in theorizing creolization against a discourse of cultural nationalism and ethnic purity: "From the viewpoint of ethnic absolutism, this [theorizing of creolization] would be a litany of pollution and impurity."[28] Therefore, the theory of creolization carries within itself the power to subvert cultural codes, and it is in this specific context that I use the term: namely to address the ways in which these authors who operate from the periphery of the European canon challenge—through complex textual and linguistic strategies—the cultural hegemony of the center.

Consider an example that I came across while doing research on Condé's novel, as I realized that the language used by the historical Tituba in the documents of her deposition stands in stark contrast to that used by Miller's Tituba in *The Crucible*. The historic Tituba speaks formal English, with no indication of pidgin in it—a sign of Tituba's acculturation to English culture, as she had had an English mistress before being sold to Reverend Samuel Parris. By contrast, Miller's Tituba speaks in a jarring dialect that becomes a sign of her lack of adaptability, her derangement, and her "primitive" nature. Miller strips Tituba from her voice, alienating her and forcing her estrangement through language.

In *The Post-colonial Studies Reader,* Bill Ashcroft, Gareth Griffiths, and Helen Tiffin write:

> Language is a fundamental site of struggle for post-colonial discourse because the colonial process itself begins in language. The control over language by the imperial center—whether achieved by displacing native languages, by installing itself as a "standard" against other variants which are constituted as "impurities," or by planting the language of empire in a new place—remains the most potent instrument of cultural control.[29]

Within this framework, creolization is a tool with which these novelists challenge the power dynamics of the language of the center: English in Danticat's and Morrison's case, and French in the case of Condé. Through the use of their respective vernaculars in their texts, these authors are able

---

28. Paul Gilroy, *The Black Atlantic: Modernity and Double Consciousness* (Cambridge, MA: Harvard University Press, 1993), 2.
29. Bill Ashcroft, Gareth Griffiths, and Helen Tiffin, *The Post-colonial Studies Reader* (London: Routledge, 1995), 283. **(done)**

to "do violence" and disturb colonial linguistic standards, thus staying true to their hybrid cultural systems.[30] Danticat, for example, effectively negotiates her status in her text as both an insider and an outsider to the American metropolis by injecting French and Creole into her narrative to articulate her transnational experience as a Haitian American. Morrison uses African American vernacular transcription to convey her African American roots and cultural heritage. The switch from the standard to the vernacular form conveys a separation between two social worlds, but also between two modes of writing: oral and written. In *Paradise,* history merges with storytelling to communicate the complexity of the African American historical experience. Storytelling disrupts the linearity of traditional historical narratives and their claim to "truth." In *I, Tituba,* Condé uses the strategies of glossing and untranslatable words to communicate her cultural distance from French. Significantly, what the reader encounters in Condé's account of Tituba is an English-speaking heroine whose story is mediated through Condé in French. This is further complicated by Condé's use of French Creole in the novel to reassert the Caribbeanness of Tituba, who most probably spoke Creole English (if any), not French, since she was from Barbados. Again, like Morrison's text, Condé's account challenges the articulation of a coherent historiography of African diaspora histories.

Another facet of creolization is intertextuality. All three authors reference biblical narratives and classical literary texts in order to construct new modalities for their female protagonists. Patrick O'Donnell and Robert Con Davis describe intertextuality as "boundary-crossing," which in the process "creates crises, aporiae, ideology wherever it goes—for as inherent in the nature of signs, the intertextual relation generates the deferral and rewriting of 'parent' texts."[31] The texts of Danticat, Morrison, and Condé exhibit a tension between the present and the past, and rewrite/modify the "parent" text in order to disrupt existing authorities and formulate new meanings in their respective texts. They use a variety of biblical literature from the Old Testament to the Gnostic Gospels to Apocryphal texts. Danticat often evokes Vodou symbols and Haitian folk stories to revise Haiti's religious and cultural traditions. The story of the bleeding woman, who goes to the Vodou loa Erzulie for assistance,

---

30. I borrowed the expression "to do violence" from Maryse Condé, who uses it in reference to Jacques Roumain, in Balutansky and Souriau, *Caribbean Creolizations,* 103.

31. Patrick O'Donnell and Robert Con Davis, eds., *Intertextuality and Contemporary American Fiction* (Baltimore: Johns Hopkins University Press, 1989), xiv.

is uncannily similar to the story of the bleeding woman in the book of Mark in the Bible. Both women bleed for twelve years, both visit doctors to no avail, and both seek the help of a divine power who heals them. Here, Danticat transforms the biblical story and associates the power of healing with a female Vodou loa, generating a narrative reflective of the historical and cultural symbiosis between Christianity and Vodou, and celebratory of healing as part of a religious tradition that is both female and Africanist.

Morrison engages with the Exodus narrative to explore the tension between the categories of the oppressed and the oppressor and to challenge official narratives of history. The journey of the people of Ruby is described as a religious exodus. Morrison's examination of the Exodus narrative is highly political, since it has been historically appropriated both by black Americans and by white settlers. For white settlers America was Canaan, while for the enslaved the image was reversed: America was Egypt, the land where they have been enslaved and dehumanized. The way each group appropriated the story of Exodus reflects the way each group viewed itself and located itself within history. However, while the Exodus narrative lives in American consciousness as a narrative of resistance to oppression, *Paradise* explores a façade of the Exodus narrative that is seldom talked about, which is how Exodus also represents a narrative of oppression, since the Israelites end up adopting the same attitude as their Egyptian oppressors toward "the indigenous" when they cross to Canaan. Through the lens of Native Americans (who are the indigenous in this scenario) the founding fathers were not the oppressed ones, but the oppressor. The people of Ruby show exactly that. They reenact the same violence against the Convent women. They become the oppressor.

Condé remains most irreverent in her revisionist strategies. Her deployment of intertextuality reflects a comic sensibility. One cannot read Tituba "seriously"—at least not entirely. She is both a heroine and a mock-heroine. She moves from being the ultimate black heroine with celebrated wisdom and supernatural powers to a parody of herself and a vulgar manifestation of the occult woman. Tituba's random encounter in jail with Hester, the heroine of Nathaniel Hawthorne's *The Scarlet Letter,* is another example of Condé's use of intertextuality to communicate the inconsistencies of Tituba's story, and ultimately suggests the impossibility of full historical recovery of diasporic experiences. Even more, Tituba's and Hester's encounter becomes a parody of twentieth-century cross-racial friendships, with Hester as a middle-class white liberal woman, and Tituba as a poor black woman. As will be explained in more detail in a subsequent chapter, Hester's clichéd and radical feminist views are a meditation on the historical tension between white and black feminists in the United States.

In their revisionist strategies, these authors also make a radical intervention in the way we read black women's fiction. They make a break with traditional black female fictional narratives and create narrators and protagonists with unreliable voices who exhibit stereotypical notions of the ethnic other, playing on readers' expectations, and challenging them into delving below the surface of their texts. In fact, these authors' narrators and protagonists weave their own stories and fabricate their own truths. Danticat generates a new meaning for the word Caco, a scarlet bird: "Our family name, Caco, it is the name of a scarlet bird. A bird so crimson, it makes the reddest hibiscus or the brightest flame trees seem white" (150). Marie-Jose N'Zengou-Tayo, who researches the origins of "Caco," tells us that she never found any associations of the word Caco with birds.[32]

In a similar fashion, Condé's Tituba is constantly challenging her readers by exhibiting the very preconceptions she is expected to resemble. This is exemplified by her utilization of pseudo-scientific names to refer to her plants, such as "passionflorinde," "Populara indica," and "Prune taureau," which is meant to delude the reader about her "serious" and "credible" knowledge of plants and the art of healing.

Morrison's *Paradise* is a masterpiece in the way it challenges readers not to take her characters for granted. In fact, Morrison constructs multiple voices and realities. When the bodies of the assaulted Convent women mysteriously disappear, Morrison brings together a multiplicity of voices, reporting different and contradictory versions of the women's disappearance: "The story was being retold; . . . people were changing it to make themselves look good . . . enhancing, recasting, inventing misinformation (297). Again this unreliability of narrators communicates these authors' sophisticated use of literary techniques and strategies to resist reductive readings and interpretations of black women's fiction.

These various narrative strategies allow these authors to insert their voices into the colonial discourse and disturb its dynamics. Cultures of the African Americas are still often seen as "naïve," "polluted," or "illegitimate." Whenever a new literary voice emerges in the African Americas, critics are quick to situate him or her within the European literary canon, as if these authors can only be legitimate if they are seen in relation to

---

32. Marie-Jose N'Zengou-Tayo, "Rewriting Folklore: Traditional Beliefs and Popular Culture in Edwidge Danticat's Breath, Eyes, Memory, and Krik? Krak!" *MaComère* 3 (2000): 123–40, 125.

European literary foremothers and forefathers. While the novel form is indeed a European form, these authors offer a new aesthetics that emerges from complex and distinctive contexts of meanings. The creolization in these texts, textual and linguistic, then, is an evolving process that challenges the articulation of coherent historiographies; it expresses a quest for wholeness against fragmented social and political realities. It is also "the explosion of cultures" that celebrates the literary imagination beyond national, cultural, or linguistic boundaries. In fact, given the transnational scope of the action and identity issues explored by Danticat, Morrison, and Condé, it can be argued that the texts themselves demand such an approach. These authors highlight the interconnectedness of African diaspora cultures and challenge the separatism of essentialist historical and cultural discourses. One of the important contributions of this study is to illustrate the shared thematic concerns and narration strategies to be found when one adopts a transnational comparative framework, as too often, in both scholarly conference panels and publications, the studies of African American and Afro-Caribbean authors, on the one hand, and Francophone and Anglophone Caribbean authors, on the other hand, remain bound off from one another.

Diaspora consciousness and literary expression

While this study is concerned with late twentieth-century diasporic literary narratives, the search for cultural and religious diasporic connections in literature of the African Americas is certainly not new. Edwidge Danticat's *Breath, Eyes, Memory,* Toni Morrison's *Paradise,* and Maryse Condé's *I, Tituba* join a rich heritage of works by female authors that reaches at least as far back as Pauline Hopkins's *Of One Blood,* and forward to contemporaries such as Ishmael Reed,[33] Paule Marshall, Gloria Naylor, and Jewell Parker Rhodes, who look to Africa and other parts of the African Americas for inspiration.

What is impressive about the writers at the heart of this study is that unlike many of their contemporaries who offer readers a relatively smooth bridge between African and African diaspora identities by way of their heroic central characters' engagement with African diaspora religious

---

33. This section focuses on fictional works by women writers of the African Americas, with the exception of Ishmael Reed, whose influential novel, *Mumbo Jumbo,* shares similar intellectual and thematic concerns with the authors discussed in this book, especially Morrison, that are worth exploring here.

modalities/rituals, Danticat, Morrison, and Condé craft considerably more complicated (sometimes even vexed) relationships with "Africa" and the historical past in their portrayals of African diaspora religions in novels that center on women who struggle for a sense of psychic wholeness with only partial success. They explore African diaspora religions not simply as sites of recovery for a pure, organic sense of heritage, but rather as indicative of the larger processes of recovery and loss, continuity and transformation, that have characterized the formation of African diaspora identities historically and in the present moment. One other important element that distinguishes these authors' works is their insistent concern with women's spirituality, as they speak to historical silences that owe to confluences of race and gender-based oppression. Danticat, Morrison, and Condé also engage much more grippingly with the historical traumas of African diaspora history than does their more unabashedly satirical and playful peer Reed, for instance. This introductory chapter will elaborate these and similar comparative threads of discussion in order to contextualize the selected novels of Danticat, Morrison, and Condé and consider them in relation to this larger body of African diaspora literature. This work also attempts to establish the thematic terrain these authors share with their peers while also making a case for the qualities that make *Breathe, Eyes, Memory, Paradise,* and *I, Tituba* especially nuanced and significant in their conceptualization.

Pauline Hopkins's *Of One Blood* (1903) is one of the earliest texts of the twentieth century by a female author that initiates the discussion of African diaspora female consciousness. Hopkins constructs Africa as a necessary catalyst for African American psychological and spiritual transformation. The novel combines an American with an African setting, telling the story of a mixed-race character, Reuel Briggs, who goes on an archeological trip to Ethiopia. His trip becomes a vehicle for a cultural and racial awakening. Hopkins's African American male protagonist is even crowned king of ancient Ethiopian civilization. While Hopkins challenges discourses about Africa's backwardness and lack of history, her approach remains affected by the "civilizing mission in Africa" at the turn of the century.[34]

Nevertheless, Pauline Hopkins remains ahead of her time as she considers the necessity of deconstructing a stereotypical view of Africa. Perhaps most significantly, Hopkins goes as far as reconstructing Ethiopian

---

34. Although Hopkins boldly suggests that the origins of Western civilization are African, she also sees Western civilization as essential to the restoration of Africa's former glory. Briggs is there ultimately to reign over Africans, and teach them about Christianity.

civilization as female-centered and matriarchal. The protagonist's sense of spirituality is linked to his mother's, a descendant in a long line of Ethiopian kings: "He remembered his mother well. From her he had inherited his mysticism and his occult powers. The nature of the mystic within him was, then, but a dreamlike devotion to the spirit that had swayed his ancestors; it was the shadow of Ethiopia's power."[35] Hopkins's novel prompts the discussion about the significance of Africa in the construction of African American consciousness, as she also pushes the notion about Africa as the axis of black female spirituality. It would be decades before other African diaspora women writers would take on in a sustained way the themes that Hopkins initiated.

Song of Solomon, another of Morrison's seminal works, offers an interesting comparison with *Of One Blood.* In a similar vein, Morrison creates a dialogue with the African heritage and ancestry and makes this connection necessary for the construction of an African American spiritual consciousness. In Morrison's typical fashion, her novel merges Judeo-Christian, Greco-Roman, and Gullah traditions. Specifically, *Song of Solomon* connects with the ancestral Gullah myth of the flying Africans, expressing a continuity between African and African American traditions. Like Hopkins, Morrison's novel focuses on the African American male consciousness and the necessity for African American males to spiritually connect with their heritage; yet, it is the female characters who are the carriers of the wisdom of the ancestors. Like Reuel's mother, Morrison's women are spiritually grounded and in touch with their heritage. The impressive Pilate Dead, who was born without a navel, is an example of the female folk figure who has magical powers and wisdom and understands the importance of keeping a link with the past and her ancestors.

Ishmael Reed's influential and provocative novel *Mumbo Jumbo,* set in the 1920s, stimulates the discussion around African diaspora consciousness in a different way. The novel is a criticism of the Harlem Renaissance and its failure to keep its promise of a distinctive form of African American aesthetics. Reed writes outside a Eurocentric discourse and conjures Africanist beliefs and myths to create a tradition that can stand against the Judeo-Christian tradition. Like Danticat, Morrison, and Condé, Reed conjures African diaspora religions and uses Vodou and Egyptian mythology against a Judeo-Christian discourse, that he sees, as conspiring to destroy black cultural aesthetics. The novel's title is ironic. Reed redefines "mumbo jumbo" and commemorates it as rich alternative of cultural, reli-

---

35. Pauline Hopkins, *The Magazine Novels of Pauline Hopkins* (Oxford: Oxford University Press, 1988), 558.

gious, and musical forms outside the parameters of Western civilization. Reed's engagement with Africanist traditions is strategic. His commitment to Vodou tradition and aesthetics is reflected in his form of writing. In an interview he comments: "I call [black writing] *Vodoun* or 'VooDoo,' because this is what *Vodoun* does, it mixes many traditions. It may have an African base, but it's adaptable, eclectic. It's able to blend with Christianity, with Native American forms, and with many others. I try to do the same in my art."[36]

Like the works of the three authors at the heart of this study, Reed's imaginative construction of African American identity is interwoven with Africanist spiritual modalities, customs, and folklore. Like Danticat, Morrison, and Condé, Reed works to free the reader from the cultural and intellectual domination of Judeo-Christianity, and like their novels, Reed's *Mumbo Jumbo* is highly sophisticated in the way it constructs these different cultural traditions to present an imaginatively rich cultural mosaic. Reed's blending of Egyptian Gnosticism and Candomblé, for instance, is reminiscent of Morrison's conflation of the same traditions. Reed identifies Bessie Smith and Josephine Baker, two jazz icons, with Erzulie, who is described as the descendant of Isis; in Morrison's *Paradise,* Isis and Yemanja (the Candomblé orixa of the sea) are associated with the Virgin Mary. Yet, unlike Reed's satirical rendering of history, these authors realistically engage with issues of female suffering and construct religiosity as a necessary site for healing.

Danticat, Morrison, and Condé are also in dialogue with other contemporary authors who engage specifically with black female spirituality, such as Paule Marshall in *Praisesong for the Widow* (1983), Gloria Naylor in *Mama Day* (1988), and Jewell Parker Rhodes in *Voodoo Dreams* (1993). Yet, the novels of this project remain distinct in the extent to which they question and critique Africanist traditions. What makes *Breath, Eyes, Memory, Paradise* and *I, Tituba* intellectually challenging is the way they operate against a simplistic discourse of Africanism. Condé comments in an interview: "To love Africa is not easy. You have to understand it thoroughly, and nobody takes the trouble to do that. People just celebrate it without really knowing exactly what it is and what it means."[37] Condé refers to a trend of writing that romanticizes Africa and its cultures. For Condé, Africa is more than just a symbol and an imagined home. Condé

---

36. Bruce Dick and Amritjit Singh, Conversations with Ishmael Reed, Literary Conversations Series (Jackson: University Press of Mississippi, 1995), 136.
37. Barbara Lewis, "No Silence: An Interview with Maryse Condé," *Callalo* 18.3 (1995): 543–50, 548

lived in Africa for several years, and unlike many authors of the diaspora, Condé *writes* about Africa. Indeed, her works *Segou I and II,* which depict the turbulences of a precolonial era of the kingdom of Segou, present-day Mali, represent a significant contribution to African diaspora literature, where Condé indirectly connects the struggle of Africans to the fate of the people of the diaspora.

While *Praisesong for the Widow* shares similar concerns with the works of Danticat, Morrison, and Condé, Marshall's vision remains fundamentally different, as the novel's protagonist, Avey Johnson, starts a journey that turns out to be a Middle Passage in reverse, taking her on a psychological and spiritual quest that connects her to her African roots and ancestry. The novel sets the tension between Western and Africanist traditions. Avey's process of transformation is realized when she reconnects with the ancestral myth of her people. Gloria Naylor's *Mama Day* also evokes black female spirituality as embodied in the character of Mama Day, whose conjure powers are deeply embedded in ancestral wisdom. George, her niece's fiancé, a man who does not acknowledge a worldview outside the parameters of an urban Western tradition, is put to test by Mama Day; she makes him undergo a ritual that involves going to the chicken nest—a symbol of the female power throughout the novel—which George fears. While this ritual could be his rite of passage into accepting Mama Day's spiritual powers, George, who refuses to follow the instructions, ends up dying in the process, thus failing to acknowledge an Africanist spiritual and magical tradition.

Like Marshall and Naylor, Jewell Parker Rhodes also emphasizes the importance of Africanist traditions and the connection to the ancestors. Her novel *Voodoo Dreams,* set in antebellum Louisiana, tells the life of the Voodoo queen Marie Laveau. Conjure in the novel becomes validated against Christianity, providing meaning, assistance, and support in the lives of female characters, while Catholicism is seen as an oppressive tool that the ruling classes use against oppressed blacks.

Like Marshall, Naylor, and Parker Rhodes, the authors at the center of this study participate in a discourse of female empowerment through connection to Africanist cultural traditions, but unlike characters in the works of the former, the characters in *Breath, Eyes, Memory, Paradise,* and *I, Tituba* are not driven by a fully realized quest to find meaning in the African past and heritage. The novels of Danticat, Morrison, and Condé are unusual in the sense that they subject these traditions to a critical lens, expressing a sophisticated concern with the socially constructed nature of historical consciousness and of religious traditions themselves.

Theoretical perspectives

This study uses a multiplicity of critical voices from biblical criticism, feminist theology, literary theory, cultural studies, history, anthropology, sociology, and translation studies. This array of voices is certainly needed to make sense of women's diasporic experiences. In fact, the texts discussed in this study demand such an approach. These are creolized texts, rich and vibrant in their vision, and therefore require a "creolized" approach that considers multiple disciplinary modalities to both encompass and map out a terrain for a conceptual exploration of African diaspora women's spirituality.

The novels of Danticat, Morrison, and Condé are more than just literary texts; they are sites of political contestation. This subversive aspect, which characterizes much of postcolonial and African diaspora literature, is best expressed by Gayle Jones, who describes the process as "decolonization." In her essay "Re-Imagining the African-American Novel: An Essay on Third World Aesthetics" she writes: "A novel is colonized, for example, when patterns of stories and patterns of ideas in stories and how stories are made from one storytelling tradition are imposed upon another storytelling tradition." She explains: "Novels are patterns of ideas that take place in time and space and that deal with perspective. In liberating themselves, colonized people also liberate their stories."[38] This study aims to conceptualize the various ways in which these authors "liberate their stories."

The authors in this study clearly stage a subversion of existing cultural codes, yet their works are not merely countercultural, as they do not subscribe to the binary of European versus African. These authors engage with the cultures of the African Americas as creole cultures. As Edward Glissant explains in *Poétique de la relation*, "If we assume that métissage is generally the result of an encounter and a synthesis between two different components, it seems to us that creolization is métissage without limits, the elements of which are manifold, its outcomes unpredictable."[39] Paul Gilroy also echoes Glissant in *The Black Atlantic*, as he sees the creolization theory as necessary to challenge the idea of cultural nationalism and ethnic purity. Gilroy goes even further, by essentially placing the African diaspora at the heart of modernity, arguing that "the black Atlantic"

---

38. Gayle Jones, "Re-Imagining the African-American Novel: An Essay on Third World Aesthetics," *Callalloo* 17.2 (1994): 511.

39. Glissant, *Poétique de la relation*, 46–47. Translated in Kathleen M. Balutansky and Marie-Agnès Sourieu, ed. *Caribbean Creolization*, 1.

is an integral part of what constitutes the cultures of the modern world. Both Glissant and Gilroy provide a solid ground for this study's conceptualization of the African diaspora and its "unpredictable outcomes" as articulated by Danticat, Morrison, and Condé.

The question of survivals, continuities, and transformation still preoccupies the field of African diaspora religions. This work is not so much concerned with continuities with the past as it is concerned with diaspora as a condition and a process. In their *Creole Religions of the Caribbean: An Introduction from Vodou and Santeria to Obeah and Espiritismo*, Margarite Fernández Olmos and Lizabeth Paravisini-Gebert describe African diaspora religions as "fundamentally complex, pluralistic, and integrationist."[40] Joan Dayan's *Haiti, History, and the Gods* and Rachel Harding's *A Refuge in Thunder: Candomblé and Alternative Spaces of Blackness* further explore this tension at the heart of diaspora by examining the violence and persecution that characterizes African diaspora religions. Dayan's impressive scholarship argues that the terror and violence of colonial Haiti deeply shapes Vodou cosmology and folktales, as Vodou monsters, ghosts, and evil spirits articulate the transformative character of Haitian Vodou and its internalization of the language of Christian demonology.

Harding equally raises similar questions about the violence embedded in diasporic histories and the struggle of people of African descent between assimilation to the Christian "norm" and resistance to it. Significantly, Harding uses police records to make sense of the history of nineteenth-century Candomblé, which was outlawed in Bahia. By demonstrating the complex colonial power relations negotiated through religious ritual, Dayan and Harding help illuminate this study's engagement with African diaspora religions, as they both radically undercut a superficial and romanticized vision of African diaspora religions as harmonious models of hybridity.

This project is also part of the ongoing discussion about the implications of looking—and not looking—toward Africa as the original homeland. Wilson Moses's *Afrotopia: The Roots of African American Popular History* is important for understanding the way the authors at the heart of this study conceive of diasporic linkages. As they resist an essentializing of diasporic experiences, Danticat, Morrison, and Condé articulate diaspora through their shared strategies of resistance to European cultural hegemony, echoing Moses in his argument that while Afrocentric movements

---

40. Fernández Olmos and Paravisini-Gebert, *Creole Religions*, 4.

rely on pseudo-history and mythology in the construction of the African past, they are a necessary reaction to Europe's intellectual discourse of universalism that seals Europe, and constructs it as impermeable to African influences. Moses uses the expression "vindicationist tradition," which he defines as "the project of defending black people from the charge that they have made little or no contribution to the history of human progress," contending that "teachers at all levels should attempt to exploit the more elevating and universalistic messages of the vindicationist tradition, and—even more important—its hostility to racism."[41]

In this regard, this study's approach has also been influenced by scholars of African history and religions such as E. Bolaji Idowu and V. Y. Mudimbe, who question the simplification and the exoticization of Africa's history and traditional beliefs. Significantly, Mudimbe looks at the way the colonizing structure in Africa generated a dichotomizing process that has reshaped African beliefs and created very simplistic oppositions between "traditional" and "modern," "pagan" and "Christian." Mudimbe examines the way Christian discourse worked to suppress African traditional religions by promoting Christianity as the only form of "Truth." He writes that "Eurocentric discourses speak about neither Africa nor Africans, but rather justify the process of inventing and conquering a continent and naming its 'primitiveness.'"[42] For his part, Idowu believes that the colonial indoctrination has been effective in suppressing African traditional beliefs, observing that "the cultures of Africa are not simple but complex, so are the systems of belief. In the past this complexity has led scholars to take refuge in insulting terms like 'amorphous,' 'savage,' 'barbarous' to describe what they really did not understand."[43] Idowu's and Mudimbe's scholarship provides a solid platform from which the novels treated here may be understood to construct and engage with African beliefs.

This study belongs to a trend of writing that engages with female spirituality as it intersects with gender, race, and sexuality. To this end, it joins the work of Charles Long in *Significations* who highlights the epistemological dilemma of those who are racially positioned outside the Christian West and develops the concept of "theologies opaques" as deconstructive theologies, or "theologies that undertake the deconstruction of theology

---

41. Moses, *Afrotopia*, 21, 43.
42. V. Y. Mudimbe, *The Invention of Africa: Gnosis, Philosophy, and the Order of Knowledge* (Bloomington: Indiana University Press, 1988), 20.
43. E. Bolaji Idowu, *African Traditional Religion: A Definition* (London: SCM Press, 1973), 78.

as a powerful mode of discourse."[44] In "The Spirit of the Holy Ghost Is a Male Spirit: African American Preaching Women and the Paradox of Gender," Wallace Best joins Long in acknowledging the discourse of racial superiority embedded in the history of the Christian West, but focuses more specifically on the interaction of race with gendered body politics. Wallace draws attention to the interaction between black female spirituality and sexuality, contending that "although black male ministers are sexual and desexualized, the black female preacher evokes the body and sex in a way the black male preacher does not. Her body is objectified, her sexuality is at issue, and the nature of her desire is held suspect."[45]

Marie Griffith and Barbara Dianne Savage explain in *Women and Religion in the African Diaspora* that their approach to studying women's religious experiences in the diaspora "is not wholly celebratory, as if women's engagement with religion were always and everywhere liberating, nor is it entirely critical, as if religion tended uniformly to reinforce women's oppression."[46] Their words echo my project's resistance to romanticizing black female spirituality. However, as this study follows in the footsteps of Griffith and Savage and refuses to construct African diaspora women's spirituality as prophetic or liberating, it is more concerned with the strategies the authors in this body of work use to unsettle traditional discourses of female spirituality.

Accordingly, this study is also influenced by Joan Dayan's "Caribbean Cannibals and Whores" and Jeffrey B. Russell's *A History of Witchcraft*. Dayan's essay examines the extreme idealization and de-idealization of womanhood in Caribbean literature in the images of virgins and whores or cannibals, and the way this mythologizing of Caribbean women has conveniently contributed to the obscuring of women's lived experiences. For his part, Russell explains that this familiar dichotomy of the virgin and the whore has its roots in Christian theology that associates women with the body and carnality, and men with spirit and divinity. He writes that "as the power of the Virgin Mother grew, so did the power of the hag . . . the European witch, then, must be understood not just as a sorceress, but as the incarnation of the hag. She is a totally evil and depraved person under the domination and command of Satan."[47] Thus, the symbol of the witch as a hag, a cannibal, a temptress but also as a healer and prophetess remains central to this work's meditation on the politics of

---

44. Long, *Significations*, 195.
45. Best, "The Spirit of the Holy Ghost," 111.
46. Griffith and Savage, *Women and Religion*, xi.
47. Russell, *A History of Witchcraft*, 118.

female empowerment, as the liberatory potential of the witch simply lies in her capacity to resist idealization.

To this end, I also draw on Naomi R. Goldenberg's *Changing of the Gods,* Mary Daly's *Beyond God the Father,* and Elaine Pagels's *Gnostic Gospels.* While, like Russell's, these works have been useful in the way they challenge Judaism and Christianity as discourses that have historically suppressed the complexity of the feminine principle of the Goddess Cult, they also open up the discussion about contemporary appropriation (as well as misappropriation) of ancient history in the ways articulated in Helene P. Foley's "A Question of Origins: Goddess Cult Greek and Modern" and Michael Allen Williams, *Rethinking "Gnosticism": An Argument for Dismantling a Dubious Category.*

The authors in this work merge fantasy, myth, folklore, and legends in their novels to unsettle traditional narratives of history. In this regard, Hayden White's *The Content of the Form* and Joseph Roach's *Cities of the Dead* provide a solid platform for the exploration of the different ways Danticat, Morrison and Condé challenge linear narratives of history. White questions the objectivity of historical narratives and undercuts the rigid distinction between historical discourse as truth, and literature as a fictional narrative, while Roach proposes a new way of reading silenced histories—through an examination of performances as sites of memory, arguing that "performances carry with them the memory of forgotten substitutions," especially in relation to the genocidal histories of Africa and the Americas.[48]

While the discipline of literary studies often defines literature in national terms, this study is transnational in its scope. In its comparative framework, it is concerned with examining narrative genres beyond nation-state. It is informed by diasporic experiences of crossings, displacement, and resettlement that make up "the black Atlantic." In addition to moving beyond national boundaries, this book also crosses linguistic boundaries as it connects the Anglophone, the Francophone, and the creole worlds of the African Americas, exploring the way in which the authors in this study disrupt the dominant literary canon and use language as a powerful tool to signify difference. Their texts are a constant act of cultural translation. I draw on *The Empire Writes Back: Theory and Practice in Post-colonial Literatures* by Bill Ashcroft, Gareth Griffiths, and Helen Tiffin, to explore the various strategies postcolonial authors use to disrupt the language of the center, and Glissant's *Poétique de la relation,*

---

48. Roach, *Cities of the Dead,* 6.

which sees the process of creolization, linguistic and cultural, as carrying within itself the potential to subvert cultural and linguistic hegemony.

There has been a growing body of work in the last fifteen years in the area of African diaspora religions. Authors such as Dayan in *Haiti, History, and the Gods* (1998) and Harding in *A Refuge in Thunder* (2000) follow a historical approach to African diaspora religions, while Voeks in *Sacred Leaves of Candomblé* (1997), Murphy in *Working the Spirit* (1995), and Yvonne Daniel in *Dancing Wisdom: Embodied Knowledge in Haitian Vodou, Cuban Yoruba, and Bahian Candomblé* (2005) pursue an anthropological approach. These are significant studies that I draw on in my analysis. Yet, this study's approach belongs to a very limited body of work in its attempt to follow a literary and cultural analysis, since the prevalent trend in studying African diaspora religions has been until recently almost always strictly historical or anthropological.

Therese Higgins's *Religiosity, Cosmology, and Folklore: The African Influence in the Novels of Toni Morrison* (2002), La Vinia Delois Jennings's *Toni Morrison and the Idea of Africa* (2009), and Judylyn Ryan's *Spirituality as Ideology in Black Women's Film and Literature* (2005) are three examples from the relatively new area of African diaspora religions in literature. Both Higgins and Jennings focus on religiosity in Toni Morrison's work, while Ryan explores spirituality in black women writers and filmmakers such as Toni Morrison, Ntozake Shange, Maya Angelou, Julie Dash, and Euzhan Palcy. Even here, my approach offers a different mode of analysis. Unlike Higgins, who makes an argument for an organic continuity with a relatively homogenized African heritage in Morrison's work, this study argues that the novels examined are more accurately understood as acts of self-conscious reclamation of specific religious systems that are used strategically to reflect on issues of identity.

In a similar vein, this book joins the important work of La Vinia Jennings in recognizing the importance of Africa and African religious symbols in Toni Morrison's fiction. However, it extends existing scholarship by examining how Morrison interweaves elements of both Candomblé and Gnosticism to comment on the possibilities and constraints on women's spirituality and agency. Equally important, Higgins's and Jennings's studies of religiosity are focused on single authors, whereas I look at different authors in a comparative fashion. As for Ryan's work, my approach remains fundamentally different from hers in the sense that it deals with spirituality strictly as a historical, political, and cultural construct, while Ryan reflects on the importance of spirituality as epistemology and as a "life force."

The authors in this book share a unique vision that allows them to look at the lives of African diaspora women with naked honesty and insight. Danticat, Morrison, and Condé go beyond a simplistic recovery of African diaspora women's histories, striking a delicate balance between the necessity to create a narrative of female empowerment without falling into essentialist ideologies. While these works burst with powerful female figures—witches, goddesses, healers, priestesses, spirits—they also remain honest in reminding us of the silences surrounding African diaspora women's realities, addressing their experiences with social violence, often a result of a gendered religious discourse that constructs women as "of the flesh" and therefore spiritually inferior. The following chapters provide a detailed analysis of each of these novels in order to respect the integrity of each novel's engagement with specific religious traditions, framework, and historical period. Chapter 2, "In the Spirit of Erzulie: Vodou and the Re-imagining of Haitian Womanhood in Edwidge Danticat's *Breath, Eyes, Memory*," articulates the struggle of Haitian women in a patriarchal society where ideas of womanhood become very rigidly defined. Danticat evokes the many manifestations of the Vodou loa Erzulie, in order to protest the violence committed against Haitian women. The novel ends with a spiritual vision that defies patriarchal notions of female propriety as the red-eyed Vodou loa Erzulie symbolically emerges in the body of the deceased Martine. The victimized and passive Martine is symbolically transformed into a powerful and enraged Jezebel-like spirit. Danticat's narrative is embedded in a Haitian worldview shaped by Vodou signs and cosmology and their liberating potential for women. What is distinctive about *Breath, Eyes, Memory* is the way its characters evolve between geographic borders, cultures, and languages, articulating a uniquely diasporic and transnational vision.

As its title implies, chapter 3, "'Thunder, Perfect Mind': Candomblé, Gnosticism and the Utopian Impulse in Toni Morrison's *Paradise*," explores the prospect of utopian communities. The novel centers on the struggle between two communities: the black patriarchal and strictly Christian community of Ruby and the neighboring female community that inhabits a former convent, whose religious beliefs are subtly, but identifiably connected to Candomblé and Gnosticism. The women's community is accused of practicing magic and witchcraft, which threatens the town's moral values and begins to exemplify wickedness for the community of Ruby. Ostensibly to keep the town's strict Christian morals intact, the men of Ruby ride out to the convent and massacre its residents. My intention is to consider how the three religious discourses—Christianity,

Candomblé, and Gnosticism—interact in the novel. Both Candomblé and Gnosticism develop in Morrison's text as alternative spaces for the exploration of female spirituality, allowing for a sense of identity that stands in opposition to the exclusionary politics of Ruby's Christianity. Morrison also merges elements of Gnosticism with Candomblé. The novel's epigraph refers to the mysterious Gnostic poem "Thunder, Perfect Mind," which evokes the Egyptian goddess Isis, who, in her ambivalence, also alludes to the Candomblé priestess Consolata.

Chapter 4, "Conjuring History: The Meaning of Witchcraft in Maryse Condé's *I, Tituba, Black Witch of Salem*," examines Condé's fictional account of the slave Tituba, who was accused and tried for witchcraft during the famous Salem witch trials of 1692. Tituba's confession of witchcraft launched one of the worst witch cases in early American history. However, her story remains marginalized within the large volume of literature produced on the witches of Salem. Set in Barbados and the Massachusetts colony, Condé's novel is an attempt to rewrite Tituba's story and restore it to public memory. The narrative develops around the meaning of witchcraft and its association with black and white identities. By self-consciously playing on the stereotype of the black witch as sexually open, in harmony with nature, and in touch with the spiritual world, Condé is mockingly exhibiting simplistic preconceptions of the ethnic woman. Condé portrays a black heroine who in fact practices a white model of sorcery extracted from Western seventeenth-century books published in America and England. In this way, the novel subtly plays on reader expectations and provides an ambiguous model of spirituality that allows for a continuous interrogation of black female subjectivity.

By way of conclusion, this project offers a meditation on "the return of the witch" and the way these authors opt for an afterlife for their female subjects in order to challenge a silenced history beyond the grave. The female characters of Danticat, Morrison, and Condé return to reclaim their respective histories. Thus, as it engages with diaspora women's spirituality, my book ultimately aims at addressing and redressing the historical, cultural, and social inequities that stifle women's silenced histories and search for wholeness. While African diaspora women's experiences articulate the violence, displacement, and fragmentation at the heart of diaspora, the liberating potential of their creolized practices clearly communicates their quest for wholeness.

2

In the Spirit of Erzulie

Vodou and the Reimagining of Haitian Womanhood in Edwidge Danticat's *Breath, Eyes, Memory*

> The story was that there was once a woman who walked around with blood constantly spurting out of her unbroken skin. This went on for twelve years. The woman went to many doctors and specialists, but no one could heal her. The blood kept gushing and spurting in bubbles out of her unbroken skin, sometimes from her arms, sometimes from her legs, sometimes from her face and chest. It became a common occurrence, soaking her clothes a bright red on very special occasions—weddings and funerals. Finally, the woman got tired and said she was going to see Erzulie to ask her what to do. After her consultation with Erzulie, it became apparent to the bleeding woman what she would have to do. If she wanted to stop bleeding, she would have to give up her right to be a human being. . . . What form of life do you want to take?" asked Erzulie. "Do you want to be a green lush plant in the garden? Do you want to be a gentle animal in the sea? A ferocious beast of the night?" The woman thought of all the animals she had seen, the ones that people feared and others that they loved. She thought of the ones that were small. Ones that were held captive and ones that were free. "Make me a butterfly," she told Erzulie "make me a butterfly." A butterfly you shall be," said Erzulie. The woman was transformed and never bled again.
>
> —Edwidge Danticat, *Breath, Eyes, Memory*

THIS STORY sets the tone for this chapter, which examines the representation of womanhood in Edwidge Danticat's *Breath, Eyes, Memory* (1994).[1]

---

1. Subsequent references to Edwidge Danticat, *Breath, Eyes, Memory (New York: Soho Press, 1994)* will appear parenthetically in the text.

The novel is about the coming of age of a young Haitian immigrant, Sophie Caco, who leaves Haiti to join her mother in the United States. The novel moves between two settings, New York and Haiti. Through Sophie and her female generational line (her mother, her aunt, and her grandmother) the novel articulates the struggle of Haitian and Haitian American women with rigid patriarchal values, and forms of sexual abuse that have been internalized by the women themselves. The Caco women all share the experience of having been "tested," a practice that involved daily checks on their intact hymens. They also "do the testing," thus also perpetuating the practice themselves.

The story above of the bleeding woman is about female transformation. It articulates women's struggle for liberation and the high price they have to pay to achieve it. The woman in the story had to give up her human form and become a butterfly in order to stop her suffering. The bleeding of women, especially in religious literature, is often a symbol of female sexuality closely tied to puberty and menstruation. Similarly, bleeding also marks the Caco women's struggle with their womanhood and sexuality and expresses their desire for transformation. Sophie uses a pestle to rape herself in order to stop the practice of testing, covering her bed sheets in blood. She sees her act of self-violence as a symbol of her transformation from a passive victim of testing to someone in control of her sexuality. Bleeding also marks the terrible death of Martine, Sophie's mother. Martine stabs herself and bleeds to death when she realizes she is pregnant. Tragically, like the bleeding woman in the story, Martine also has to give up her human form to achieve liberation. Sophie reports at her burial: "She is going to be a star. She is going to be a butterfly or a lark on a tree. She is going to be free" (228). Religiosity and female religious figures become empowering forces in these characters' struggle for liberation, playing a key role in the process of reconstructing female identity. Specifically, the many manifestations of the Vodou loa of love, Erzulie, become measures against which Haitian womanhood is being contested, interrogated, but also celebrated in the novel. The goddess Erzulie, who can represent an impossible ideal of womanhood, also offers the possibility of liberation for the Caco women.

Danticat dedicates her story to "the brave women of Haiti, grandmothers, mothers, aunts, sisters, cousins, daughters, and friends on this shore and other shores. We have stumbled but we will not fall," reclaiming Haitian history through Haitian women's stories. She uses Haitian cultural symbols that have historically been associated with a male heroic discourse, to create a space for women's empowerment. Caco, the female characters' family name, for instance, is embedded in Haitian history of struggle and resistance. The word refers to nineteenth-century peasant soldiers who fought against corrupt Haitian governments. Through the name Caco, Danticat is reclaiming women's contribution and involvement in the Caco resistance movement, opening the past to reinterpretation, and telling Haitian history from a specifically female perspective.

The novel tells the story of the four female generations of the Caco family. The grandmother Ife, the daughters, Atie and Martine, the granddaughter Sophie and the great granddaughter Brigitte. At the center of the novel is Martine's story. Back in Haiti, Martine was raped by a member of the Tonton macoutes, a rural militia group installed by the Duvalier regime and notorious for its violence and systematic rape of women. This resulted in Martine getting pregnant and giving birth to Sophie. Haunted by the violent memory of her rape, Martine escapes to the United States and works to provide for her family in Haiti. Yet, Martine never gets rid of the ghosts of her past and has nightmares frequently. After getting pregnant a second time by her Haitian lover in New York, unable to bear the pregnancy that reminds her of her past trauma, Martine stages her own death in the bathroom by stabbing her stomach seventeen times with a rusty knife.

Martine's story speaks of the tragedies of Haitian women where rape has been systematically used by successive governments to exercise control over the female body. The reader is constantly reminded of the presence of the Macoutes through the various scenes of violence Sophie describes from the very start of the novel. When young Sophie is leaving for New York, she sees a riot on the way to the airport where people are being killed, and when she returns many years later she sees the Macoutes abusing and killing innocent peasants. In folk stories, the Macoutes are bogeymen who instill terror in children. They retain a mythical dimension in the Haitian consciousness, which conveys the extent to which they inspire fear and terror in people. In the light of this state of violence imposed on women, and the systematic rape by the Macoutes, chastity, virginity, and female sexual purity assume a special importance. When Sophie protests against the testing to her grandmother, the latter replies: "From the time a girl begins to menstruate to the time you turn her over to her husband, the mother is responsible for her purity. If I give a spoiled daughter to her husband, he can shame my family, speak evil of me, even bring her back to me" (157). These patriarchal standards perpetuated by the women themselves make it even more difficult for women to break from this cycle of oppression imposed by strict societal rules.

In the novel, historical trauma, like genetic data, is passed down from one female generation to the next. Each generation carries the burdens and the pains of the previous one. Sophie talks about what it means to be diagnosed with "chagrin" or sadness, which is more than just an emotion, but a physical illness. She reports: "to my grandmother, chagrin was a genuine physical disease. Like a hurt leg or a broken arm" (24). All the Caco women carry their historical chagrin passed on from one generation to the next. When Sophie asks her mother about testing, her mother replies, "I did it because my mother done it to me. I have no greater excuse" (170). However, the story of the Caco women is not a story of victimhood. As Danticat establishes in her dedication: "We have stumbled but we will not fall." Ultimately, the painful experiences of these women are empowering examples of survival.

This chapter explores the way Danticat evokes the many manifestations of Erzulie to examine the personal, social, economic and cultural realities of Haitian womanhood. Haitian Vodou symbols, figures, and stories as revisited by Danticat to articulate the complex experiences of Haitians and Haitian immigrants in the United States especially as they relate to a Haitian collective memory of the U.S. invasion of Haiti in early twentieth century, as well as a resulting discourse of exoticization of Haitian immigrants in the United States. I argue that while Danticat experiments with ideas of the Haitian Indigenist movement, a black consciousness literary movement of the 1920s, her vision articulates a transnational reality as her characters continue to navigate between various geographic settings, cultures, and languages.

THE PRIMARY mechanism by which Danticat enables her characters to survive and move beyond their traumatic experiences is by evoking images of the Vodou loa Erzulie, the Haitian loa of love who in her many reincarnations articulates the cultural, racial, and social realities of women in Haiti. She is known as "the tragic mistress," "the black Venus," and "goddess of love," but the three main manifestations of Erzulie are: the pale Erzulie; Freda, the lady of luxury and love who is the ideal for men and a symbol of purity served by the Haitian elite and young virgins. Erzulie Danto, a black Madonna always depicted holding a child, who is a symbol for overworked single mothers; and Erzulie Jewouj, the red-eyed loa of fury and vengeance who belongs to the militant Petro family of loa.[2] In *History, Haiti, and the Gods* Joan Dayan argues that Erzulie is the

---

2. Joan Dayan, "Erzulie: A Women's History of Haiti," *Research in African Literatures* 25.2

most contradictory of the Vodou loa: "A mystery of love, assistance, and beauty, she appears at night to her devotees in the form of a pale virgin. As spirit of vengeance, she is fiercely jealous and sometimes punishes wayward devotees with death, impotence or frigidity."[3]

Erzulie, clearly a loa who resists idealization, allows women in the novel to express and celebrate their womanhood beyond the rigid constraints of a social discourse that confines them into symbols of purity and perfection. According to Karen McCarthy Brown, Erzulie becomes "the mirror that gives objective reality to what would otherwise remain, as it does in so many cultures, women's silent pain and unhonored power."[4] Haitian Vodou here represents an alternative space where black womanhood can be examined challenging a patriarchal discourse that has suppressed the complexity of Haitian womanhood. Brown observes:

> The adaptability of Vodou over time, and its responsiveness to other cultures and religions, the fact that it has no canon, creed, or pope; the multiplicity of its spirits, and the intimate detail in which those spirits reflect the lives of the faithful—all these characteristics make women's lives visible within Vodou in ways they are not in other religious traditions.[5]

The spirit of Erzulie follows Danticat's female characters throughout the narrative, challenging, provoking, inspiring, and protecting them. In Haitian Vodou, the loa Erzulie is also identified as the Virgin Mary. The many Catholic lithographs of the Virgin Mary become representations of Erzulie: the pale Erzulie Freda becomes the *Mater Dolorosa* who is depicted as a white-skinned young girl wearing pearl and gold jewelry, and her heart pierced with a golden sword, and the dark-skinned Erzulie Danto becomes *Mater salvatores* depicted as a black virgin holding a child, two scars on her right cheek, and a halo around her head.[6] Sophie refers to this syncretism as doubling. She writes, "Erzulie, our goddess of love who doubled for us as the Virgin Mother" (113). However, "unlike the Mary of Mainstream Catholicism, who offers an impossible ideal of perfectly

---

(1994): 5–31, 6. See also Dayan, *Haiti, History, and the Gods* (Berkeley: University of California Press, 1998), 59.

3. Dayan, *Haiti, History, and the Gods*, 59.
4. Karen McCarthy Brown, *Mama Lola: A Vodou Priestess in Brooklyn* (Berkeley: University of California Press, 1991), 221.
5. Ibid.
6. For details, see Dayan, *Haiti, History, and the Gods*, 59; and Leslie G. Desmangles, *The Faces of the Gods: Vodou and Roman Catholicism in Haiti* (Chapel Hill: University of North Carolina Press, 1992), 138–41.

submissive (and virginal) motherhood for emulation, the Ezili are much closer to the human drama. In addition to providing examples of love, care, and hard work, they model anger—righteous and raging—power and effectivity, sensuality, sexuality, fear, frustration, need and loneliness."[7]

In *Breath, Eyes, Memory*, Danticat revises Vodou symbols and creates a new symbiosis between Erzulie Jewouj (red eyes) and Jezebel. Thus, the fierce Erzulie Jewouj who doubles as Jezebel at the end of the narrative, provides an alternative space for womanhood against the virginal and passive standards imposed by Erzulie/Mary binary. When Sophie rebels against the practice of testing by deflowering herself, she is rebelling against a passive, domesticated and asexual ideal of womanhood. Breaking from the practice of testing was "like breaking manacles" (130), reports Sophie. However, what seems like a physical act of liberation does not free her from her emotional trauma and still does not allow her to take control of her sexuality. Sophie's quest for a sense of wholeness remains a central concern in Danticat's novel, articulating Haitian women's struggle against historical trauma and strict societal roles. Her psychological journey can be traced through the way she relates, interrogates, resists, interprets, and identifies with Erzulie in her extreme manifestations of both purity and sensuality, love and fury. Her struggles with these seemingly contradictory manifestations of Erzulie attests to her psychological struggle with the different facets of her womanhood. In Sophie's imagination Erzulie Freda is the ideal mother she would have liked to have, as she reports:

> As a child, the mother I had imagined for myself was like Erzulie, the lavish Virgin mother. She was the healer of all women and the desire of all men. She had gorgeous dresses in satin, silk, and lace, necklaces, pendants, earrings, bracelets, anklets, and lots and lots of French perfume. She never had to work for anything because the rainbow and the stars did her work for her. Even though she was far away, she was always with me. I could always count on her. (59)

The image of the lavish, rich, and glorious Erzulie, who did not need to work, stands in sharp contrast with Martine, who lives in a grim area of Brooklyn and works two jobs to support herself and Sophie. Martine cannot possibly live up to this unrealistic image of womanhood. Sophie also imagines her mother to be always present with her, a wish Martine cannot fulfill. Because of their economic situation, many Haitian women have to

---

7. Brown, *Mama Lola*, 221.

leave their children behind and immigrate to the United States to make a better life for them. Sophie's fantasy painfully highlights the reality of most Haitian female immigrants who come from poor backgrounds and, forced by their economic situations, have to endure separation from their children. Atie tells Sophie: "In this country there are many good reasons for mothers to abandon their children" (20). What is even more ironic is that Martine, a victim of rape, struggles with this ideal of motherhood in more than one way. When she gets pregnant the second time, the memory of her rapist comes haunting her. Martine imagines the fetus torturing her, and tragically stabs herself to death to end her mental torture. She tells Sophie: "Yes, I am sure it [fetus] spoke to me. It has a man's voice, so now I know it's not a girl. I am going to get it out of me, I am going to get it out of me, as the stars are my witness" (217). Martine's violent act de-idealizes motherhood and poignantly sheds light on women's emotional and mental trauma that results from sexual violence and that is seldom spoken about.

Erzulie Freda, this lavish pale-skinned loa, also represents white and upper middle-class standards of beauty that most Haitian women cannot live up to. In the novel we see how Martine tries to change the shade of her skin when she buys "facial cream that promised to make her skin lighter" (51). For poor Haitian women, Freda represents an unattainable image of womanhood. Martine, who is aware of her peasant background, is trying to do her best to hide it and live up to the image of a sophisticated Freda. Even her answering machine message, for instance reflects "Impeccable French and English, both painfully mastered, so that her voice would never betray the fact that she grew up without a father, that her mother was merely a peasant, that she was from the hills" (223).

Most working-class Haitians cannot afford to serve this difficult loa who demands perfume, silk, and expensive jewelry. Expectedly, most of Freda's followers are the Haitian elite. Karen McCarthy Brown explains: "The women of the elite are the contemporary incarnations of the mulatto mistress of the slave era, the famed Creole beauties who lent erotic charm to the outsider's image of colonial Haiti. Ezili Freda rides the current of this particular ideology of female beauty and worth."[8] Alourdes, the working class Haitian priestess who lives in Brooklyn, and the subject of Brown's study, explains to Brown that it is hard for working-class women to serve Freda: "'When you have Freda you always got to be clean—twenty-four hours a day! Perfume . . . Jewelry . . . fancy!'"[9] Alourdes tells

---

8. Brown, *Mama Lola*, 248.
9. Ibid., 249.

Brown that "when she called Freda, the spirit refused to stay because Alourdes had not yet taken a bath that day."[10] This description of Erzulie is a commentary on the class system and the economic realities of Haitian and Haitian American women. Curiously, neither Sophie nor Martine seek the protection of Erzulie Danto, the black goddess and the fierce mother who provides solace and care for her devotees, despite the fact that she is closer to their reality. Danto's followers are mainly single working-class black women who identify with her industrious nature and her struggles as a single mother.

When Sophie subsequently visits Haiti, her grandmother gives her the statue of Erzulie Freda she had on her dresser, telling her "my heart weeps like a river for the pain we caused you," referring to the testing Sophie had to endure. Sophie recounts: "I held the statue against my chest as I cried all night" (157). This is a cathartic moment for Sophie who finally faces her sexual inadequacy caused by the practice of testing. To exorcise her pain, Sophie takes that same statue of Erzulie to use in her session in therapy with her sexual phobia group which consists of an Ethiopian, a Chicana, and their therapist, a Santeria priestess. The statue of Erzulie Freda that soars over these sexually abused women in their therapy session ironically highlights their reality that could not be furthest removed from the ideals of sexual purity and virginity expressed through Erzulie Freda. Sophie reports, "I pondered what it [the statue of Erzulie] meant in terms of my family" (202). Here, Sophie struggles to exorcise the image of womanhood associated with Freda as oppressive and damaging to women. The session is reminiscent of both Vodou and Santeria ceremonies, with all members of the group wearing white scarves and dresses. The association of Vodou and Santeria with therapy is an important one that introduces African diaspora religions as traditions of healing, and challenges the idea in popular culture that associates these belief systems with harm and black magic.

Sophie keeps struggling against the passive images of womanhood as represented by Erzulie Freda until the close of the narrative. Her perception of her sexuality is also strongly tied to her mother's rape. As a result, she finds herself unable to have a healthy sexual relationship with Joseph. She contends:

> After Joseph and I got married, all through the first year I had suicidal thoughts. Some nights I woke up in a cold sweat wondering if my

---

10. Ibid.

mother's anxiety was somehow hereditary or if it was something I had "caught" from living with her. Her nightmares had somehow become my own. (193)

During her therapy session, her therapist tells her that she has a "Madonna complex" and asks her to think of her mother as a sexual being and imagine her in the sexual act. Sophie reports: "I tried to imagine my mother, wincing and clenching her teeth as the large shadow of a man mounted her. She didn't like it. She even looked like she was crying" (210). Sophie continues to see her mother as a victim of sexual abuse, and only frees herself from this image after her mother's death which becomes a catalyst to her change. At the funeral, Sophie dresses her mother in bright red for her burial:

> I picked out the most crimson of all my mother's clothes, a bright red, two-piece suit that she was too afraid to wear to Pentecostal services. It was too loud a color for a burial. I knew it. She would look like a Jezebel, hot-blooded Erzulie who feared no men, but rather made them her slaves, raped them, and killed them. She was the only woman with that power. (227)

Sophie lets go of her Madonna complex and celebrates a different facet of her mother in the image of the hot-blooded Erzulie and Jezebel as a symbol of female strength and sensuality. This image replaces the image of passive sexuality that characterizes Mary/Freda. Dayan reports that Erzulie Freda and Erzulie Jewouj are the two extreme representations of this goddess:

> It is as if the two extremes of love and restraint, enacted for the community by the generosity, tears, and surrender of Ezilie Freda, lead to a more savage transformation: the flowers, perfume, and basil of Ezilie Freda turn into (or merge to form) the blood, flesh, and dirt of Ezilie-Jewouj.[11]

Martine also evokes Marinet Bwa-chech, another fierce female spirit of the night. Dayan comments that "for some Haitians, the beautiful coquette is linked to the terrifying Marinet-bwa-chehe, who evolves as another aspect of Ezilie. Ezilie, the gracious mulatto . . . turns into the cunning and can-

---

11. Dayan, *Haiti, History, and the Gods,* 106.

nibal woman of the night, Marinet, the spirit of the bush."[12] Thus, Martine, the male's victim, is transformed into a fierce spirit of the night who turns men into her victims. Even the letters that constitute Martine's name suggest that duality of Martine/Marinet. Both Marinet and Jewouj are also truer to the Caco women's working class roots as they clearly defy middle and upper class ideals of women's decorum and respectability.[13]

Through Erzulie, Danticat is rewriting a historical narrative inspired by allegories and images of Vodou to allow for the transformation of her female protagonists' consciousness. Danticat evokes Erzulie and makes her necessary for the transformation of Sophie, in the same way Erzulie is necessary for the transformation of the bleeding woman in the story quoted at the outset of this chapter. Danticat reasserts women's liberation via Jezebel and Erzulie Jewouj, manifestations that are furthest removed from patriarchal standards of women's propriety and purity. In doing this, Danticat does not attempt to reinforce the dualism of the virgin and the whore, but instead, change a long masculinist discourse that constructed an unrealistic image of womanhood in these reductive dichotomies. Danticat celebrates women beyond their simplistic representation in dominant narratives as objects to be either desired or feared. She redefines black female heroism by conjuring up female protagonists who in their complexity and ambivalence challenge these social constructions and refuse to be victimized by them.

BREATH, EYES, MEMORY is a celebration of the culture of Haitian peasantry in its use of cultural and religious symbols derived from Vodou, a religion that forms an important part in the lives of Haitian rural masses. However, Danticat's engagement with Haitian culture goes beyond simply celebrating its symbols. Danticat's novel is a revisionist project that fashions a new reality for Haitian women. Danticat uses various textual strategies to modify, unsettle, and disturb dominant narratives of Haitian history. Her use of the technique of naming, for instance, conveys her complex process of reimagining of Haitian historical and cultural narratives. The Caco women are connected in a long chain, each bearing the legacy of their past—both in its agony and in its heroism—in their names: Ife, Atie, Martine, Sophie, and Brigitte. Sophie refers to her daughter as

---

12. Ibid.
13. For more on how Erzulie in her various manifestations reflects the politics of class in Haiti, see Joan Dayan, "Caribbean Cannibals and Whores," *Raritan* 9.2 (1989): 63–67.

"part of this circle of women from whose gravestones our names had been chosen" (233).

Atie, an unusual female name, is a literary invention reminiscent of the Vodou loa Ati-Bon Legba, the most important loa in Haitian Vodou. He is the opener of the gates and the one who controls communication between the human and the spirit world. Legba's symbol is the cross; he is known as the loa of the crossroads who facilitates communication between the human and the spirit world, but also among human generations. When Sophie first returns to Haiti for a visit, Atie waits for her in the crossroads, Legba's domain: "Tante Atie was standing at the crossroads" (100). Without Legba, no communication between the two worlds is possible. Legba is "the interlocutor, the interpreter, the principle of crossing and communication with the divine world."[14] Legba, thus, is the one who owns the power of language and communication. Like Legba, Atie owns the gift of language and communication, "I always felt, I did, that I knew words in my head. I did not know them on paper. Now once every so often, I put some nice words down. Louise, she calls them poems" (103).

Like Legba, who hides an amazing strength under his frail appearance of an old man leaning on a cane, Atie, despite her seemingly vulnerable character is the one who has the potential as a writer to carry the legacy of the Caco women and of Haitian women in general. Her writings allow her to subvert a patriarchal narrative of female victimization, as the poem she writes about her best friend and lover Louise demonstrates: "She speaks in silent voices, my love. I drink her blood with milk, and when the pleasure peaks, my love leaves" (135). Atie's poem which refers to the bond between herself and Louise correlates with the folk story in the novel about the man who ends up killing his virgin bride in their wedding night because she does not bleed. Both the poem and the folk story evoke the drinking of blood with milk, a ritual traditionally meant to confirm and celebrate the chastity of men's untouched brides. The man in the story "bought a can of thick goat milk in which he planned to sprinkle a drop of her [his bride] hymen blood to drink" (154). The story finishes tragically. The bride does not bleed on her wedding night. Desperate for her hymen blood, the man cuts her between the legs, after which she bleeds uncontrollably and dies. In contrast to this story, the drinking of blood and milk, in Atie's poem, becomes a metaphor for love and intimacy. Danticat here breaks the narrative of female victimhood and rewrites the ritual as a symbol of intimacy. She also opens up a space outside the constraints

---

14. Desmangles, *The Faces of the Gods*, 99.

of heterosexuality where the ritual is reimagined as an expression of love between two women.

Through her ability to write, Atie has the potential of becoming the voice of thousands of Haitian peasant women whose stories have not been told. Atie's poem most of all attests to her taking control of her own body and sexuality, when she realizes the demands Haitian society puts on her:

> [E]ach finger had a purpose. It was the way she had been taught to prepare herself to become a woman. Mothering. Boiling. Loving. Baking. Nursing. Frying. Healing. Washing. Ironing. Scrubbing. It was not her fault. Her ten fingers have been named for her even before she was born. Sometimes, she even wished she had six fingers on each hand so she can have two left for herself. (151)

Atie regains control over who she is by breaking the silence and deciding to write about her experiences. Sophie tells her disproving grandmother, "I think it is very good that she [Atie] has learned to read. . . . It's her own freedom" (119).

Danticat here emphasizes language as a potentially liberating force for Haitian women, while at the same time articulating the tension between oral and written traditions. Grandmother Ife, who belongs to the old generation of Haitian peasant women, does not approve of Atie's efforts to read and write. She does not understand the power of the written word and the importance of recording one's history by writing it. When Atie insists on going and listing her name in the city archives, Ife comments "If a person is worth remembering. . . . People will remember. It need not be cast in stone" (129). Atie's insistence on listing her name is an attempt to record her story against a patriarchal culture that tends to de-emphasize women's contributions. While oral history is important—Vodou is a wonderful example of cultural retention and preservation of important episodes of Haitian history—Danticat seems to suggest that women need to write their stories to fill in the gaps in Haitian history where women's voices have not been recorded. One still wonders who was the mambo who started the Haitian revolution alongside Boukman, for instance, and what her name was. Both oral and written histories are necessary to preserve women's roles and contribution.

Ife's name comes from Ile-Ife, which in Vodou mythology refers to the original home for all beings in Africa. It is where creation started. It is the holy city where the loa reside.[15] Grandmother Ife therefore repre-

---

15. Ibid., 158.

sents the origins. Through her spirituality which is firmly grounded in an African belief-system, she preserves the link with the African past and the ancestors. This diasporic consciousness remains highly important to the Caco women's sense of cultural and historical identity, as they continue to communicate with their ancestors beyond the traditional parameters of life and death. Atie tells Sophie while they are in the cemetery: "Walk straight, you are in the presence of family" (149). This again shows that the Caco women are joined in a strong cultural chain beyond the limitations of physical death. Danticat's act of writing is in itself a spiritual act of communicating with her past and her ancestors as she informs us in an interview: "I write to communicate with my ancestors."[16]

Guinea is the place where the Caco women will meet again when they die, a place that Sophie describes as "where all the women in my family hoped to eventually meet one another, at the very end of each of our journeys" (174). Guinea is Africa, which is described in Vodou cosmology as a place under water where one goes after their death to join their ancestors. It is a resting place, somewhat like the concept of heaven in Christianity.[17] Here, Danticat evokes Vodou, not as ceremonies of dark magic, as low-budget Hollywood films want us to believe, but as a an empowering belief system that allows for the preservation of the past, providing Danticat's female protagonists with a diasporic vision necessary to their quest for spiritual wholeness.

Danticat also communicates the importance of Vodou in preserving oral history. However, she does not romanticize oral narratives and is cautious of the role folk stories play in perpetuating cultural standards that can be oppressive to women. Ife in the novel is a "tale master" who through storytelling preserves Haitian oral culture, but she belongs to the old generation that adheres to traditional norms and does not see a way out of oppressive practices against women in Haiti. She apologizes to Sophie about testing, but does not see any other choice but to perpetuate the practice. She starts her stories with the proclamation: "Let the words bring wings to our feet" (123), referring to the potential stories can have in terms of offering freedom to women, but her stories ironically are stories that warn and caution women about the danger of freedom. Ife's story about the little girl who outsmarted the lark that wanted to take her away from her home and village, is an example of folk stories that are used as a

---

16. Edwidge Danticat, "Three Young Voices" (interview), *Essence*, May 1996.
17. Alfred Metraux, *Voodoo in Haiti* (New York: Shocken Books, 1972), 91–92. See also Desmangles, *The Faces of the Gods*, 69; Brown, *Mama Lola*, 223; Joseph Murphy, *Working the Spirit: Ceremonies of the African Diaspora* (New York: Beacon Press, 1995), 28–29.

reprimanding tool to teach young girls about self-restriction. The message is that women's freedom is a dangerous tool that always ends with harsh punishment.

It is Danticat who is the real "tale master." She is the one with the power to give wings to the stories and turn them into liberating tools for women. Danticat revises Haitian folk stories told by grandmother Ife and rewrites them as stories of courage and resistance. In this process, Haitian folk stories acquire a fresh outlook that expresses a new generation of Haitian women's interpretation of their own culture. The stories of female evil spirits such as the loup-garou and the platonade become empowering examples of female folk figures who rebelled against societal rules, despite the resulting harsh punishment. The platonade, for example, was "a loose woman who made love to the men she met by a stream and then drowned them in the water" (118), and the loup-garou was a woman "who flew without her skin at night, and when she came back home, she found her skin peppered and could not put it back on. Her husband had done it to teach her a lesson. He ended up killing her" (150).[18] While these stories refer to the high price women pay for their freedom, they are stories of women who are rebelling against tradition. These stories about women's transformation create a space where gender dynamics can be contested. They interrogate the place of women in Haitian society, but also in Haiti's historical, literary, and cultural discourses.

The names of the younger Caco women are also symbols that conjure powerful figures and attest to Danticat's employment of religious symbols to rewrite her female characters as heroic figures. Sophie's name comes from Sophia, referring to the goddess of wisdom, a black goddess who appears in biblical, Apocryphal, and Gnostic texts. According to Gnostic texts, Sophia is the first universal creator. She is the creator of men and women and of the material world. She is a divine feminine entity who enlightens human beings and gives them wisdom. Sophia is also associated with the black Egyptian goddess Isis. Sophia, most importantly, expresses the complexity of the feminine element. Somewhat like Erzulie in Vodou, she is portrayed variously as a hag, queen of heaven, a harlot, and a faithful wife.[19] Sophie in the novel is the black goddess who enlightens the

---

18. Loup-garou or Lougawou in Creole are creatures of the night. They are similar to werewolves. Danticat also refers to lougawou women in "Nineteen Thirty-Seven," in *Krik? Krak!* (New York: Soho Press, 1991). Joan Dayan, who explores the history of torture in Haiti, argues that these folk stories grew out of Haiti's colonial history, where slave men and women were punished by having their skin peppered. See Dayan, *Haiti, History, and the Gods*, 265.

19. See Caitlin Matthews, *Sophia, Goddess of Wisdom: The Divine Feminine from Black Goddess to World Soul* (London: Mandala, 1991), 11 and 15–19, on Sophia as "goddess of wis-

younger generations of Haitian women about their womanhood. Sophie is the first one in her family line who breaks the practice of testing. Unlike her mother and grandmother, Sophie swore to never put her daughter Brigitte through testing. Instead, Sophie passes on her wisdom to Brigitte. She liberates herself from the rigid patriarchal values that defined her sexuality and passes on a healthy image of womanhood to her daughter.

The last in the female line of the Caco women is Brigitte, the future carrier of the Caco women's legacy. When Ife first sees Brigitte she comments in wonderment: "The tree has not split one mite. Isn't it a miracle that we can visit with all our kin, simply by looking into this face?" (105). Brigitte evokes the Haitian loa Grande Brigitte, also spelled Brijit, the loa of the dead and the guardian of the cemetery.[20] Brigitte is the guardian of her family's history. In a symbiotic relationship characteristic of Vodou, Brigitte, a variation of Brigit, also evokes the Celtic goddess and Catholic saint, known as "Mary of the Irish,"[21] who is "a bridge between this world and the world beyond."[22] In both traditions, Brigitte conveys this connection between the present and the past, between the world of the living and the world of the ancestors. Both as goddess and saint, Brigit is the patroness of poetry and learning, an allusion to the possibility of Brigitte inheriting the gift of poetry and learning from Atie.[23]

MANY HAITIANS and Haitian Americans were unimpressed with Danticat's novel, disputing the practice of testing, and arguing that Danticat is giving Haitian culture a bad reputation. Danticat's choice of a sensitive subject matter and a discussion of female sexuality may not have gone down well with some Haitian Americans, especially conservative middle-class Haitians. With that in mind, it is important to consider the ritual of testing, not necessarily as a Haitian practice, but also as an authorial strategy that allows Danticat to explore practices of sexual abuse. The familiarity Danticat has with Haitian culture allows her to construct stories, practices, rituals that may seem Haitian in origins, but are sometimes the product of her own invention, especially that she writes primarily for a North American readership that is not familiar with Haitian culture. It

---

dom" and as a "black goddess." For more on Sophia as the first creator, see Elaine Pagels, *Gnostic Gospels* (1979; London: Penguin, 1990), 76.
   20. Metraux, *Voodoo in Haiti*, 114.
   21. Sean Duinn, *The Rites of Brigid: Goddess and Saint* (Dublin: Columbia Press, 2005), 10.
   22. Ibid., 8.
   23. See Duinn, *The Rites of Brigid*, 56–62, for more on Brigid's attributes both as goddess and as saint.

is necessary for the reader not to assume Danticat's role as simply a transmitter of Haitian culture. While this strategy significantly allows Danticat to rewrite Haitian women into history, it also challenges the reader into delving beyond a surface reading into an engagement with Haitian culture as both revised and reimagined by Danticat.

When asked in an interview about testing and if it is a common Haitian practice, Danticat was vague. She explains that the Caco family is not meant to be typically Haitian: "The family in the book was never meant to be a 'typical' Haitian family, if there is ever a typical family in any culture. The family is very much Haitian, but they live their own internal and individual matriarchal reality."[24] It is possible that the practice of testing is constructed by Danticat as a way to shock her readers into an engagement with Haitian women's experiences with sexual abuse and violence both in private and public spaces. When asked about the origins of the practice of testing, Danticat reports that it is an ancient practice that dates back to the Virgin Mary. The practice is mentioned in the Book of James of the Apocryphal gospels, one of the earliest surviving documents that attest to Mary's perpetual virginity. The story goes that Mary's midwife, Salome, doubted her virginity and after birth tested it only to realize that she was in fact a virgin and therefore converted to Christianity.[25] Either invented as an authorial strategy or reflective of Haitian reality, through an examination of Mariology and how it relates to her own family, the practice of testing also allows Danticat to critically engage with representation of womanhood in the Judeo-Christian discourse.

Interestingly, the discussion around testing, or what Sophie calls "the virginity cult," can also be countered by the figure of the djablesse in Haitian folk culture, who threatens the very idea of virginity. Dayan writes: "In Haiti it is no good to be a virgin, no matter what the priest, nuns, or prospective partners will tell you. One of the most feared ghosts is the djablesse. Haitians will tell you that she wanders in forests and cities, condemned to walk for a number of years for the sin of having died a virgin."[26] Dayan's point is also supported by Alfred Metraux's *Voodoo in Haiti*. In a section entitled "The Fate of the Soul after Death," Metraux talks about the wandering souls of those who die virgins: "From fear of the terrible ordeal which awaits virgins in the after life—the woman who

---

24. Edwidge Danticat, "A Conversation with Edwidge Danticat," October 29, 2008, http://www.randomhouse.com/vintage/danticat.html, 1.
25. Ibid., 2.
26. Dayan, "Erzulie," 25–26.

washes a virgin's corpse is asked to deflower the body before burying it."²⁷ This shows that Danticat's novel is in a constant process of revising Haitian folk culture.

The story of the bleeding woman who goes to Erzulie, with which I opened this chapter, is an example of intertextuality that shows another facet of Danticat's revisionary narrative. The story is uncannily similar to the story of the bleeding woman in the book of Mark in the Bible. Both women bleed for twelve years, both visit doctors to no avail, and both seek the help of a divine power who heals them. Compare Danticat with its biblical referent:

> And a woman was there who had been subject to bleeding for twelve years. She had suffered a great deal under the care of many doctors and had spent all she had; yet instead of getting better she grew worse. When she heard about Jesus, she came up behind him in the crowd and touched his cloak, because she thought, "If I just touch his clothes, I will be healed." Immediately her bleeding stopped and she felt in her body that she was freed from her suffering.²⁸

Here Danticat transforms the biblical story and associates the power of healing with a female Vodou loa, generating a narrative reflective of the historical and cultural symbiosis between Christianity and Vodou, and celebratory of healing as part of a religious tradition that is both *female* and *Africanist*.

In a similar manner, Danticat also revises the concept of the Marassa, or the Vodou twins to interrogate family ties and closeness among the Caco women. When Martine finds out about Sophie's relationship with Joseph, she tells her: "The love between a mother and daughter is deeper than the sea. You would leave me for an old man who you didn't know the year before. You and I we could be like the Marassas" (85). The Marassa, according to Maya Deren, celebrate "man's twined nature: half matter, half metaphysical; half mortal, half immortal; half human, half divine."²⁹ Deren explains that the metaphysical nature of the Marassa is reflected in the importance given to twins in Vodou tradition who "are understood as two parts of a whole, hence sharing one soul."³⁰ In the same vein, Alfred

---

27. Metraux, *Voodoo in Haiti*, 258.
28. Mark 5:25–29.
29. Maya Deren, *Divine Horsemen: The Living Gods of Haiti* (New York: McPherson, 1970), 38.
30. Ibid., 39.

Metraux describes how "even death does not break the ties which link twins together. The survivor puts to one side, for the deceased, a symbolic portion of whatever he eats or receives by way of presents."[31]

The Marassa reflect the struggle of the Caco women with the nature of their closeness and intimacy. Martine's desire for closeness with Sophie is pathological, and contradicts the concept of the Marassa in Vodou. Martine wants to control Sophie's freedom and prevent her from emotional growth. She also imposes the practice of testing on her causing her to rape herself in order to end the practice. There are early indications in the novel that articulate Sophie's fear of her mother's desire for closeness. She has recurring nightmares about her mother trapping her: "she would try and squeeze me into the small frame so I could be into the picture with her. I would scream until my voice gave up" (8). In another instance, Sophie describes: "She opened her arms like two long hooks and kept shouting out my name. Catching me by the hem of my dress, she wrestled me to the floor" (28). The Marassa who symbolize the closeness of the twins and the union of two energies, are ironically used not to convey the closeness of mother and daughter, but rather to interrogate it. However, it is Sophie and Atie who represent the healthy energy of the Marassa, a sense of an unthreatening closeness based on affinity and respect. They are both poets and share appreciation for language. Atie is always present in Sophie's mind. When she first meets Joseph she remembers Atie's words: "Tante Atie once said that love is like rain. It comes in a drizzle sometimes. Then it starts pouring and if you are not careful it will drown you" (67). Sophie also compares Joseph with Mr. Augustin, her aunt's former lover.

The name Caco is another example of the way Danticat is constantly generating meaning through cultural and linguistic constructions. While the name refers to the Caco guerilla, Danticat generates a new meaning for the word, a scarlet bird: "Our family name, Caco, it is the name of a scarlet bird. A bird so crimson, it makes the reddest hibiscus or the brightest flame trees seem white" (150). Sophie surely cannot be trusted as a reliable source of Haitian culture. In her reading of the novel, Marie-Jose N'Zengou-Tayo tells us about the origins of the name: "'Caco' is the name of a tiny red ant whose bite burns terribly. Through analogy, people gave the name to nineteenth-century peasant soldiers who defeated successive Haitian governments. We don't find the association of 'Caco' with

---

31. Metraux, *Voodoo in Haiti*, 149.

a bird in the literature."[32] Danticat here fashions a new meaning for her female protagonists, challenging cultural traditions defined by patriarchal standards, and celebrating the powerful voices of marginalized Haitian women.

DANTICAT'S NARRATIVE is reminiscent of the Haitian literary movement of the 1920s, a black consciousness movement called Indigenism. Authors of the 1920s—such as René Depestre, who lived through the U.S. occupation of Haiti and who was one of the leading figures of Indigenism—found it necessary to go back to the African roots, celebrate Vodou as the organic religion of the masses, and connect to the land and the plight of the peasant class. They used literature as a form of cultural resistance against the degradation caused by American occupation. According to Joan Dayan, the indigenous movement marked a turning point in the forming of a national Haitian literary identity that recognized an African heritage long despised and scorned in favor of a European literary discourse.[33]

Like the Haitian authors of the 1920s, Danticat uses Haitian cultural heritage as a way to give voice to Haitian rural classes against their omission from Haiti's historical and cultural discourses. Her novel celebrates working-class women both in their struggles and triumphs, and the symbols she uses are deeply embedded in the culture of rural Haiti, where her ancestors came from. Atie conveys this sentiment when she tells Sophie, "We are a family with dirt under our fingers. Do you know what that means? That means we worked the land. We are not *educated* . . . we, daughters of the hills, old peasant stock, *petit soyèt,* ragamuffins" (20). Danticat is acutely aware of the importance of recording the stories of rural Haitians, whose voices do not get heard in either their own nation's political discourse or in the pages of Western literature. In *After the Dance,* a travelogue that records her journey through Carnival, Danticat describes the reality of the peasantry as

> mocked in comic television or theater programs, which poke fun at their lack of comfort or familiarity with urban settings, or they are revered in folkloric dances when people dress up in what once was their daily

---

32. Marie-Jose N'Zengou-Tayo, "Rewriting Folklore: Traditional Beliefs and Popular Culture in Edwidge Danticat's *Breath, Eyes, Memory,* and *Krik? Krak!*" *MaComère* 3 (2000), 3, 125.

33. See Joan Dayan, introduction to A *Rainbow for the Christian West,* by René Depestre, trans. Joan Dayan (Amherst: University of Massachusetts Press, 1977), 8.

garb. . . . Still they are like Maroons in their own country, excluded from any national decision-making process, remaining symbols more than anything else.[34]

Danticat's comment further emphasizes the necessary task of recording the lives of the marginalized Haitian peasantry, communicating through Atie, for instance, the importance of reading and writing as a way to end the silence surrounding the experiences of peasant Haitian women. Danticat is highly aware of her working-class background and consciously uses it to talk about the realities of working-class Haitian women both in Haiti and in the United States. In an interview with the *New York Times* she notes: "This friend of mine kept saying that in Haiti his mother had a maid, but here his mother is a maid. I can be friends with women that, if we lived in Haiti, our paths would never cross. People where I was from were the maids."[35]

Significantly, Caco, the family name Danticat gives to her female characters, refers to the peasant guerilla that was wiped out by the U.S. Marines during the American occupation of Haiti from 1915–1934.[36] The occupation threatened Haitians' pride of their history of independence, and used forced labor which brought memories of slavery and oppression under Colonial France. A discourse of exoticization went hand in hand with the occupation, manifesting itself in tales of cannibalism and ceremonies of black magic supplied by both the Marines and American visitors who were intrigued by the island.[37] African American authors such as Zora Neale Hurston, Langston Hughes, and James Weldon Johnson visited Haiti during the occupation and wrote about it. Johnson objected to the U.S. discourse of paternalism and made a case for Haitians' right to self-governance. He questioned the United States' dubious accomplishments in Haiti, exposing the brutal treatment of Haitians by the Marines, comparing the Marines' use of forced labor to a slave regime that destroyed the peasantry's way of life. In his article "Self-Determining Haiti," Johnson writes: "By day or night, from the bosom of their families, from their little farms or while trudging peacefully ion the country roads, Haitians were seized and forcibly taken to toil for months in far sections of the country.

---

34. Edwidge Danticat, *After the Dance: A Walk through Carnival in Jacmel, Haiti* (New York: Crown, 2002), 57–58.
35. Gary Pierre-Pierre, "At Home with Edwidge Danticat: Haitian Tales, Flatbush Scenes," *New York Times*, January 26, 1995: 1, section C.
36. See Mary A. Renda, *Taking Haiti: Military Occupation and the Culture of the U.S. Imperialism, 1915–1940* (Chapel Hill, University of North Carolina Press, 2001).
37. Ibid., 33.

Those who protested or resisted were beaten into submission."[38] Hughes was also critical of the U.S. actions in Haiti. He wrote about the condition of the peasantry and the way they were exploited by both the Americans and the Haitian upper classes: "Haiti was a land of people without shoes. . . . Barefooted ones tending the rice and cane fields under the hot sun, climbing the mountain slopes, picking coffee beans, wading through surf to fishing boats on the blue sea. All of the work that kept Haiti alive, paid the interest on American loans, and enriched foreign traders, was done by people without shoes."[39]

In contrast to Johnson and Hughes, Hurston's *Tell My Horse* expresses a rather conservative view of the occupation. She portrayed a violent Haiti and saw the U.S. intervention as necessary. Hurston's description of the Caco does not differ much from that of the Marines' accounts. She refers to them as "knife-men." They are cowardly, corrupt, and bloodthirsty.[40] Hurston observes about the end of the occupation and its destruction of the Caco resistance: "This was the last hour of the last day of the last year that ambitious and greedy demagogues could substitute bought Caco blades for voting power. It was the end of the revolution and the beginning of peace."[41]

Hurston's political conservatism was also accompanied by sensationalized accounts about Haitian culture, reinforcing an exotic discourse of otherness. Hurston's ethnographic work on Vodou lacks the objectivity of responsible ethnographic scholarship she is known for. She writes tales about zombies and secret sects and their cannibalistic practices. Her accounts about Vodou cosmology and practices are both very generic and generalized. While Hurston contributed to an imperialist discourse of primitivism about Haiti, Hughes could not have been more aware of these sensational accounts about Haiti, especially in relation to Vodou. Hughes comments insightfully: "Real Voodoo dances are not easy for tourists to see. I saw only one, deep in the woods. . . . The songs were monotonous chants punctuated by long wails. The dancers danced themselves into a kind of trance, not unlike that of our Deep South revivals."[42]

Danticat consciously conjures the period of occupation in order to challenge narratives of exoticism and paternalism about Haiti that even

---

38. James Weldon Johnson, "Self-Determining Haiti: The American Occupation," *The Nation* 111.2878 (August 28, 1920): 237.
39. Langston Hughes, I *Wonder as I Wander* (New York: Rinehart, 1956), 27.
40. Zora Neale Hurston, *Tell My Horse: Voodoo and Life in Haiti and Jamaica* (New York: Harper and Row, 1990), 66–68.
41. Ibid., 72.
42. Hughes, I *Wonder as I Wander*, 22.

major authors such as Hurston could not escape. By drawing on the name Caco, she evokes peasant resistance that forms an important part of the Haitian consciousness. This movement, which was started in the nineteenth century by the peasantry, was a reaction against exploitation by corrupt governments and urban elites in Haiti who wanted control over agriculture and economic production. Historically, it was the peasantry in Haiti who carried the spirit of the Haitian revolution and fought to keep economic autonomy against those who were in power. Significantly, Charlemagne Caco, the name Danticat gives to Sophie's grandfather, refers to the historical figure of Charlemagne Peralte who was one of the two leaders of the Caco resistance assassinated in 1918 by the U.S. Marines. Johnson writes about Peralte: "If anyone doubts that the 'caco' hunting is the sport of American Marines in Haiti, let him learn about the death of Charlemagne,"[43] who was tried by a marine court for his involvement with the Caco and sentenced to five years of slave labor. After escaping he went back to working with the Caco, and not long after that, he was tracked and shot by the Marines. Johnson describes how Charlemagne "met his death not in an open fight, not in an attempt at his capture, but through a das tard deed. While standing over his camp fire, he was shot in cold blood by an American Marine officer who stood concealed by the darkness. . . . This deed, which was nothing short of assassination, has been heralded as an example of American heroism."[44]

The suppression of the Caco resistance, which Hurston describes as the end of war and the start of peace, sadly, had deadly effects on the peasantry, as it allowed for the emergence of a centralized government control over the rural masses. Thus, in succeeding to destroy the Caco bands, the U.S. Marines also succeeded in suppressing the voice of the rural masses and with it the freedom of speech.[45] Hence, Danticat's rewriting of this episode of Haitian history is even more significant as she conjures up the voices of the peasantry who are not just silenced by Haiti's national discourse, but also within a U.S. narrative of national heroism.

The U.S. occupation of Haiti remains present in Haitians' historical consciousness. Haiti's revolutionary history and its reputation as the first independent black republic in the Western hemisphere were challenged by the U.S. occupation. Haiti was forced to face a form of American neocolonialism that imposed social structures similar to those of French colonial Haiti. Mary A. Renda reports that during the nineteen years of the

---

43. Johnson, "Self-Determining Haiti," 13.
44. Ibid.
45. Renda, *Taking Haiti*, 36.

U.S. presence in Haiti: "Marines installed a puppet president, dissolved the legislature at gunpoint, denied freedom of speech, and forced a new constitution on the Caribbean nation—one more favorable to foreign investment."[46] René Depestre lamented the situation as: "the sacred soil of Dessalines profaned, the oath of January violated with the complicity of the so-called elites, the occupying Yankees dancing the polka, the waltz and the quadrille . . . the peasants deported in masses, returned to slavery and forced labor."[47] The U.S occupation brought class divisions similar to those that had defined colonial Haiti, with an elite minority at the top of the ladder who have historically supported and accepted a foreign presence in Haiti, and who felt more cultural affinity with the Europeans, and a majority of rural masses who have been historically suspicious of foreign presence in Haiti. The following conversation about the U.S occupation of Haiti, which takes place in a Haitian restaurant in New York where Sophie, her mother, and her mother's boyfriend, Marc go for dinner, indeed reflects these dynamics between the elite and the peasantry, and conveys that this part of Haitian history remains vivid in the Haitian mind many decades after the occupation:

> "Never the Americans in Haiti again," shouted one man. "Remember what they did in the twenties. They treated our people like animals. They abused the *konbit* system and they made us work like slaves." "Roads, we need roads," said another man. "At least they gave us roads." (54)

This passage shows the contradictory views that Haitians have in relation to the U.S. presence in Haiti. While the American occupation carried out public work projects such as the building of roads, they used the forced labor system as peasants were caught, roped, brought to prisons, and forced to work. Ultimately, it was the peasantry who suffered the most from the U.S. occupation, which only worked to reinforce the gap between the elite and the rural majority.

The U.S. Marines' presence also set the groundwork for the presence of successive corrupt political regimes in Haiti, including two Duvalier dictatorships and a series of post-Duvalier military regimes. Sophie poses the question: "Who invented the Macoutes? The devil didn't do it and God didn't do it" (138). This question is at the core of Danticat's novel,

---

46. Ibid., 10.
47. Depestre, A *Rainbow for the Christian West*, 5–6.

since the Macoutes are the ones accountable for the tragedy of the Caco women and their dispersal. Martine, who was raped by a Macoute, has never recovered from the trauma that eventually leads to her suicide. This affects Sophie too, who struggles with her sexuality and relationship to her husband.

Danticat's meditation on the Haitian past also works to reflect on the present. As part of her strategy of naming, Danticat evokes the figure of Jean-Jacques Dessalines to engage with the reality of violence that still plagues Haiti. Dessalines (1758–1806) was the first president and emperor of Haiti who was assassinated and mutilated by Haitian soldiers. The character Dessalines in the novel is a coal vender who gets cruelly beaten and killed by the Tonton macoutes. More so than any other Haitian leader, the historical Dessalines remains a very powerful symbol in the Haitian imagination, especially to the Indigenist movement. Dessalines represented everything the Indigenists believed in. He advocated racial equality and changed blackness in Haiti into a positive symbol. Dessalines also wanted to break the class hierarchy and empower the rural masses by allowing them access to land ownership, a right that was traditionally only reserved to the Haitian elite. Unlike other Haitian leaders who shunned Vodou and made Catholicism the official religion of the state, Dessalines remained close to Vodou as the true religion of the masses. No wonder then that Dessalines was made into a god, a Vodou loa, by Vodou practitioners, thus becoming an everlasting presence in Haitian memory.[48]

Louise, Atie's friend, announces in the novel the death of the coal vender Dessalines: "They killed Dessalines." "Who killed Dessalines?" asks the grandmother. "The Macoutes killed Dessalines" (138). Danticat here is reenacting a powerful moment in Haitian history and in the Haitian popular imagination: the tragic death of the historical Dessalines who was cruelly shot and mutilated by soldiers. Significantly, Danticat is drawing a parallel between Haiti's past and present. However, far from painting an image of a disempowered Haiti, by evoking the name of Dessalines Danticat is also resurrecting the figure of Dessalines and celebrating him in public memory.

While Danticat's novel evokes traits of the Haitian nationalist movement of the 1920s, she also challenges the movement's masculinist trend that often suppresses women's achievements. Through the Caco women, Danticat reclaims women's contribution to Haiti's history of resistance.

---

48. Dayan, *Haiti, History, and the Gods*, 16–28.

Moreover, Danticat's daring engagement with female violence and sexual oppression also challenges the romanticization of Haitian womanhood found in the Indigenist male literary discourse, where women are often mythologized into either symbols of purity or aggressive sexuality, which alienates their actual experiences with sexual violence and oppression.[49] Thus, while Danticat celebrates the Haitian Indigenist movement for its progressive vision especially in terms of its focus on reclaiming Haiti's cultural identity, she goes a step forward and inscribes Haitian women's stories into Haiti's discourse of heroism and resistance.

DANTICAT DOES NOT subscribe to simplistic notions of place. The United States is not constructed as a site of liberation against Haiti's oppressiveness, nor is Haiti romanticized as the lost homeland against an American exile. Sophie's reality embodies a transnational experience rooted in cultural mixing and ambivalence both toward the homeland and the adopted country. Both Haitian and American values are contested in the novel. Sophie, for example, is aware of the U.S. isolationist policies toward its minorities and feels a sense of alienation both as a black woman and as a Haitian immigrant. However, both places also offer the possibility of liberation.

Sophie and Martine's experiences in the United States reflect the complex experiences of Haitian immigrants, as the relationship between the United States and Haiti has been a complicated one historically. Negative accounts about Haiti are still vividly present in American popular culture. With the flow of Haitian immigrants to the United States during the 1970s and 1980s, Haitians became associated with the image of the helpless refugee and were frequently referred to as "boat people." Haitians who were fleeing the Duvalier dictatorship—which was long supported by U.S. money—were not granted political asylum, and filled up refugee camps.[50] Haitians also became stigmatized as AIDS carriers, a claim that

---

49. Notably, male authors of black consciousness movements have been traditionally uneasy about talking about women abuse and saw women authors who spoke of these problems as betraying a nationalistic discourse of unity. Indeed, the indigenist movement remains progressive in terms of its focus on reclaiming a sense of cultural identity tied to the uniqueness of the Haitian historical experience; nevertheless, the movement is problematic in the way it represents womanhood. See Miriam Chancy's discussion of Edwidge Danticat and Nadine Magloire in *Framing Silence: Revolutionary Novels by Haitian Women* (New Brunswick, NJ: Rutgers University Press, 1997), 105–33.

50. Ronald Fernandez argues that despite the fact that Haitians were running away from the cruelty of the Duvalier and post-Duvalier regimes, the United States refused to consider them political refugees and give them asylum. He reports that the INS since 1970 refused 95 percent of

did not have any factual grounds, but was supported at the time by federal and national organizations. Sophie refers to this reality when she describes how "Many of the American kids even accused Haitians of having AIDS because they had heard on television that only the 'Four Hs' got AIDS—Heroin addicts, Hemophiliacs, Homosexuals, and Haitians" (51). Sophie's experience is congruent with the historian Flore Zéphir's analysis:

> Perhaps more than any other group, Haitian immigrants became the victims of strong attacks, the more ferocious of these being their characterization as AIDS carriers. Indeed on March 4, 1983, the U.S. centers for disease control (CDC) identified four AIDS high-risk groups: homosexuals, Haitians, hemophiliacs, and heroin users, thus imposing membership into this infamous "Four-H-Club" on Haitians. Following the CDC's exclusionary lead, the United States Public Health Service recommended that Haitians not donate blood, and, in consequence, school blood drives blatantly excluded Haitian teenagers. Those recommendations were taken seriously, and Food and Drug Administration (FDA) issued an original stipulation preventing Haitians who had come to the United States after 1977 from donating blood. The discriminatory policies did not stop here, and in February 1990, the FDA's paranoia reached its climax when this time it issued a ruling prohibiting all Haitians from giving blood.[51]

Danticat must have been acutely aware of this reality, especially as someone who grew up in the Flatbush neighborhood of Brooklyn in the 80s where there is a major concentration of Haitian immigrants and also demonstrations in the city against these discriminatory acts. In *After the Dance* she writes: "AIDS is a painfully complicated issue for us Haitians."[52] Through Martine and Sophie's process of integrating in the larger American society, Danticat records a transnational experience from a perspective that takes into account the complex realities of Haitian immigrants in the

---

Haitian applications for asylum. He writes: "As a final assault on reason and the humanitarian principles of refugee law, President Carter (and President Reagan) continued to offer economic, political, and military assistance to the Duvalier dictatorship. Thus, 'Baby Doc' and General Cedras picked the people clean, killed or imprisoned anyone who got in their way, and often turned a blind eye to the boat people who, if they reached shore or a coast guard cutter, would still be presumed to be economic migrants." Ronald Fernandez, *America's Banquet of Cultures: Harnessing Ethnicity, Race, and Immigration in the Twenty-First Century* (London: Praeger, 2000), 83.

51. Flore, Zéphir *The Haitian Americans* (London: Greenwood Press, 2004), 81.
52. Danticat, *After the Dance*, 137.

United States, a result of an ongoing discourse of cultural othering that reinforced an image of Haitians in the American mind as a primitive and diseased people.

Through Sophie's experiences, Danticat's novel questions the U.S integration policies toward its minorities and further complicates Sophie's transnational identity as a Haitian American. Sophie's access to the American dream is embodied in her ability to pursue an education, something her mother and aunt could not afford in Haiti. Yet, the experience of education is also tainted by harsh racism and a sense of alienation imposed on her by her American peers: "Outside the school, we were 'the frenchies,' cringing in our mock-catholic- school uniforms as the students from the public school across the street called us 'boat people' and 'stinking Haitians'" (66). Sophie here sheds light on a discourse of both exoticization and victimization that has been associated with Haitians. Perhaps the contestation of the United States as a liberatory site is most apparent in Sophie's description of her mother when she arrives in New York. Sophie is struck by how frail and exhausted her mother who works two jobs looks:

> She did not look like the picture Tante Atie had on her night table. Her face was long and hollow. Her hair had a blunt cut and she had long spindly legs. She had dark circles under her eyes and, as she smiled, lines of wrinkles tightened her expression. Her fingers were scarred and sunburned. It was as though she had never stopped working in the cane fields after all. (42)

The grim and unfriendly Brooklyn's landscape where her mother lives also stands in high contrast with the landscape in Croix De Roses in Haiti, where neighbors gathered in the evenings for potlucks. Sophie reports: "The streets we drove down now were dim and hazy. The windows were draped with bars; black trash bags blew out into the night air. There were young men standing on street corners throwing empty cans at passing cars" (43).

Sophie's encounter with Joseph, a middle aged African American jazz musician, breaks the cycle of alienation that she feels, and allows her to discover new cultural connections in the United States. Her relationship with Joseph develops out of a diasporic awareness based on a shared past and legacy. When she meets him he tells her, "'I am not American . . . I am African-American.' 'What is the difference?' 'The African. It means you and I, we are already part of each other'" (72). Her encounter with Joseph opens up an alternative space for new cultural associations. A diasporic African identity takes priority over an American one. Even Sophie's mother only feels strongly connected to American culture when she listens to Negro spirituals as the following conversation that takes place between Joseph, Martine, and Marc shows:

> Joseph began to hum a spiritual. *Oh Mary, Don't weep!*
> "That's a Negro spiritual," said my mother.
> "It sounds like *Vaudou* song," said Marc. "He just described a *Vaudou* song. *Erzulie, don't you weep,*" he sang playfully.
> "I told you I could have been Southern." My mother laughed. "Do you have a favorite Negro spiritual?" Joseph asked my mother. "I sure do."
> "Give us a rendition," urged Marc. . . . "Sometimes I feel like a motherless child / A long ways from home." (215)

Here Southern African American and Haitian cultures are brought together, not as incongruous but as similar and complementary. Negro spirituals are like the songs dedicated to Vodou gods and goddesses, and Mary of Negro spirituals is also Erzulie. Both songs—a plea to Mary and Erzulie not to weep—reflect a universal image of women's suffering.

Sophie also forms a connection with other minorities in her therapy group, which consists of immigrant minorities. Perhaps in evoking the experiences of minorities, Danticat is revealing an image of an isolationist America that is falling short from including its minorities. Nevertheless, these connections are forged in the United States, which is also a testimony to a diverse American culture. These encounters open up spaces where other forms of cultural connections and association are taking form. Danticat's portrayal of a Dominican character as Sophie's therapist allows her to symbolically address the historical tension between Haiti and the Dominican Republic, suggesting a possibility of recovery and reconciliation. African diaspora religions are also emphasized as spaces of healing. Under the guidance of their therapist, a Santeria priestess, the therapy group members perform rituals reminiscent of both Santeria and Vodou. Again, the religious and cultural affinity between Haiti and the Dominican Republic is emphasized. Thus, while Sophie's adopted homeland can be alienating, it also provides a space for her to forge other cultural connections through Joseph and her sexual phobia group. The United States even offers space for addressing the possibility of historical reconciliation between Haiti and the Dominican Republic, conveyed in the diaspora and symbolized in the relationship between Sophie and her Dominican therapist. This shows that Danticat does not subscribe to simplistic notions of place.

Perhaps the value of Danticat's engagement with transnationalism resides in an unresolved sense of belonging that emerges from ambivalence both toward the homeland and the adopted country. Sophie cannot and perhaps does not need to make a choice between America and Haiti. While both places can represent a sense of oppressiveness, both offer possibilities for liberation. The United States, despite its ostracizing policies, is a place that has the potential of making Sophie happy and giving her a sense of belonging. When Joseph, her husband, asks her to move with him to Providence, Sophie reflects: "I was immediately fascinated by the name. Providence. Fate! A town named for the creator, the Almighty. Who would not want to live there?" (70). The U.S. thus acquires a positive association and becomes a place of divine intervention.

THE BODY OF criticism surrounding Danticat's *Breath, Eyes, Memory* often reflects a preoccupation regarding how to situate the novel politically. Where does Danticat's loyalty reside? Does her novel belong to the genre of literature of exile? Or does the novel exhibit traits of migrant literature? Is it more accurate to situate her within a Haitian nationalistic discourse? Or does the novel display transnational tendencies? Does Danticat show an affinity with Haitian literary discourses or with American ones? Perhaps it is inevitable to ask these questions when one deals with an author who feels at ease both toward her Haitian and American identities, who is comfortable with English, Creole and French. But perhaps, what makes it hard to pin down Danticat is the fact that her criticism of Haitian traditions does not fully imply a total embrace of the United States. Unlike many authors who deal with issues of migration and place, Danticat does not construct the United States as a liberating space against Haiti's oppressiveness. Her work demands open-mindedness in terms of classification. While some critics place her work within a nationalistic discourse thus oversimplifying identity politics in the novel, others who see the novel as transnational are quick to make predictable judgments rooted in a desire to always see the West as a liberatory space.

In her article "From Literature of Exile to Migrant Literature," in which she compares Danticat's *Breath, Eyes, Memory* and Julia Alvarez's *Yo!*, Carine M. Mardorssian maintains that Danticat's novel "retains a nationalistic focus that belies the Haitian writer's classification as 'transnational' and 'migrant.'"⁵³ She writes that in Danticat's novel "what matters is not what America is but Haiti's absence. What grounds Sophie's and her mother's identity crisis is the country and traditions they left behind. Where they landed only plays a secondary role as the opposite term in the Haiti/US dyad."⁵⁴ On the other hand, Michael Dash's *Haiti and the United States: National Stereotypes and the Literary Imagination* adopts Edward Glissant's concept of "errance" or errancy to refer to work by Haitian Americans such as Edwidge Danticat and Dany Laferrière. Dash writes that "the idea of 'errancy' undermines the often reductionist discourse of self vs. other, center vs. periphery, authentic vs. alien. As the old foundational myths recede, a new fluid identity, no longer based on an originary discourse, frees the individual to conceive himself or herself in terms of a groundless cosmopolitanism."⁵⁵

Unlike Mardorssian, Dash argues that what distinguishes Danticat from a Haitian nationalistic discourse is her ability to embrace the United States as a liberatory site rather than a threatening and pathological space. He writes that Danticat's characters "are caught between the nightmare of patriarchal, authoritarian Haiti and the liberating anonymity offered by the American city. The dominant culture of Haiti in this novel is oppressively masculine . . . in contrast, the experience of New York that is conveyed is a liberating one and enhanced by the restorative masculine presence of the jazz musician, Joseph."⁵⁶ Dash's approach is rather contrived. While he promotes the idea of errancy and fluid identity, he falls into the same problematic dualities of reductionist discourses where America acquires the potential to fully liberate Sophie. Dash fails to see that the United States, like Haiti, represents an oppressive force in Sophie's life. Sophie's description of New York where her mother lives is rather grim and far from being a site of freedom. Sophie's connection to Joseph is also complex in terms of how she relates to him sexually.

Danticat's novel is transnational in its refusal to oversimplify the experiences of Haitian Americans. Neither Haiti nor the United States are easily embraced. Yet, Danticat's attitude is ingrained in a real sense of commitment to both Haiti and the United States. Danticat interrogates a roman-

---

53. Carine M. Mardorssian, "From Literature of Exile to Migrant Literature," *Modern Language Studies* 32.2 (2002): 15–33, 19.
54. Ibid., 28.
55. J. Michael Dash, *Haiti and the United States: National Stereotypes and the Literary Imagination* (1988; London: Macmillan, 1997), 153.
56. Ibid., 160.

ticized concept of errancy or the transnational subject as a wanderer. The following conversation between Joseph and Sophie is a tongue in cheek comment where she humorously challenges this idea:

> "It is ok not to have your future in a map," he [Joseph] said. "The way you can flow wherever life takes you."
> "That is not Haitian," I said. "That's very American."
> "What is?"
> "Being a wanderer. The very idea." (72)

Yet, the aspect of the novel that is most reflective of a sense of transnationalism is Danticat's conscious play on language. In her use of English, French and Creole, Danticat articulates the paradoxes and complexities of her transnational identity. When asked why she chose to write in English, Danticat explains: "English was as much an act of personal translation as it was an act of creative collaboration with the new place I was in. My writing in English is a consequence of my migration, in the same way that immigrant children speaking to each other in English, is a consequence of their migration."[57] Danticat's novel therefore is already an act of translation, and acts of translation, both linguistic and cultural, always involve either a movement from the author to the reader where the foreign text or culture is assimilated, or a movement from the reader to the author where the reader is made to progress toward the unfamiliar text or culture. Within the context of postcolonial translation where power differentials are involved, the second process is seen as more ethical, since it necessarily involves engaging the reader with difference and otherness.

Danticat successfully engages the American reader in this process by constantly making them move toward the unfamiliar: Haitian and Haitian American cultures. Danticat does that explicitly when she breaks the flow of English with French and Creole words, and implicitly, by transposing French and Creole syntax on English. While the reader feels a sense of familiarity with the language, the unfamiliar structure and terminology signal to them that they are entering unfamiliar territory. As these linguistic shifts indicate a movement from one culture to another, they also signal a physical movement from the United States to Haiti or vice versa. For instance, in her trip to Haiti, once Sophie reaches the shores of Haiti, the linguistic structure changes immediately as the flirtatious tap-tap driver

---

57. http://www.randomhouse.com/catalog/display.pperl?isbn=9780375705045&view=auqa (June 4, 2009).

declares to her: "I would crawl inside your dress and live there. I can feed on your beauty like a leech feeds on blood. I would live and die for you. More than the sky loves its stars" (93).[58] This change in the syntax signals a cultural and geographic change. The reader becomes acutely aware that Danticat is taking them to another place, another culture, and another language, all while using English.

The translation of *Breath, Eyes, Memory* into French by Pygmalion ignores the complexity of Danticat's linguistic strategies and the political choices she makes through language.[59] The catchier and more dramatic title "Le cri de l'oiseau rouge" (The Cry of the Red Bird) is already an indication of the shift that is occurring in the translation to French, where the focus is more on the suffering of the Caco women, as the red bird refers to the family name. This title also suggests victimization, which goes against Danticat's attempt to create a narrative of empowerment as the Epigraph suggests. The English title, however, is less specific, referring to time and memory indicating broader experiences of movement and migration. On the front cover of the Livre de Poche (pocket book) edition, Danticat's first name is even misspelled as "Edwige"—signaling negligence.[60] The translation of Creole terms and expressions is clumsy and clearly shows that the metropolitan translator, Nicole Tisserand is not familiar with Haitian culture nor made an effort to research it. According to Marie-Jose N'Zengou-Tayo and Elizabeth Wilson in "Translators on a Tight Rope" the name "Enough-boys" (6), for instance, which is translated as "Assez–de-gars" (17), should have been translated more accurately as "Acélhomme," as found in Haitian literature.[61] There is no doubt that the task of Nicole Tisserand is complex, given that she is dealing with a double translation, since Danticat is already translating aspects of Haitian culture into English. For example, the proverb "crabs don't make papayas" (45), which comes from the Creole saying "joumou pa donnen kalbas" (pumpkins don't produce calabashes), is translated as "les crabes

---

58. Tayo and Wilson note that the driver's speech is reminiscent of Emilie Roumer's poem "Marabout de mon coeur." Significantly, Roumer was also a member of the Indigenist movement. See Marie-José N'Zengou Tayo and Elizabeth Wilson, "Translators on a Tight Rope: The Challenges of Translating Edwidge Danticat's *Breath, Eyes, Memory* and Patrick Chamoiseau's *Texaco*," *Traduction, terminologie, rédaction* 13.2 (2000): 75–105.

59. Edwidge Danticat, *Le cri de l'oiseau rouge*, trans. Nicole Tisserand (Paris: Pygmalion, 1995). See Tayo and Wilson, "Translators on a Tight Rope," 79–90, for a detailed discussion of Tisserand's problematic use of tense and translation of expressions and proverbs which shows her unfamiliarity with Haitian culture.

60. Edwidge Danticat, *Le cri de l'oiseau rouge* (Paris: Livre de poche, 1995).

61. Tayo and Wilson provide specific examples to support this point: "Translators on a Tight Rope," 88.

font pas de papayas" (45). While the translator is not expected to go back to the original proverb, Tayo and Wilson propose that in cases like this "a translator's note reminding readers of the original would have been relevant."[62] This of course demands a degree of familiarity with Haitian culture on the part of the translator.

It is clear that the French packaging and translation strategies ignore the Caribbean experience and deal with Danticat's text plainly as an American text. This is also indicated by the back cover of the Livre de poche where Danticat is simply described as "American talent," rather than Haitian American: "Elle (Danticat) figure aujourd'hui parmi les espoirs les plus prometteurs de la littérature américaine" [She is today one of the most promising talents in American literature]. It is problematic that the French translation ignores the specifics of Danticat's novel both as a Caribbean and a postcolonial text that uses linguistic strategies characteristic of postcolonial authors. Even as Danticat's acts of translation, cultural and linguistic, express a political choice, the translation to French does not deal with the particularities of Danticat's text as transnational—both Caribbean and American. But perhaps this negligence exhibited toward Danticat's work and the resistance to her Caribbeanness reflects a long ongoing attitude in France toward Caribbean authors. The translation of *Breath, Eyes, Memory* to French, while allowing the novel to reach a vast Francophone audience, thus giving the novel a global quality, does not do justice to the novel; instead, it reduces the work in terms of its literary qualities.

Breath, Eyes, Memory ends with Sophie running to the canefields—a charged cultural and historical symbol for Haitian peasantry, but also the place where Sophie's mother was raped—with her grandmother asking her "Ou libéré?" (Are you free?) (233). This question remains at the heart of Danticat's novel which articulates Haitian and Haitian American women's experiences of transformation, emphasizing the necessity of addressing historical, cultural and psychological trauma. By giving voice to Haitian women's silenced histories, Danticat is creating a liberatory space that challenges a Haitian masculinist discourse that failed to address the realities of Haitian women, especially peasant women whose experiences have been repressed within Haiti's nationalist discourses, but also in Western literary representations. In her attempt to capture the history of women in Haiti and reclaim their contribution to Haiti's narratives of resistance, Danticat constructs a rich cultural myriad of folk stories, Vodou symbols,

---

62. Tayo and Wilson, "Translators on a Tight Rope," 89.

and folk songs interwoven to create a space for the celebration of the culture of Haitian peasantry long ignored. In her visit to Haiti to attend and write about carnival, Danticat writes: "I want to spin my own story."[63] In *Breath, Eyes, Memory* Danticat indeed spins her own story about Haitian and Haitian American women's experiences, addressing through Vodou, the possibility of women's heroic return as angry spirits, larks or butterflies.

---

63. Danticat, *After the Dance*, 34

3

"Thunder, Perfect Mind"

Candomblé, Gnosticism, and the Utopian Impulse in Toni Morrison's *Paradise*

> Whether they be the first or the last, representing the oldest black families or the newest, the best of the tradition or the most pathetic, they had ended up betraying it all. They think they have outfoxed the Whiteman when in fact they imitate him. They think they are protecting their wives and children, when in fact they are maiming them. . . . Unbridled by Scripture, deafened by the roar of its own history, Ruby, it seemed to him, was an unnecessary failure. How exquisitely human was the wish for permanent happiness, and how thin human imagination became trying to achieve it. Soon Ruby will be like any other country town: the young thinking of elsewhere; the old thinking of regret. The sermons will be eloquent but fewer and fewer will pay attention or connect them to everyday life. How can they hold it together, he wondered, this hard-won heaven defined only by the absence of the unsaved, the unworthy and the strange?
>
> —Toni Morrison, *Paradise*

MORRISON'S *Paradise* (1999) is the last part of a trilogy that Morrison started with *Beloved*, followed by *Jazz*. The three novels focus on the issue of excessive love that leads to violence. Morrison claims that while in *Beloved* she examines maternal love, and in *Jazz* she writes about erotic love, *Paradise* is about "the love of God . . . the passionate, even excessive devotion to God as is manifested in how we construct paradises."[1] She

---

1. "A Conversation with Toni Morrison," http://go.borders.com/ features/mmk98004. xcvDecember 16, 2000), 3.

contends that what started the latter novel was the desire to explore the exclusionary politics involved in the construction of utopian communities:

> The isolation, the separateness, is always a part of any utopia. And it [the novel] was my meditation . . . and interrogation of the whole idea of paradise, the safe place, and the place full of bounty, where no one can harm you. But, in addition to that, it's based on the notion of exclusivity. All paradises, all utopias are defined by who is not there, by the people who are not allowed in.[2]

Morrison's *Paradise* provides a critical reading of American history referencing and revising a myriad of religious narratives and traditions beautifully interwoven in order to initiate a conversation about what constitutes a utopia.

While the body of criticism on *Paradise* remains mainly focused on racial and gender representations in the novel, this chapter will address the construction of religiosity and the way Morrison uses various religious discourses to question and counteract the exclusionary notion of paradise in Judeo-Christianity, especially as a male-centered discourse. In an interview with the *New York Times,* Morrison comments: "All paradises are described as male enclaves, while the interloper is a woman, defenseless and threatening."[3] Afro-Brazilian religion Candomblé and Egyptian Gnosticism serve in the novel as alternative spaces, offering a liberating model of spirituality for women. Morrison's investigation takes the form of an examination of two communities, the black patriarchal and strictly Christian community of Ruby; and the neighboring female community whose religious beliefs are unclear on a surface reading, but which, as my research demonstrates, have their origins in Candomblé and Gnosticism. I will argue in this chapter that the female community practices a mixture of Candomblé and mystic Gnosticism. My intention is to consider how the three religious discourses–Christianity, Candomblé, and Gnosticism—interact in the novel.

Paradise begins in 1976 and then reaches back to slavery, Reconstruction, Civil War, black exodus from the South, and extends forward to the Civil Rights and Black Power movement. It depicts the people of Ruby

---

2. Elizabeth Farnsworth, "Conversation: Toni Morrison," *Online Newshour,* March 9, 1998, 1.

3. Dinitia Smith, "Toni Morrison's Mix of Tragedy, Domesticity, and Folklore," *New York Times,* January 8, 1998, http://www.nytimes.com/library/books/01898toni-morrison-interview.html, 2 (accessed December 16, 2000).

who are descendants of a group of African American pilgrims who were forced to migrate after the Civil War, and their exodus from Louisiana and Mississippi to the Oklahoma territory. After being rejected by a frontier settlement of light-skinned blacks, they negotiated the right to land from Native Americans and built their own town and proclaimed it to be "the one black town worth the pain."[4] As a reaction to the emotional injury of being rejected by their own race—an episode of their history they call the "Disallowing"—these black pilgrims established strict blood rules and turned their town into a black utopia defined by racial purity and stern Christian moral values. The progressive Reverend Richard Misner, and a relatively new member of Ruby, wonders about this black utopia which was initially founded to protect its members against racial injustice, but has grown prejudiced and desolate with time: "How can they hold it together . . . this hard-won heaven defined only by the absence of the unsaved, the unworthy and the strange?" (306).

In 1976, Ruby is a troubled town with a tense conflict between the old generation who wants to hold on to the values of their forefathers, and the young generation, who already affected by the Black Power movement, wants to break the isolation of their town and engage with the bigger political scene. Gender dynamics are also very rigidly defined in Ruby. The women operate under strict patriarchal values, which is also starting to take its toll on the community's sense of well-being. Seventeen miles from Ruby, there is the Convent, which assumes a mission of sheltering injured outcast women who have lost their way. It is inhabited by four female boarders, Mavis, Gigi, Seneca and Pallas, and Consolata, who runs the place. Consolata, who has spent most of her life in the Convent, was taken as a child from the streets of Brazil and brought to the United States by Mary Magna, the Catholic nun who managed the Convent, at that time a Catholic school devoted to the evangelizing of Native American girls. After the Catholic school failed, Consolata and Mary Magna became the only residents of the Convent. Consolata takes care of Mary Magna, grows food to sell to drivers by and the people of Ruby, and opens the door of the Convent to lost and abused women who need care and shelter.

Mavis is first to arrive in the Convent. After accidentally suffocating her newborn twins in the back of her husband's Cadillac, Mavis flees, terrified of the reaction of her abusive husband and her children who she believes are plotting to kill her. Mavis is haunted by the ghosts of

---

4. Toni Morrison, *Paradise* (London: Chatto & Windus, 1998), 5. Subsequent references will appear parenthetically in the text.

her dead twins who she hears laughing and singing all over the Convent. Gigi, who arrives in the Convent next, is also haunted. Gigi, who was part of the Black Power movement, is troubled by the image of a well-dressed boy who was shot during a confrontation between the police and the Black Panthers in Oakland, as he was spitting blood in his hands in an effort not to ruin his shoes. Seneca, whose name suggests Native American origins, is a traumatized twenty years old, who was abandoned by her mother when she was five, and raised in foster homes. Seneca started cutting herself after being sexually abused by one of the boys in the shelter. As an adult, Seneca becomes involved in abusive relationships, with her boyfriend, and with a rich woman who uses her as a sex toy. The last of the women to arrive in the Convent is sixteen years old Pallas. After falling in love with Carlos, the maintenance man at her school and an aspiring sculptor, Pallas leaves the home of her rich father, and goes with Carlos to stay with her mother, a painter who lives in an artist colony. When she discovers her mother and Carlos having an affair, Pallas drives off, and ends up in the Convent after being raped by a group of guys in a truck.

The Convent, which has over the years provided shelter for various members of Ruby's community, gradually starts to represent a place of evil and destruction to the town, because of its female residents' unconventional behavior, as they embody a life style that does not conform to the town's strict politics of respectability. To the people of Ruby, the Convent women are: "go-go girls: pink shorts, skimpy tops, see-through skirts; painted eyes, no lipstick; obviously no underwear, no stockings. Jezebel's storehouse raided to decorate arms, earlobes, necks, ankles and even a nostril" (156–57). The women also challenge the town's religious values: "Before these heifers came to town this was a peaceable kingdom. The others before them at least had some religion. These here sluts out there by themselves never step foot in church and I bet you a dollar to a fat nickel they ain't thinking about one either" (276). The female residents become scapegoats to the men of Ruby who project the failure of their town on them: "If they stayed to themselves, that'd be something. But they don't. They meddle. Drawing folks out there like flies to shit and everybody who goes near them is maimed somehow and the mess is seeping back into *our* homes, *our* families" (276). The Convent, also a refuge to Ruby's women from the heavy patriarchal demands of their town, highlights the failure of the men's ability to shelter their women. Ostensibly, in order to keep their town's utopian morals intact, the men ride out to the Convent and massacre its female residents.

The massacre of the Convent women is reminiscent of the witch-hunts of early European and American history, where women were being executed under the pretext of sexual deviancy and practices of dark magic. Like these early societies, the men of Ruby, uncomfortable with the Convent women's sexuality and ambiguous model of spirituality, accuse them of perversion and satanic practices. They are "obviously not nuns, real or even pretend, but members, it was thought, of some other cult. Nobody knew" (11). The men thus feel justified in their doing. After the shooting, the bodies of the Convent women mysteriously disappear in the surrealist manner of a witch tale, only to reappear in another realm, as spirits, strong and triumphant.

The two communities represent very different models of spirituality. One, male-centered, unaccepting of otherness, and sees violence as a holy act against evil, and the other, represented by the Convent female residents who articulate an inclusive model of spirituality that focuses on psychological healing and inner growth expressed through both Candomblé and Gnosticism. The Convent women, however, do not represent a perfect model of spirituality. In fact, they are far from being perfect. While they are racially diverse and not strictly bound to an institutionalized religion, they are impractical women who have refused to take control of their lives. Whereas Ruby's people, while strictly religious and color-conscious, they are hard working, proud and protective of their community.

Nevertheless, I argue that what sets the two communities apart is Ruby's sacrilegious act of violence against innocent women, which marks Ruby's transformation from a society whose history has symbolized the triumph of the oppressed and the marginalized in the face of racial injustice to a society that perpetuates violence against those who are different. In one of her interviews Morrison states that the question which initiated her novel was "how do fierce, revolutionary, moral people lose it and become destructive, static, performed—exactly what they were running from?"[5]

Through the Convent women, Morrison constructs a specific model of spirituality that challenges the nature of the male god in Judeo-Christianity as wholly good and masculine, evoking archetypal goddesses, ambivalent in character. The dualities of good/evil, body/spirit, and virgin/hag are challenged by the ambivalent feminine principle of ancient religions and early forms of Christianity.

---

5. A. J.Verdelle, "Paradise Found: A Talk with Toni Morrison about Her New Novel," *Essence*, February 1998, 78–79.

MORRISON'S EXPLORATION of the all-black community of Ruby allows her to reflect on the history of colonial America and its white founding fathers. Morrison depicts an all-black community's migration to the West, and their pursuit for new territory. Like the old fathers, who left the South for Oklahoma after Reconstruction when they were reduced from holding positions in office to field labor, their descendants perform a second exodus after World War II when violence against African American war veterans mounted, moving deeper in Oklahoma and founding Ruby. While trying to replicate the legendary exodus of their old fathers, the people of Ruby develop a colonial attitude toward the land. Like white pilgrims, they are determined to lay claim to the land, and create their own utopian community in the American West. They establish their town on land that was previously owned by Native Americans, as they "made their way west of the unassigned lands, south of Logan County, across the Canadian River into Arapaho territory" (14). They spend sixteen months negotiating the right to the land "to finally have it free and clear" (99). The black pilgrims reenact the attitude of white colonialists toward the land, and instead of feeling humbled by the overpowering landscape, they want to conquer it: "Here freedom was a test administered by the natural world that a man had to take for himself every day. And if he passed enough tests long enough, he was king" (99). Their relationship to the landscape reflects a sense of alienation from their culture and past history. Wilderness which once provided for slaves a safe place and a shelter from the eyes of the white slaveholders becomes a place to be conquered by violence.

These black pilgrims also develop a discourse of otherness in relation to Native Americans. Kristin Hunt argues, for example, that "one gets the sense that the Arapaho culture has been lost, conquered and replaced by the black townships and others."[6] However, while hardly visible in the ways of life of the black town, the landscape becomes a constant reminder of their presence in Ruby, and their historical presence in the West. Anna the shopkeeper, for instance, draws on their eternal presence in Ruby: "A mineral scent was in the air, sweeping down from some Genesis time.... The same wind that once lifted streams of Cheyenne/ Arapaho hair also parted clumps of it from the shoulders of bison, telling each when the other was near" (186). Nathan, the oldest male in Ruby, also recalls his conversation with a Native American about the harvest "Was an Indian

---

6. Kristin Hunt, "Paradise Lost: The Destructive Forces of Double Consciousness and Boundaries in Toni Morrison's *Paradise,*" in *Reading under the Sign of Nature: New Essays in Ecocriticism,* ed. John Tallmadge and Henry Harrington (Salt Lake City: University of Utah Press, 2000), 117–27, 120.

come up to me in the bean row. Cheyenne, I believe. The vines were green, tender. The blossoms coming out all over. He looked at the row and shook his head, sorrowful-like. Then he told me too bad the water was bad" (205). Here, the Cheyenne man shows an intimate and well-informed understanding of the landscape and passes his knowledge on to Nathan. Such moments are tragically few in Ruby, however. More often, by keeping the Native Americans' presence to the margins, the people of Ruby parody the West's colonial attitude toward Native American culture.

Morrison also draws on the myth of the Wild West and challenges its traditional representation in the American imagination as an exclusively white world. Through the "imperfect" genealogy of Ruby, a community obsessed with racial purity, Morrison parodies the history of the American West and its attempt to preserve an exclusively white image, overlooking the presence of Native Americans and African Americans. In fact, the genealogy of Ruby shows their racial mixing with Native Americans in the Blackhorses whose name and physical features suggest this connection. William Loren Katz claims that the misrepresentation of the West as entirely white "had no room for people of color and was not subject to Indian claims. But it became the version that ultimately reached hundreds of millions of minds."[7] The experience of the people of Ruby mirrors the experiences of many African American groups who settled in the West and whose experiences have been repressed. Morrison here reasserts the participation of African Americans and Native Americans in the making of the history of the West. Even more, she writes African American presence back into history of the American West even as she also shows how African Americans too participated in erasures of the Native American presence from the West and from America's collective memory.

The all-black families visualize their history and their claim to the land through the lens of the Exodus narrative. Like the Israelites who fled from their enslavement in Egypt, this group of pilgrims leaves the south in search of their own Canaan. When Zechariah, the founding father, is praying for a sign of deliverance, a mystic figure appears to him and leads the group to what will become their first town, Haven. The figure clearly alludes to Moses:

> "He is with us," said Zechariah. "He is leading the way." From then on the journey was purposeful, free of the slightest complaints. Every now

---

7. William Loren Katz, *The Black West: A Documentary and Pictorial History of the African American Role in the Westward Expansion of the United States* (New York: Touchstone, 1996), xiii.

and then the walking man reappeared: along a riverbed, at the crest of a hill, leaning against a rock formation. Only once did someone gather courage to ask Big Papa how long it might take. "This is God's time," he answered. "You can't start it and you can't stop it." (97–98)

Here, The black pilgrims are enacting the dynamics of the Exodus where the claim to the land becomes justified through God's will.

Morrison's use of the Exodus narrative originates from an old black tradition where biblical imagery, especially the Exodus narrative has been employed by African Americans since early slavery. Albert J. Raboteau comments in his "African-Americans, Exodus, and the American Israel" that "no single symbol captures more clearly the distinctiveness of Afro-American Christianity than the symbol of Exodus."[8] It "contradicted the claim made by white Christians that God intended Africans to be slaves. It seemed to prove that slavery was against God's will and that slavery would inevitably end, although the when and the how remained hidden in the divine providence."[9] The black families of Morrison's novel, like many African American groups, took ownership of the Exodus story and found refuge in its biblical imagery. Being identified with Israel and with the Israelites as divine people discarded the racist discourse which justified their oppression in favor of a message of liberation.

Significantly, the biblical story remains highly charged since it is a text that has been appropriated both by black Americans and by white settlers who saw themselves as the Israelites and America as their Canaan. Raboteau explains: "From the earliest days of colonization, white Christians had represented their journey across the Atlantic to America as the exodus of a New Israel from the bondage of Egypt into the Promised Land of milk and honey."[10] The Exodus narrative and its twofold interpretation clearly relates to Morrison's use of dualities to shed light on the paradoxes of America's national discourses. The Exodus narrative becomes fundamentally ambiguous as it is adapted by both the oppressed and the oppressor. For white settlers America was Canaan, while for the enslaved the image was reversed: America was Egypt, the land where they have been enslaved and dehumanized. Raboteau comments: "White Christians saw themselves as the New Israel; slaves identified themselves as the

---

8. Albert J. Raboteau, "African-Americans, Exodus, and the American Israel," in *African-American Christianity: Essays in History*. ed. Paul E. Johnson (Berkeley: University of California Press, 1994), 13.
9. Ibid.
10. Ibid., 9.

old."[11] It is highly ironical to note that while the two communities shared one country and one religion they had two different, if not contradictory views of history. The way each group appropriated the story of Exodus reflects the way each group viewed itself and located itself within American history.

Thus, the Exodus narrative remains inherently problematic. While it contains a message of liberation and deliverance, it inevitably justifies violence and conquest of those who are different. Let's analyze the part of the Exodus story where God warns the Israelites who crossed over into Canaan not to mix with the indigenous people:

> And I will set your bounds from the Red sea even to the sea of the Philistines, and from the desert to the river: for I will deliver the inhabitants of the land into your hand; and you shall drive them out before you. You shall make no covenant with them, nor with their gods. They shall not dwell in your land, lest they make you sin against me: for if you serve their gods, it will surely be a snare to you. (Exodus 23:31–33)

God had also given them the right to cleanse the land through the spilling of blood:

> When the Lord your God shall bring you into the land where you go to possess it, and has cast out many nations before you, the Hittites, and the Girgashites, and the Amorites, and the Canaanites, and the Perizzites, and the Hivites, and the Jebusites, seven nations greater and mightier than you; And when the Lord your God shall deliver them before you; you shall smite them, and utterly destroy them; you shall make no covenant with them, nor show mercy to them. (Deuteronomy 7:1, 2)

The same story is echoed in *Paradise*. In Ruby, nearly a full century after its establishment, the founders' descendants participate in the massacre of those who are different—the Convent women. They justify this act by seeing themselves as the chosen people of God and their violence as an act of moral purification.[12]

---

11. Ibid.

12. The massacre of the Convent women is also reminiscent of a witch-hunt, which Exodus specifically warns about: "Thou shall not suffer a witch to live" (22:18). Jeffrey B. Russell informs us that in the late Middle Ages, this stern passage from Exodus was used to torture and execute women accused of witchcraft, and for the men of Ruby, the Convent women are "bitches more like witches." Jeffrey B. Russell, A *History of Witchcraft: Sorcerers, Heretics, and Pagans* (London: Thames and Hudson, 1980), 276, 53.

Thus, while the Exodus narrative lives in American consciousness as a narrative of resistance to oppression, *Paradise* explores this other façade of the Exodus narrative (seldom talked about) which is how Exodus also represents a narrative of oppression, since the Israelites end up adopting the same attitude as their Egyptian oppressors when they cross to Canaan—the people of Ruby show exactly that. Robert Allen Warrior, who meditates on the implication of the Exodus narrative for Native Americans, states in his essay "A Native American Perspective: Canaanites, Cowboys and Indians" that Native Americans are the Canaanites, about whom Yahweh warns the Israelites:

> As a member of the Osage Nation of American Indians who stands in solidarity with other tribal people around the world, I read the Exodus stories with Canaanite eyes. And, it is the Canaanite side of the story that has been overlooked by those seeking to articulate theologies of liberation. Especially ignored are those parts of the story that describe Yahweh's command to mercilessly annihilate the indigenous population.[13]

Through the lens of Native Americans, the founding fathers were not the oppressed ones, but the oppressor. They did not include other groups in their utopian vision, just as the town of Ruby did not include the Convent women in theirs.

The role the Exodus narrative rhetorics played in distancing Native Americans also led indirectly to a violent process of Christianizing Native American children, which was at the heart of America's colonial enterprise, and an integral step into "civilizing" and "pacifying" Native Americans. Significantly, the Convent which initially used to function as a Catholic school for Native American girls, reflects this reality:

> It was an opportunity to intervene at the heart of the problem: to bring God and language to natives who were assumed to have neither; to alter their deities, their clothes, their minds; to help them despise everything that had once made their lives worthwhile and to offer them instead the privilege of knowing the one and only God and a chance, thereby, for redemption. (227)

---

13. Robert Allen Warrior, "Canaanites, Cowboys and Indians," in *Christianity and Crisis*, September 11, (1989): 261–65, 262.

Morrison's words illuminate on Warrior's discussion about the dilemma Native Americans encounter in situating themselves within a Euro-American nationalist discourse. For Native Americans, the Exodus narrative is clearly a narrative of conquest, and not deliverance.[14]

Warrior insightfully proposes an alternative reading of the Exodus narrative, a reading that puts the story of the Canaanites at its center, rather than suppress it. He argues that the Exodus story should be read as it is, as a narrative of *both* deliverance *and* conquest; the deliverance of the Israelites and the conquest of the Canaanites:

> As long as people believe in the Yahweh of the deliverance, the world will not be safe from Yahweh the conqueror. But perhaps, if they are true to their struggle, people will be able to achieve what Yahweh's chosen people in the past have not: a society of people delivered from oppression who are not so afraid of becoming victims again that they become oppressors themselves, a society where the original inhabitants can become something other than subjects to be converted to a better way of life or adversaries who provide cannon fodder for a nation's militaristic pride.[15]

This unwillingness to deal with the Exodus as both a narrative of deliverance and conquest is at the heart of America's visionary ideals, where the construction of an American national discourse necessarily excludes the histories of its minorities that challenge the Euro-American interpretation of the Exodus story as a narrative of liberation.

Morrison's reconsideration of the concept of utopia or the Promised Land is ultimately a reconsideration of history as a closed territory. Frances Fitzgerald's *Cities on a Hill*—the title of which is taken from John Winthrop's words to the Puritans—investigates the way Americans have consciously continued to build utopian communities four centuries after Winthrop's words. Fitzgerald draws upon America's visionary tradition through a case study of four different groups from the 1970s and the 1980s who set boundaries for themselves and created their own separatist communities. She argues:

---

14. Ironically, the history of the Convent attests to the failure of discourses of conquest. The practices of the Convent women articulate the triumph of Candomblé as an inclusive religion that celebrates elements of African, Native American, and Christian traditions, over an orthodox Judeo-Christian discourse forced on Native American girls. Consolata herself, the Convent leader, who is Brazilian in origins, and whose features suggest a Native American background, transitions from Catholicism to an embracing of her spiritual and magical powers in Candomblé.

15. Warrior, "Canaanites, Cowboys and Indians," 264.

From a European perspective this was an absurd enterprise. Man could change the political system by reform or revolution; he could change the social system by changing the means of production. But he—or she—could not erase history or pull himself up by his own bootstraps. Yet Americans characteristically continued to try. That individuals could start over again, and if necessary reinvent themselves, was one of the great legends of American life.[16]

Like Fitzgerald's communities, Morrison's fictional black families also attempt to reinvent themselves and forge their "promised land" in isolation from others. They create a heroic narrative which celebrates their achievements and suppresses the histories of those who are different. They believe that they are the chosen people of God and use religion to justify their violence against the Convent women.

These utopias are set for failure because they loose the capacity for self-criticism. This is apparent in the relationship between the old and new generations in Ruby. Ruby's elders refuse to listen to the voices of the new generation and want their children to become a replica of themselves, thus loosing all capacity to honestly and openly deal with their own history:

[T]hey pulled their stock of stories tales about the old folks, their grands and great-grands; their fathers and mothers. Dangerous confrontations, clever maneuvers. Testimonies to endurance, wit, skill, and strength. Tales of luck and outrage. But why were there no stories to tell of themselves? About their own lives they shut up. Had nothing to say to pass on. As though past heroism was enough of a future to live by. As though, rather than children, they wanted duplicates. (161)[17]

This black utopia, inspired by the biblical narrative of the Exodus, becomes mythologized, and therefore, impermeable to change or criticism. Instead of dealing with their reality, the black community elevate their history and construct an edited version of it, as in the case of Zechariah, the Morgans' grandfather and the town's founding father. Before reinventing himself, Zechariah was known as Coffee and had a twin brother named Tea. Both twins were made an object of amusement by a group of whites

---

16. Frances Fitzgerald, *Cities on a Hill* (London: Picador, 1987), 23.
17. There are other doubles in the novel: Mavis's baby twins whom she kills by mistake, but who come back and haunt her; Billie Delia, the daughter of the town's schoolteacher who is tormented by her love for two brothers and can never decide which to choose. The duality is also expressed through structure; the novel's last two chapters, for example, are both entitled "Save-Marie."

who asked them to dance. Tea accommodated the whites and danced, unlike Coffee who refused and as a consequence got shot in the foot. Coffee cut all his links with his brother after this incident, and reinvented himself as Zechariah, repressing the memory of his twin forever. The absence of this story from the town's public memory articulates the attitude people of Ruby have about their history, being selective, and only writing a narrative that can glorify their achievements.

Morrison's portrayal of the all-black community becomes a sobering critique of essentialist discourses in the United States, both black and white. By exploring how each group locates itself within American history, Morrison is implicitly questioning the Euro-American official narrative of history even as she also pushes revisionary African American counter-narratives toward greater complexity. The Exodus narrative becomes particularly interesting when one considers the time period the novel ends, which is 1976, the height of Black Power movement which challenges the African American traditional adaptation of the Exodus narrative. The identification with the Israelites is replaced by identification with Egypt (the land of the oppressor) and its civilization. In *Afrocentrism* Stephen Howe argues: "Appropriation of the Exodus narrative, with its liberatory identification with slaves escaping oppression, has now been replaced by a fixation of the supposed glories of pharaonic Egypt–an identification, in effect, with the oppressors."[18] Here again, the ideological line between the oppressed and the oppressor becomes blurred. The attempt to recover Black history and gain pride has developed into the very essentialist concepts Black Nationalism initially condemned. Morrison's community who are proud of their dark skin and who refuse to accept white racism, develop the same strict blood rules as their oppressors and start to look down on those with different skin complexions. They even end up exterminating the neighboring female community, because the women do not share their same values.

In her seminal work, *Playing in the Dark*, Morrison writes:

> I do not want to alter one hierarchy in order to institute another. It is true that I do not want to encourage those totalizing approaches to African-American scholarship which have no drive other than the exchange of dominations—dominant Eurocentric scholarship *replaced* by dominant Afrocentric scholarship.[19]

---

18. Stephen Howe, *Afrocentrism: Mythical Pasts and Imagined Homes* (London: Verso, 1998), 109.

19. Toni Morrison, *Playing in the Dark: Whiteness and the Literary Imagination* (London: Picador, 1993), 8.

In her depiction of Ruby, Morrison intentionally confuses the boundaries of black vs. white, the oppressed vs. the oppressor, and the true believers vs. the nonbelievers. The result is a rich parable of American history: a black utopia that is territorial, color-conscious, lives in fear of miscegenation, and in denial of Native American presence. In her article "The Scripture of Utopia" Patricia Storace writes: "Toni Morrison is relighting the angles from which we view American history, changing the very color of its shadows, showing whites what they look like in black mirrors."[20] Morrison marginalizes whiteness in order to critique an American national discourse and its repression of the African American presence. Morrison begins her novel with "they shoot the white girl first," but withholds the information about which of the Convent women is white. She explains in an interview with Paul Gray published in *Time* magazine her reason behind constructing the Convent women in a way that prevents the reader from identifying their color: "I did that on purpose,'" Morrison says. "I wanted the readers to wonder about the race of those girls until those readers understood that their race didn't matter. I want to dissuade people from reading literature in that way." Then she adds that she wants to make the readers aware that "race is the least reliable information you can have about someone. It's real information, but it tells you next to nothing."[21]

Morrison's concern with creating a language unburdened by racial categories has been one of the focal points of her critical work as well as her fiction. She writes: "The kind of work I have always wanted to do requires me to learn how to maneuver ways to free up the language from its sometimes sinister, frequently lazy, almost always predictable employment of racially informed and determined chains."[22] Morrison writes against an American literary discourse, which, in its attempt to ignore the issue of race, has created a manipulative language which has contributed in enforcing racial boundaries rather than attempting to bridge them. She condemns white American critics in their tendency to assume that race is irrelevant to American literature claiming that a "criticism that needs to insist that literature is not only 'universal' but also 'race free' risks lobotomizing that literature, and diminishes both the art and the artist."[23]

Morrison's "Recitatif" (1983), the only short story ever published by the author, provides a useful comparison to *Paradise* in its racial dynamics

---

20. Patricia Storace, "The Scripture of Utopia," *The New York Review* 14 (1998): 64–69.
21. Morrison, *Playing in the Dark*, 4.
22. Ibid., xiii.
23. Ibid., 12.

and further communicates Morrison's preoccupation with racial representations in literature.[24] The story charts the developing relationship of two friends, Roberta and Twyla, who first meet in an orphanage when they are eight years old. We know that they are from two different races but we do not know which one of them is black and which one is white. Both girls leave the shelter eventually, and keep meeting again in different stages of their lives. While each meeting provides new information and reveals more about the girls' personalities and social status, the reader remains confused as their racial identities remain undisclosed. But after a continuous attempt to code and decode the characters one realizes that perhaps by pulling the reader into this confusion Morrison wants them to free themselves from previous assumptions about race.

Both *Paradise* and "Recitatif" are a meditation on America's racial politics, and remain challenging in the way they disturb the racial boundaries of black/white identities. Morrison continues to push the envelope, writing a parable of cross-racial representation. Her marginalization of whiteness is a sharp criticism of the American national discourse and its suppression of the experiences of its minorities.

DESPITE being overpowered by Ruby's patriarchal system, the women of Ruby are constantly disrupting the town's official male narrative. Their voices allow Morrison to comment on the official discourse of Ruby, and even ridicule it, purposefully filling the gaps left out by the men and creating an alternative version to the town's male-authored narrative. They piece together the fragmented stories and the conflicted versions of the past challenging the men's mythologizing of their history.

Patricia, the schoolteacher, who takes the role of a historian, is constantly faced with silence and resistance from the founding fathers who want to keep their town's heroic narrative intact. The twins Steward and Deacon, for instance, are constantly trying to cover the story of their great grandfather, Zechariah, the founder of the town and Moses-like figure who has been mythologized in the town's official history. Zechariah, who was previously named Coffee, leads the black families in their sacred journey and renames himself after Zechariah, "the witness to whom God and angels spoke on a regular basis" (192), but what remains suppressed of Zechariah's story is that he was once accused of malfeasance in office

---

24. Toni Morrison, "Recitatif," in *Ancestral House: The Black Short Story in the Americas and Europe*, ed. Charles H. Rowell (Boulder, CO: Westview Press, 1995), 422–36, 423.

during Reconstruction, and was "an embarrassment to the Negroes and both a threat and a joke to whites" (302). The town's attempt to control Zachariah's story and construct a heroic version of the past is analogous to the Euro-American nationalist discourse and its control of America's foundation myth.

Another example of the town's attempt to control its official history is the symbolism attached to the town's communal oven. After moving from Haven, the town their forefathers founded, the men disassemble the communal oven that had been once the center of the town's life and take it with them to their new town, Ruby. The Oven is marked with a strict religious motto "Beware the Furrow of His Brow." This motto is a reminder of their forefathers' journey and struggle. The Oven's motto causes a generational debate. The young generation asserts that the Oven's motto should read "Be the Furrow of His Brow" instead of "Beware the Furrow of His Brow," arguing that "No ex-slave would tell us to be scared all the time. To 'beware' God. To always be ducking and diving, trying to look out every minute in case He's getting ready to throw something as us, keep us down" (84). This reaction represents the militant rhetoric of the 1960s where Christian theology was being challenged, and viewed as part of the slaveholder's mentality. The older generation, however, believes that the existing motto preserves the memory of their forefathers, and thus are unprepared to listen to the young generation and seas their ideas as a threat to community's sense of cultural identity. Steward threatens the youngsters: "If you, any one of you, ignore, change, take away, or add to the words on the mouth of that Oven, I will blow your head off just like you was a hood-eye snake" (87).

The desperate attempt of the founders of Ruby to control the Oven's motto expresses their desire to control the town's official history, and protect the official version of the past. The Oven, traditionally a feminine symbol of nurture and womanhood, turns into a masculine and public icon, epitomizing patriarchy and religious intolerance, signaling Ruby's men's desire to control the feminine. Soane, who recalls the women's disproval of the men's attempt to transform the Oven into a public icon, recounts:

> The women nodded when men took the Oven apart, packed, moved, and reassembled it. But privately they resented the truck space give over to it—rather than a few more sacks of seed, rather than shoats or even a child crib. Resented also the hours spent putting it back together—hours that could have been spent getting the privy door on sooner. (103)

Soane criticizes the impracticality of the men's actions, and their rigid attitude toward their history. She comments: "A utility became a shrine" (103), referring to how the Oven which was a symbol of their communal values turned into an empty public icon. Dovey also sheds light on the men's militant attitude in relation to the intergenerational dispute over the Oven's motto. She believes that "'Furrow of His Brow' alone was enough for any age or generation. Specifying it, particularizing it, nailing its meaning down, was futile. The only nailing needing to be done had already taken place. On the cross. Wasn't that so?" (93). Dovey here expresses a better and wiser understanding of her community's history and an interpretation of Christian theology that is based on tolerance and understanding. Yet, within the town's dynamics, where women are not expected to voice their political opinions, the feminine wisdom and knowledge gets lost, and the men of Ruby refuse to listen. The community of Ruby fails to reach integrity because of the suppression of women's voices from the political scene. It is thus ironic to note that Ruby where women's voices remain silenced is named after a woman—again, another empty symbol.

The men also attempt to control the town's genealogy. It is clear that their sense of identity rests on their racial purity and strict rules against miscegenation. The town's citizens are described as "8-R. An abbreviation for eight-rock, a deep deep level in the coal mines" (193). They are a "Blue black people, tall and graceful, whose clear, wide eyes gave no sign of what they really felt about those who weren't 8-rock like them" (193). Their internalized racist ideology is reflected in the way they view those who are not dark skinned, like Patricia. When Patricia's father, Roger, decides to bring her and her mother, Delia, a light-skinned woman he falls in love with, to the town, Steward, one of the leaders of Ruby, contemptuously comments, "He's bringing along the dung we leaving behind" (201). Patricia's father was never forgiven by the black community for betraying the racial code. Patricia knows that Ruby's sense of identity rests on their racial purity. She is aware that they will never accept her because she is the embodiment of what they all fear: the transgression of racial boundaries. This fear of miscegenation echoes that of White America, turning their town into a shadow image of what they really despise.

The men of Ruby develop their strict blood rules as a reaction to the discrimination they experienced during Reconstruction, not only from whites, but also from other light skinned African Americans who looked down on them:

> For ten years they had believed the division they fought to close was

free against slave and rich against poor. Usually, but not always, white against black. Now they saw a new separation: light skinned against black. Oh, they knew there was a difference in the minds of whites, but it had not struck them before that it was of consequence, serious consequence, to negroes themselves. Serious enough that their daughters would be shunned as brides; their sons chosen last; that colored men would be embarrassed to be seen socially with their sisters. (194)

This episode of their history that marked them profoundly and which they coined the "Disallowing" has become mythologized in their collective consciousness and remains central to their sense of identity, turning their dark skin color into a sign of superiority against those who are different.

Patricia realizes to her surprise that to this highly color-conscious male community, women remain their main source of worry since preserving the purity of their black blood can only happen by controlling the women's sexuality. She wonders: "Did they really think they could keep this up? The numbers, the bloodlines, the who fucks who?" (217) The men of Ruby are proud of the fact that ostensibly "there wasn't a slack or sloven woman anywhere in town" (8). Deacon describes their black utopia as a place where women adhere to their traditional roles as housewives: "quiet white and yellow houses full of industry; and in them were elegant black women at useful tasks; orderly cupboards minus surfeit or miserliness; linen laundered and ironed to perfection; good meat seasoned and ready for roasting" (111). This shows that the construction of their utopia is based on a typically patriarchal attitude toward women and explains the threat that they feel from the Convent women who exemplify everything that the men of Ruby despise. They are independent, self-sufficient and they don't need men. They are described by the males of Ruby as "Not women locked safely away from men; but worse, women who chose themselves for company, which is to say not a Convent but a coven" (276).

In contrast with the racially pure people of Ruby, who are highly conscious and proud of their blackness, the Convent women are racially ambiguous. The Convent women also represent a community that is sexually unattached, which further threatens Ruby's moral values which rest on the suppression of their women's sexuality. They are described as "Bodacious black Eves unredeemed by Mary" (18), and their Convent is a place with "not a cross of Jesus anywhere" (7). Deacon, one of Ruby's leaders, once had an affair with Consolata, but now sees her as a "Salome from whom he had escaped just in time" (280). During one of their meetings Consolata bites Deacon's lip and licks the blood from it. As a result, the affair ends as Deacon is revolted, if not threatened, by her aggressive sexuality.

The criticism of the religious outlook of Ruby's males is a criticism of an orthodox Judeo-Christian discourse and its suppression of feminine power, a point that becomes clearer when one considers the counterpoint offered by the Convent community. The men of Ruby refer to the Convent in derogatory terms as a coven. Yet, outside an orthodox Christian discourse a coven is a feminist symbol of women's empowerment that dates back to ancient history where women's spiritual power was recognized, and the feminine principle was embraced and celebrated. Covens are places that emphasize community life and provide a space for female psychological and spiritual growth and transformation.

The Convent/coven, shunned by Ruby's men, becomes a sole shelter for the women of Ruby from the patriarchal setting of their town. Lone Dupres, an older resident of Ruby and the town's once midwife, describes how the women of Ruby are always walking between Ruby and the Convent: "It was women who walked this road. Only women. Never men. For more than twenty years Lone had watched them. Back and forth, back and forth: crying women, staring women, scowling, lip-biting women or women just plain lost" (270). The women walk to the Convent seeking help and comfort. Arnette, distressed by her unwanted pregnancy, delivers her still born in the Convent with the help of its women, Billie Delia, judged by her town because of her light color complexion, only feels comfortable around the Convent women. Sweetie, traumatized and run down by the demands of her sick babies, also walks to the Convent where the women treat her fever. While the convent/coven fulfills a fostering function that Ruby is unable to fulfill for the women, it is also a feminine symbol of nurturing where the women of Ruby like Soane often stop by to buy food supplies homemade and homegrown by Consolata.

The absence of the feminine in Ruby is most expressed through Dovey's imagining of a stranger, who appears one day in the yard of her deserted house, and who she feels she can share her most intimate thoughts with, something she cannot do with her husband: "Thing was, when he came, she talked nonsense. Things she didn't know were in her mind. Pleasures, worries, things unrelated to the world's serious issues. Yet he listened intently to whatever she said. By a divining she could not explain, she knew that once she asked him his name, he would never come again" (92). Dovey's stranger articulates her yearning for intimacy. Her fantasies about the stranger become an escape from the standards of propriety and respectability put on her in Ruby. The Convent women, in contrast, break all rules of respectability. The Convent provides them with a space where they can express their emotions openly, and exhibit a freedom that seems outrageous to the males of Ruby.

MORRISON'S TEXT revises archetypal female goddesses of early Christianity and ancient religions in order to rewrite female spirituality into contemporary religious and social discourses. Significantly, Morrison starts her book with a Gnostic poem delivered in the voice of a female divine power:

> Thunder, Perfect Mind
> For many are the pleasant forms which exist in numerous sins,
> And incontinencies, and disgraceful passions and fleeting pleasures,
> which (men) embrace until they become sober
> And go up to their resting place.
> And they will find me there,
> and they will live,
> and they will not die again.[25]

This poem was found among 52 Gnostic manuscripts at Nag Hammadi in Egypt in 1947. It represents a vision of paradise, a place where the followers of this divine power "will live, and they will not die again." The poem represents a religious discourse which contradicts that of Christianity. The divine power that offers salvation is feminine, and the salvation she suggests does not conform to the Christian concept of salvation, but instead requires the ability to embrace "incontinencies, and disgraceful passions and fleeting pleasures." The material these manuscripts embody ranges from secret gospels, poems, myths of the origins of the universe, and magic. The author, date, and place of composition of this mysterious poem are unknown, but it is generally believed that its cultural milieu is second- or third-century Alexandria. The poem has a riddling nature, expressing ambiguity and narrative indeterminacy in its extensive use of

---

25. Morrison uses these lines in her epigraph to *Paradise*. They are from "Thunder, Perfect Mind," a mysterious poem that has been found among the Nag Hammadi transcripts. Most of the information I cite here about the poem is from *Nag Hammadi, Gnosticism, and Early Christianity*, ed. Charles W. Hedrick and Robert Hodgson (Peabody, MA: Hendrickson, 1986). It is important to note that religious narratives form an important part of Morrison's fiction. For instance, *Jazz*'s epigraph is also extracted from a passage in "Thunder, Perfect Mind," *Beloved*'s epigraph is from Romans 9:25, and *Tar Baby*'s is from 1 Corinthians 1:11.

antithesis and paradoxes. The poem remains difficult to classify as it combines the style of biblical wisdom literature, the paradox of a Greek riddle as well as the self-proclamation style of the Isis aretalogy inscriptions.[26]

There have been many speculations about the identity of the female figure of the poem, but most commentators have agreed that the female figure of the poem represents the Egyptian Goddess Isis. Bentley Layton contends that "the most obvious cross-referent to the persona was Isis—an essentially Egyptian or Egyptianizing feature within Gnostic Sethianism."[27] But he also argues that the language and the style of the poem are very evocative of the Song of Eve: "The true setting of the poem may be a monologue of the saving spiritual principle, spoken from within the body of the fleshy Eve after her separation from the masculine part of the Adam androgyne."[28] Eve, separated from Adam, calls for a vision of paradise which is inclusive of both the masculine and the feminine. Morrison laments Eve's separation from Adam, and reincorporates in her novel, through the voice of the female figure, the feminine principle long absent from the Orthodox Christian discourse. The sin committed by the men of Ruby against the Convent women resides in their suppression of the feminine element.

In Consolata, Morrison creates a female figure who bears the feminine principle. From her humble beginnings as a homeless child who was taken from the streets of Brazil by Mary Magna, Consolata emerges like an ancient goddess with the power of resurrection. Like Christ, Consolata owns the ability to revive the dead by "stepping in," and uses this gift to resurrect Mary Magna: "Stepping in to find the pinpoint of light. Manipulating it, widening it, strengthening it. Reviving it, even rising, her from time to time. And so intense were the steppings in, Mary Magna glowed like a lamp till her very last breath in Consolata's arms" (247). Through Consolata, the ancient goddess materializes from antiquity to reclaim her place within a Judeo-Christian discourse that constructed the divine as a supreme male god.

Here, Morrison also challenges the Christian discourse in its condemnation of women's power. Women who own supernatural powers have

---

26. *"The Thunder: Perfect Mind,"* trans. Anne McGuire, in *Diotima: Material for the Study of Women and Gender in the Ancient World* (CG VI.2: 13,121,32), http://www.stoa.org/diotima/anthology/thunder.shtml.

27. Bentley Layton, "The Riddle of the Thunder (NHC VI, 2): The Function of Paradox in a Gnostic Text from Nag Hammadi," in Hedrick and Hodgson, *Nag Hammadi*, 37–54, quote at 52.

28. Ibid., 53.

been constantly condemned and persecuted as witches by the Church. Consolata struggles with her Catholic upbringing when she realizes she is endowed with magical powers. She is stuck within the dynamics of a religious tradition that only acknowledges male as divinity. When she resurrects Mary Magna, Consolata realizes that "she had practiced, and although it was for the benefit of the woman she loved, she knew it was an anathema, that Mary Magna would have recoiled in disgust and fury knowing her life was prolonged by evil" (247). Consolata wonders why God endows, or rather inflicts, on her such powers: "He was sometimes overgenerous. Like giving satanic gifts to a drunken, ignorant, penniless woman living in darkness unable to rise from a cot to do something useful or die on it and rid the world of her stench" (248). Consolata is torn between her devotion to Catholicism and her reality as someone endowed with supernatural powers that have been exclusively associated in Judeo-Christianity with the male God. Expressions such as "evil" and "satanic," used here by Consolata, express Christianity's radical denunciation of female powers as antithetical to Christian practices.

Outside an orthodox Judeo-Christian discourse, Consolata is a priestess and a healer, who like ancient goddesses owns the power and wisdom which enable her to cure others. Her spiritual powers allow her to save the traumatized Convent women from their hollow existence. Under her guidance, they undergo a ritualistic process which enables them to deal with their traumatic experiences. When Soane visits them from Ruby she notices the crucial difference:

> [T]he charged air of the house, its foreign feel and a markedly different look at the tenants' eyes—sociable and connecting when they spoke to you, otherwise they were still and appraising . . . how calmly themselves they seemed. And Connie—how straight-backed and handsome she looked . . . unlike some people in Ruby, the Convent women were no longer haunted. (266)

Consolata resembles the divine mother in Gnosticism that Elaine Pagels describes in her much celebrated work *The Gnostic Gospels* as the one who "enlightens human beings and makes them wise."[29] Consolata embraces the traumatized women and helps them heal their emotional wounds. This again conjures an important element of ancient religions where the emphasis is on inner growth and transformation. Pagels argues

---

29. Elaine Pagels, *The Gnostic Gospels* (1979; London: Penguin, 1990), 141.

that many Gnostic Christians, unlike Orthodox Christians, insisted that "ignorance, not sin, is what involves a person in suffering. The Gnostic movement shared certain affinities with contemporary methods of exploring the self through psychotherapeutic techniques. Both Gnosticism and psychotherapy value above all, knowledge—the self-knowledge which is insight."[30] When Mavis, one of the women taking shelter in the Convent arrives, she was surprised by the isolation of the place. She asks Consolata: "'You ain't scared to be out here all by yourselves?' Connie laughed: 'Scary things not always outside. Most scary things inside'" (39).

Consolata's philosophy of looking inwards sharply contrasts the territorial attitude of Ruby's males, where the main approach is to conquer land and acquire property. This statement encapsulates one of the main conflicts between male and female-centered religions. Judeo-Christianity belongs to a monotheistic tradition rooted in violence and conquest. Robert Allen Warrior's interpretation of the Exodus story earlier problematizes this very issue, referring to the God of the Old Testament as "God the conqueror."[31]

The character of Consolata allows Morrison to introduce a different interpretation of Christianity—one in which women have played an important part since its early existence. Pagels claims that the early Christian movement showed certain openness to women, but this situation was overturned in a remarkably short period of time, disappearing completely by the second century. She contends that among certain Gnostic groups "women were considered equal to men; some were revered as prophets; others acted as teachers, travelling evangelists, healers, priests, perhaps even bishops. . . . But from the year 200, we have no evidence for women taking prophetic, priestly, and Episcopal roles among orthodox churches.'"[32]

Consolata, like ancient goddesses, undercuts the duality of Christianity that restricted women to the idealizing passive image of the virgin mother or its shadow-image of the immoral hag. These two extremes of female representations, both disempowering to women, are at the core of orthodox Christianity. Consolata talks about her Catholic education and the Reverend Mother who taught her to suppress her sexuality: "a woman who teach me my body is nothing my spirit everything" (263). It is ironic that Mary Magna who teaches Consolata to despise her body, is clearly seduced by nine-year-old Consolata's physical beauty when she first sees

---

30. Ibid., 133.
31. Warrior, "Canaanites, Cowboys and Indians," 262.
32. Pagels, *The Gnostic Gospels*, 81.

her in the streets of Brazil, and that becomes the main reason she chooses to take her with her to the United States: "She had fallen in love with Consolata. The green eyes? The tea-colored hair? maybe her docility? Perhaps her smoky, sundown skin?" (223).

It is only when Consolata meets Deacon Morgan that she starts to struggle with the body/spirit dichotomy that Mary Magna instilled in her: "I agreed her until I met another. My flesh so hungry for itself it ate him" (263). Consolata refers to her love affair with Deacon, and the way her sexuality, repressed for too long by her Christian education, turned aggressive. As noted earlier, Consolata bit Deacon on the lip until he bled and that marked the end of their affair. Consolata instructs the women in the Convent near the end of Morrison's tale: "Hear me, listen. Never break them in two. Never put one over the other. Eve is Mary's mother. Mary is the daughter of Eve" (263). Consolata here, like the Eve and Isis of "Thunder, Perfect Mind," insists on the merging of the two opposite images of soul and body associated with Christian tradition. Jeffrey B. Russell's study of the symbolism of the feminine element in Christianity explains that

> Christianity traditionally found it difficult to accept the principle of ambivalence in the deity: the Christian God was wholly good and wholly masculine, excluding both the feminine principle and the principle of evil. Repression of the principle of evil from the godhead led to the development of the concept of the Devil. Repression of the feminine principle produced a new ambivalence of idealization and contempt.[33]

Through Consolata, who expresses her opposition to this dividing of womanhood, the novel ruptures the dualistic oppositions associated with the perception of the sinning flesh and the immaculate soul in Christianity.

While Morrison interrogates masculinist discourses and the way they suppress the feminine, she does not suggest a notion of utopia that excludes men, but rather a notion of utopia that includes both. Consolata feels powerful only when she becomes androgynous. The mystical male figure that appears to Consolata in the Convent bears a striking physical resemblance to her, the tea-colored hair, and the distinguished green eyes. Morrison describes his appearance:

> Not six inches from her face, he removed his tall hat. Fresh, tea-colored hair came tumbling down, cascading over his shoulders and down his

---

33. Russell, *A History of Witchcraft*, 117–18.

back. He took off his glasses then and winked, a slow seductive movement of a lid. His eyes, she saw, were as round and green as new apples. (252)

Consolata's experience with her double recalls Dovey's relationship with her stranger. In both cases, the women feel accepted and connected. When Consolata asks her stranger who he is, he answers: "Come on girl you know me" (252). The stranger is her masculine side, and when she recovers him she feels strong and complete in nature just like the divine of early Christianity. In the language of the Gnostics, Consolata bears the dyadic nature of God. Pagels claims that "since the Genesis account goes on to say that humanity was created 'male and female' (1:27), some concluded that the God in whose image we are made must also be both masculine and feminine—both father and mother."[34] It is this vision of utopia that Morrison embraces: a vision of spirituality that does not exclude either. The mysterious man is Adam of Eve's laments in the "Thunder, Perfect Mind" poem.

After this encounter, Consolata becomes powerful and strong enough to instruct the Convent women, and leads them into a ritual to exorcise their painful pasts. The women find it difficult to recognize the androgynous Consolata "who has the features of dear Connie, but they are sculpted somehow—higher cheekbones, stronger chin. Had her eyebrows always been that thick" (262). Following Consolata's instructions the Convent women dance all night. Through their dancing they reach an ecstatic state symbolic of their recovery. They attain self-knowledge or what the Gnostics call gnosis, which contains a major belief that remains antithetical to the institutional church's understanding of a chasm separating God from humanity. Gnostics believe that knowledge comes from within, and that the psyche bears within itself the potential for liberation or destruction.[35]

---

34. Pagels, *The Gnostic Gospels*, 72.
35. For more details about the Gnostic concept of salvation, see Pagels's *The Gnostic Gospels*. Pagels writes that "the conviction of whoever explores human experience simultaneously discovers divine reality is one of the elements that marks Gnosticism as a distinctly religious movement" (141). See also Josephine Donovan, *Gnosticism in Modern Literature: A Study of the Selected Works of Camus, Sartre, Hesse, and Kafka* (London: Garland, 1990). Gnostics, according to Donovan, believe that they belong to the realm of good or the transcendent realm, but they exist in an evil world. They feel displaced from their original world, but it is this transcendent part of their beings or "pneuma" that identifies them as beings from another world or "The Transcendent Kingdom." Donovan compares Gnosticism to Existentialism as both view humans as "fundamentally alienated: The Gnostics perceived them as thrown into a world controlled by archons; Existentialists saw them as thrown into the alienating clutches of bureaucracy or into a state of tyranny under the mores of what Heidegger called ads Man. In each vision humanity has

DURING THE 1980s Toni Morrison visited Brazil to learn about the religious practices of Candomblé, an Afro-Brazilian religion which first emerged in the era of slavery and syncretizes elements of African belief systems, Catholicism and Native American traditions. While she was there, she heard a story which turned out to be untrue about a community of black nuns who were murdered by a group of men because they were practicing Candomblé. Her trip suggests a link between the rituals practiced by the Convent women and the African-Brazilian religion. The story of the black nuns certainly resembles *Paradise*'s plot: that is, a female community with ambiguous religious beliefs massacred by a self-righteous Christian male community. Although the story was untrue, the violence it expresses certainly reflects the reality of Candomblé in Brazil, a religion that endured a history of persecution and condemnation by the Catholic Church and the State, which viewed Candomblé practices as dark magic. Rachel E. Harding reports that during the nineteenth century "authorities regularly conducted raids against black religio-cultural gatherings, often breaking or burning any ritual items they discovered and jailing participants or impressing them into military service."[36] The police harassment of Candomblé practitioners continued until mid-twentieth century. According to Brumana and Martinez, "Umbanda, together with Candomblé and the other Afro-Brazilian cults, suffered the greatest persecutions at the same time as the Brazilian Left."[37]

The religious dynamics between the Community of Ruby and the Convent women also alludes to the dynamics in Brazilian society between Catholicism and Candomblé. David J. Hess, who explores the polarities of the religious system in Brazil in *Samba in the Night,* writes:

> [a]t the European (white, privileged) end of the spectrum, the Catholic Church hierarchy (priests, bishops, and so forth) is still the province of men. At the African (black, underprivileged) end of the spectrum, women are usually the only mediums (the mothers-of-the-saints) in the most orthodox of Yoruba or Nago Candomblés. Thus, in the most general sense, the Brazilian religious system might be pictured as having two poles—a male, European, elite religion (Catholicism) versus a female, African, popular religion (Candomblé).[38]

---

been uprooted from the ground of meaning; each urges that it be re-rooted in a sacred ground" (7).

36. Rachel E. Harding, *A Refuge in Thunder: Candomblé and Alternative Spaces of Blackness* (Bloomington: Indiana University Press, 2000), 64.

37. See Fernando Giobellina Brumana and Elda Gonzales Martinez, *Spirits from the Margin: Umbanda in Sao Paulo* (Uppsala: Uppsala University, 1989), 295.

38. David J. Hess, *Samba in the Night: Spiritism in Brazil* (New York: Columbia University

Morrison's novel expresses similar polarities between the male community of Ruby and the Covent women, not in terms of racial categories (white vs. black) but in terms of the power dynamics between Ruby which represents a male, elite institutionalized religion, as opposed to the Convent women who represent an underprivileged uninstitutionalized female African-based belief system.

The Convent women, under the leadership of Consolata, undergo rituals reminiscent of Candomblé, a religion that also has women at its axis. Although the rituals of Candomblé can be both male and female directed, Candomblé remains a female-centered religion. Women were the first establishers of Candomblé temples in Brazil in the early nineteenth century, and the majority of temples are still run by women.[39] The priestesses or (mae-de-santo) "represent the principal line of communication between the material world of mortals and the spiritual world of deities."[40] Morrison's Consolata takes the role of mother-of-saints when she initiates the Convent women. Their initiation is similar to the initiation ceremony of Candomblé, where the initiates isolate themselves for months to get prepared to meet the gods or the orixas. Consolata tells the Convent women "stay here and follow me. Someone could want to meet you" (262), preparing them to meet the orixas.

After meeting the orixas, the women undergo a trance-like state reminiscent of Candomblé possession, collectively facing and exorcising their pain: "In loud dreaming, monologue is no different from a shriek; accusations directed to the dead and long gone are undone by murmurs of love. So, exhausted and enraged, they rise and go to their beds vowing never to submit to that again but knowing full well they will. And they do" (264). Mavis, haunted for so long by her twins, finally faces the fact that they are dead. Gigi, traumatized by the memory of the boy who was shot in the demonstration, symbolically witnesses the cleansing of his shirt in the dream. Seneca makes peace with her past of abandonment and stops cutting herself, and Pallas, who got pregnant after her gang rape, finally accepts her pregnancy and holds her son in the dream. Their Candomblé initiation ends with dancing, a crucial part of Candomblé ceremonies

---

Press, 1994), 144. Hess also looks at the issue of sexuality in both religions and argues: "The fathers of the Catholic priesthood are unmarried (as are gay men), whereas the women of Candomblé s are referred to as 'mothers- of-saints, a term that suggests procreation and therefore heterosexuality" (145).

39. Robert A. Voeks reports that the first houses of Candomblé were established by three freed African Nigerian women, and were dedicated to Yoruba gods and goddesses. See Robert A. Voeks, *Sacred Leaves of Candomblé: African Magic, Medicine, and Religion in Brazil* (Austin: University of Texas Press, 1997), 63.

40. Voeks, *Sacred Leaves of Candomblé*, 51.

where the possessed incarnate the deity's energy through dancing.[41] The Convent women become "holy women dancing in hot sweet rain" (283), and when they return to the house they are "tired from their night dance, but happy" (284).

Morrison engages with Candomblé as a female-centered religion to create an alternative space for female spirituality. Unlike men, women in Candomblé occupy the most important positions that demand spiritual maturity. Joseph Murphy writes: "The Candomblé belief is that men have 'hot blood.' They have neither the patience to submit to discipline of Candomblé, nor the control of their passions necessary to incarnate the spirits."[42] This is a religious discourse that contradicts Christian discourse drastically. The notion of women as the weaker sex who is not fit for priesthood is turned upside down and replaced by a discourse that does not only inserts women as equal to males but rather, favors the feminine.

Through Candomblé, Morrison is also conjuring an African diaspora religion which has developed as one of the major religious and cultural expressions of the Afro-Atlantic Diaspora. It incorporates elements of both African beliefs and Christianity, and expresses the triumph of syncretism against the intolerant policies of Catholicism. Candomblé survived the pressure of white dominant culture, and succeeded in preserving the link with West African traditions and rituals. Yet, this religion, a model of cultural continuity with Africa is scorned by the people of Ruby who adopt a colonial attitude toward the Convent women's practices and deem them as black magic. The people of Ruby are unwilling to engage with Africanist cultural and political discourses. They are, for instance, intolerant of the young generation who identifies with the Black Power movement. Patricia, the school teacher, tells Reverend Misner: "I just don't believe some stupid devotion to a foreign country—and Africa is a foreign country, in fact it's fifty foreign countries—is a solution for these kids" (210). Soane expresses a similar sense of disconnection, as Africa for her is "the seventy-five cents she gave to the missionary society collection. She had the same level of interest in Africans as they had in her: none." The community of Ruby, in their isolation, refuse to acknowledge a connection to Africa as their ancestral home and refuse to envisage their history within the larger context of the African diaspora.

---

41. Voeks contends that "the most intimate ritual act is that of being possessed by the spiritual force of the orixa, of making this energy manifest by incarnating it in one's flesh; dancing for and as an orixa" (*Sacred Leaves of Candomblé*, 124).

42. Joseph Murphy, *Working the Spirit: Ceremonies of the African Diaspora* (New York: Beacon Press, 1995), 53.

Morrison's engagement with African Diaspora traditions and discourses articulates the place Africa occupies in the African American consciousness, both as an actual place and as a symbol. It is significant to note that as the community of Ruby took their journey from the south to Oklahoma to found a home after Reconstruction, other African Americans were heading to Africa, from Oklahoma. The black families of Ruby surely must have been aware of this, but perhaps chose to suppress it from the town's official narrative. William Loren Katz reports that while "between 1890 and 1910, thirty black communities were formed in Oklahoma, the state's total black population rising by 537 percent to 137,000 people," by 1891 many blacks were under white threat to leave their Oklahoma communities, and started to head toward Africa: "It was paradoxical that as black people poured into Oklahoma others already there were forming Africa societies and preparing to leave for Africa," which they perceived as their homeland.[43] Katz informs us that "some black families sold their land for a fraction of its value, camped near the railroad stations, and began a vigil for the trains that would carry them to New York City and the ships for Africa."[44] He reports that the flight from the South to Oklahoma and Africa "was basically a response to white racism rather than a carefully reasoned nationalist movement."[45]

By reclaiming Candomblé in her exploration of African American cultural and historical identity, Morrison is drawing the link between Afro-Brazilian and African American diasporic experiences. The novel expresses this through Consolata's meeting with the people of Ruby and with Deacon. When she first visits the town and sees their celebrations, it reminds her of her childhood home, Brazil:

> A memory of just such skin and just such men, dancing with women in the streets to music beating like an infuriated heart, torsos still, hips making small circles above legs moving so rapidly it was fruitless to decipher how such ease was possible. . . . And although they were living here in a hamlet, not in a loud city full of glittering black people, Consolata knew she knew them. (226)

Consolata feels the same toward Deacon. She is attracted to him partly because of the familiarity of his skin color and his movements. She feels that being with him is being "home." She tells Mary Magna: "He and I

---

43. Katz, *The Black West*, 249–52.
44. Ibid., 254.
45. Ibid., 249–50.

are the same" (241). Again, this shows how Consolata recognizes a diasporic connection that the community of Ruby is not capable of. The Gnostic poem in the epigraph provides a framework for Morrison's utopian engagement with Africa. While the poem in its multiple religious discourses is symbolic of the relationship between different cultures, it also evokes Africa, since the poem was located in Egypt and refers to an Egyptian divine power.

Morrison's engagement with Gnosticism and Candomblé elevates these traditions and strategically position them as models of women's empowerment. Through Gnosticism, Morrison creates a female community which exemplifies the power of the feminine principle in its spirituality, tolerance, and regeneration. However, many scholars argue that early Christianity has been rather idealized in contemporary literature. According to Michael Allen Williams in *Rethinking "Gnosticism,"* this generalized view of Gnosticism as female-centered is not justified by any ancient self-definition. Gnosticism according to Williams is an umbrella term that has been used in scholarly research and popular culture to invoke a rather romanticized image of a pre-Christian tradition.[46] While on the surface, this might suggest that Morrison's novel appeals to an idealized construction of Gnosticism and elevates Gnostic literature without fully engaging with it, a close reading shows that Morrison's engagement with Gnosticism is strategic. It highlights the problematics of an orthodox Christian discourse that does not open up a space for women's spirituality in its full potential, especially as it relates to the moral dichotomies of Christian tradition that reduce women's nature to the virgin or the hag opposition. The goddesses of ancient times, either real or imagined, need to be reincarnated and incorporated into our religious and social lives.

Candomblé, which is also equally strategically constructed as a model of racial and cultural hybridity in the novel, is also questionable as a model of cultural hybridity in the light of its historical development, especially that the cultural syncretism in Candomblé was, in so many ways forced, since "first, the actors [Africans] were unwilling participants in the migration, and second, cultural retention occurred both in spite and partly as a result of barriers to diffusion that were erected by European society."[47] The merging of Catholic and African divinities was, rather, an attempt by enslaved Africans to survive the pressure of the New World. This shows that the process of interaction and the juxtaposition of Euro-

---

46. Michael Allen Williams, *Rethinking "Gnosticism": An Argument for Dismantling a Dubious Category* (Princeton, NJ: Princeton University Press, 1996), 53.
47. Voeks, *Sacred Leaves of Candomblé*, 63.

pean and African cultures in the model of Candomblé is not a process of mutual and harmonious syncretism, but a one-sided attempt from the non-white underprivileged.

Even the nature of syncretism in Candomblé can be questioned as superficial, since archetypal similarities between the orixas and the Catholic saints have been purely a matter of coincidence. In fact, most Candomblé priests, well-educated adherents, and intellectuals view this juxtaposition of religious images as a historically necessary inconvenience. Voeks reports that "such followers contend that, for political motives as well as to maintain religious orthodoxy, the black gods and white saints must be maintained in a state of spiritual segregation."[48] The symbiosis in Candomblé between Africanist and Christian symbols and images can also be seen as the triumph of the Catholic Church in implementing Christian values among the Afro-Brazilian population. The Catholic Church historically showed a calculated tolerance toward "anti-religious" rituals in its conversion policies through a gradual acculturation into Christianity. This is quite apparent in relation to Candomblé, where most adherents see themselves both as Candomblé followers and good Catholics. They attend both the Sunday mass and Candomblé ceremonies, and do not see any contradiction at all in the way they view their orixas, and in many Candomblé terrieros "baptism into the Catholic faith is a pre-requisite of initiation into Candomblé."[49]

Again, though, whether the process of syncretism was forced or spontaneous, Candomblé as a creolized religion provides a strategic model of openness that is lacking in the Judeo-Christian model exhibited by the males of Ruby. The closed-mindedness of the people of Ruby led to an attitude of self-righteousness that ended up being destructive to them and to others. Morrison's intellectual engagement with Candomblé and Gnosticism suggests a model of cultural and religious hybridity that shows diversity and openness toward others, a model much needed in contemporary American society.

Morrison's *Paradise* includes powerful archetypal Goddess-like figures, blurring them into one another, and reincorporating them against the image of a supreme male God. The novel ends with a vision of paradise where Consolata is resting on the beach with her head on Piedade's lap: "In ocean hush, a woman black as firewood is singing. Next to her is a younger woman whose head rests on the singing woman's lap" (318). This vision evokes the iconic image of the Pietà or Piety (Piedade in Portu-

---

48. Ibid., 61.
49. Ibid.

guese), which displays Jesus in Mary's arms after his crucifixion. In Morrison's rendition, the mother and son image is replaced by a mother and daughter—Consolata in Piedade's arms. The association with the ocean, the ships and the shores suggests Piedade's connection with the Candomblé Goddess, Yemanja, the patron of the sea and the protector of ships and fishermen, and with the Virgin Mary, another manifestation of Yemanja in Candomblé. Piedade, whom Morrison also describes as "black as firewood" (318), alludes to the Egyptian goddess Isis.

This vision where Yemanja, the Virgin Mary, and Isis are blurred suggests another level of syncretism across religious traditions with a focus on the feminine as a common bond. Morrison said that she intended the final word of the novel to be "paradise" with a lower case "p" and asked the publisher to make the correction for later editions. She reports: "I wanted the book to be an interrogation of the idea of paradise and . . . to move it from its pedestal of exclusion and to make it more accessible to everybody."[50] Morrison proposes a vision of paradise as an "earthly home" that is accessible to everyone, where: "sea trash gleams. Discarded bottle caps sparkle near a broken sandal. A small dead radio plays the quiet surf" (318). This far from idealistic description of the beach articulates Morrison's idea of paradise as an earthly place, rather than a "heavenly place." The beauty of Morrison's paradise is transmitted through its contradictory images, mundane and imperfect, and through its accessibility to everyone: "passengers, lost and saved" (318). The description echoes the vision of paradise in the Gnostic poem in the epigraph—a vision articulated by a female power in which paradise is a place where women's ambivalence is embraced.

---

50. Timehost, "Toni Morrison," transcript from January 21, 1998, http://www.time.com/time/community/transcripts/chattr012198.html, 6 (accessed December 19, 2000).

4

Conjuring History

The Meaning of Witchcraft in Maryse Condé's
I, Tituba, Black Witch of Salem

> "Hester interrupted me, aware of the tremor in my voice. 'What's this story you are telling me, Tituba? Isn't it yours? Tell me!' But something stopped me from confiding in her." [Hester m'interrompit, consciente de l'angoisse de ma voix: qu'elle histoire me racontes-tu là, Tituba? N'est-ce pas la tienne? Dis-moi? Dis-moi? Mais Quelque chose me retint de me confier.][1]
>
> —Maryse Condé, *I, Tituba, Black Witch of Salem*

MARYSE CONDÉ'S *I, Tituba, Black Witch of Salem* (1992) is a fictional account of the slave Tituba who was accused and tried for witchcraft during the famous Salem witch trial of 1692. The novel is set in the seventeenth century, and explores Tituba's life journey: first, her early life in Barbados, then her deportation to the Massachusetts colony in New England, and finally, her return to her homeland. The historic Tituba played a central role in the Salem witch trials. She was the first to declare her involvement in witchcraft practices in the community, and her confession launched one of the worst witch cases in early American history. However, despite the large quantity of literature produced on the witches of Salem, Tituba is barely mentioned in most scholarly accounts.[2] Tituba's

---

1. My translation.
2. A 1996 historical study by Elaine G. Breslaw, who reexamines the role of Tituba in the Salem trials, explains that Tituba's absence from historical records "stems from the dearth of

absence from historical records provides the basis for Condé's project, as she reports in an interview with Françoise Pfaff: "When the witch craze in Salem dissolved, a general pardon was granted to the accused, their possessions were returned to them, and their names were cleared, except for Tituba. We don't know what happened to Tituba after she left prison. It is believed that she was sold to pay for expenses incurred during her incarceration."[3]

A first attempt to record Tituba's story was carried out by the African American writer Ann Petry in *Tituba of Salem Village* (1964), a children's book which represents Tituba as an intelligent and persevering slave who uses her magical powers to fight oppression.[4] Unlike Condé, who wanted to explore Tituba's life, the value of Petry's novel lies in her attempt to provide a role model for young people. However, despite the differences between Petry and Condé's projects, they both use the historical Tituba as the basis for their texts and both attempt in their accounts to empower Tituba, and give her a voice against her effacement from history.

Tituba's historical confession provides the factual ground for Condé's project. In her trial Tituba tells an extraordinary story of consorting with the devil; she describes a coven in Boston, and talks about witches flying on broomsticks, manipulating her audience through her deployment of Puritan imagination. Tituba's extraordinary testimony—which turned her from a scapegoat to a central figure in the expanding prosecution of Salem—allows Condé to reflect on the concept of confession inherent in Christian discourse, and examine the politics of race, class and gender involved in Tituba's testimony.

Condé's account gives Tituba the chance to tell her "true" story, as opposed to the confession in the documents of her deposition. Tituba supposedly shares her fictional/personal "confession" with Condé, as the latter makes apparent in the preface, "Tituba and I lived for a year on

---

useful, direct information about her. Historians need reliable written, artifactual, or statistical evidence with which they can detail events or on which to base their conclusions. The absence of reliable resources often means that a particular potentially significant element has to be omitted from a study. Such has been the case for most of the underclass in history, particularly women, Africans, and American Indians." Elaine G. Breslaw, *Tituba, Reluctant Witch of Salem: Devilish Indians and Puritan Fantasies* (New York: New York University Press, 1996), xx.

3. Françoise Pfaff, *Conversations with Maryse Condé* (Lincoln: University of Nebraska Press, 1991), 60. In the same interview Condé reports how she came across Tituba's story by coincidence while undertaking research at the University of California library. She says: "I was unaware of her existence and asked about her, but I didn't find anything because nobody seemed to know her. There were historians at the institution where I was teaching at the time, but they didn't know about Tituba and were not the least bit interested in her" (58).

4. Ann Petry, *Tituba of Salem Village* (1964; New York: Harper Trophy, 1991).

the closest of terms. During our endless conversations she told me things she had confided to nobody else" [Tituba et moi, avons vécu en étroite intimité pendant un an. C'est au cours de nos interminables conversations qu'elle m'a dit ces choses qu'elle n'avait confiées à personne].[5] Here Condé becomes Tituba's confidant and the only one who knows Tituba's "true" story.

The autobiographical narrative allows Tituba to become both the narrator and the narrated, speaking directly to readers, and establishing a close intimacy with them, but it also poses the question as to whether the reader can fully trust Tituba's voice, since Tituba's autobiography may be read simply as another "confession" that is meant to manipulate the readers. I will argue that there is both a serious treatment and an undercutting of Tituba through confession. While the confessional narrative seems to reinforce Tituba's credibility, it simultaneously allows Condé to interrogate religious, racial, and historical discourses, as well as question the production of ethnicity in contemporary cultural politics by freely playing on stereotyped notions of identity.

I, Tituba provides an ambiguous model of spirituality that allows for a continuous interrogation of religious beliefs and the way they interact with gendered and racial discourses. The novel does not commit to a specific notion of religiosity, and registers a poignant criticism by playing on clichéd images of black female spirituality. While Condé celebrates Tituba's witchcraft–her magical powers, her gift of healing, her communication with the ancestral spirits—as a model of African diaspora religiosity, she is also repeating clichés about black female spirituality. Through Tituba, Condé is dealing with a complex historical character. The seventeenth-century Tituba, a Christianized Indian whose use of magic was European white magic taught to her by her English mistress, reappears in twentieth-century fiction as a black Voodoo priestess.

This model of spirituality allows Condé to interrogate the representation of ethnicity in self-referential genres of contemporary writing, and to play on the banal preconceptions of the ethnic that those who are marginal to mainstream Western culture are expected to conform to and exhibit. Yet, while on the surface Tituba seems to be displaying her otherness for

---

5. Except for the quote in note 1, all references to the novel in English translation are from the following edition: Maryse Condé, *I, Tituba, Black Witch of Salem*, trans. Richard Philcox (Charlottesville: University of Virginia Press, 1992). References to the novel in the original French, enclosed in brackets, are from the following edition: Maryse Condé, *Moi, Tituba, sorcière . . . noire de Salem* (Paris: Mercure de France/Folio Series, 1988). Subsequent references to the English and French editions of the novel will appear parenthetically in the text.

her Western audience, a detailed reading of the text shows that Tituba resists this stereotyped view of her as the other.

To highlight the novel's resistance to performing ethnicity, I use Rey Chow's critique, *The Protestant Ethnic and the Spirit of Capitalism,* which explores productionism in contemporary cultural/ethnic politics and looks at the politics of cross-ethnic representation. In a section entitled "I Confess, Therefore I am," Chow discusses the turn toward the ethnic self as a form of production. The continuous staging of the ethnic self in contemporary cultural politics, according to Chow, takes the form of confessions through self-referential genres such as autobiographies, memoirs, diaries and journals. She argues that the tendency toward self-referential genres indicates the change in the ethics of representation. Self-referentiality is seen as a way out of the problems associated with representing others or "speaking for" them. Thus, the turn toward the self, according to Chow, becomes the only "appropriate" form of representation. She contends that "self-referentiality has increasingly acquired legitimacy as a resistive, liberatory, and thus corrective form of discourse (aimed at setting us free from the fetters of conventional representation)."[6] Yet, the turn toward the self as the only legitimate form of representation is highly problematic. She argues that "the self and the so-called freedom that comes with it, a freedom that is always imagined as freedom from power and from domination, are, strictly speaking, effects of power."[7] Thus, the insistence on self-referential genres as liberatory needs to be questioned and the phenomenon of ethnic minorities turning to self-referentiality needs to be seen and understood within these power relations. Accordingly, Chow writes:

> Resorting to the self-referential gesture as an ethnic and/ or sexual minority is often tantamount to performing a confession in the criminal as well as noncriminal sense: it is to say, "Yes, that's me," to a call and a vocation—"Hey, Asian!" "Hey, Indian!" "Hey, gay man!"—as if it were a crime with which one has been charged; it is to admit and submit to the allegations (of otherness) that society at large has made against one. Such acts of confession may now be further described as a socially endorsed, coercive mimeticism, which stipulates that the thing to imitate, resemble, and become is none other than the ethnic or sexual minority herself. When minority individuals think that, by referring to themselves, they are liberating themselves from the powers that subor-

---

6. Rey Chow, *The Protestant Ethnic and the Spirit of Capitalism* (New York: Columbia University Press, 2002), 113.

7. Ibid.

dinate them, they may actually be allowing such powers to work in the most intimate fashion—from within their hearts and souls, in a kind of voluntary surrender that is, in the end, fully complicit with the guilty verdict that has been declared on them socially long before they speak.[8]

Chow's argument, which addresses the complexity and problematics of cross-ethnic representation, or what Chow calls "coercive mimeticism," allows for a different reading of Tituba's historical confession. A reading that takes into consideration the power dynamics involved in self-representation, and questions the mechanisms by which we read the ethnic other. Tituba's highly complex and sophisticated use of language in her actual confession provides the basis for Condé's aesthetics of narration. Like Tituba's confession, Condé's language remains elusive, showing how the text can mean more than one thing at a time.

Tituba manipulates the law and the judges in her trial. She responds positively to the accusations. Her confession expresses her acculturation to Puritan thought, and how she uses the Puritan imagination to manipulate her audience. Yet, what makes Tituba's testimony believable is her status as an outsider to Puritan culture. Breslaw contends: "Puritans were predisposed to believe that Indians willingly participated in Devil worship. That perception of Indians as supporters of the devil encouraged Tituba to fuel their fantasies of a diabolical plot."[9] Tituba as the other is already associated in the Puritan mind with the devil, and her confession only worked to reinforce their prejudice about the connection of otherness with witchcraft. Paradoxically, it is her acculturation to Puritan thoughts which allows her to manipulate the fears of the Puritan community and influence the Salem trial. Tituba here produces an image of herself that has nothing to do with her reality. Breslaw argues against some earlier historians who have suggested the lack of coherence in Tituba's confession. Breslaw judges that Tituba's confession

> was a carefully crafted tale that provided satisfactory answers to the questions in the seventeenth-century mind. Tituba explained the cause of the calamities. She also created a new aura of mystery about events of Salem. The more credulous the magistrates appeared to be, the more richly embroidered the tale became. The reluctant witch has captured her audience.[10]

---
8. Ibid., 115.
9. Breslaw, *Tituba, Reluctant Witch*, xx.
10. Ibid., 115.

The complexity with which Tituba displays her ethnicity in her confession allows Condé to capture her ambivalence and create a multilayered text where the politics of self-representation are constantly interrogated.

In this chapter I argue that Condé's *I, Tituba* examines the intersection of racial, religious and gendered discourses within a framework provided by Tituba's confession. Tituba's self-referential narrative destabilizes the reader and challenges them to move beyond simplistic notions of identity. I will begin by exploring Tituba's model of spirituality and its association with black and white identities, then move on to explore the way in which Tituba's witchcraft operates in the novel as a positive symbol for women's empowerment against an orthodox Judeo-Christian tradition which persecuted witches. I will then examine the novel's resistance to producing an ethnic self through a continuous parodying and ridiculing of Tituba and her supernatural powers. This will be looked at in relation to the novel's packaging and translating strategies which provide a perspective into the power dynamics involved in shaping both the French and American version of Condé's novel, further illuminating the complexity of Condé's narrative.

IT IS HIGHLY significant that Tituba appears in contemporary narratives as a woman of African descent, while in the seventeenth-century court documents, the historical Tituba is referred to as Indian.[11] Chadwick Hansen in "The Metamorphosis of Tituba" explores the shift in Tituba's racial identity and shows how Tituba's race has been gradually changed from Indian, to half-Indian half-black, to black, and how this was paralleled by a change in her practices of magic, which were originally identifiably English, but were transformed to Indian then to African. Hansen traces Tituba's representation by historians, novelists, and dramatists chronologi-

---

11. Most recent historians agree on Tituba's Indian origins based on records of Salem witchcraft. See Chadwick Hansen, "The Metamorphosis of Tituba, or Why American Intellectuals Can't Tell an Indian Witch from a Negro," *New England Quarterly* 47 (1974): 3–12; Bernard Rosenthal, "Tituba's Story," *New England Quarterly* 71 (1998): 190–203; Mary Beth Norton, *In the Devil's Snare: The Salem Witch Crisis of 1692* (New York: Knopf, 2002); Breslaw, *Tituba, Reluctant Witch;* Francis Hill, *A Delusion of Satan: The Full Story of the Salem Witch Trials* (New York: Doubleday, 2002). In her detailed inquiry into Tituba's origins, Breslaw contends that Tituba was brought to Barbados as a child from the South American mainland. Rosenthal, who draws on Breslaw's study in his essay, argues that her inquiry remains highly speculative because it assumes that Tituba was acquired by Rev. Parris in Barbados, while there is no evidence supporting that. Peter Hoffer is the only contemporary historian who argues that Tituba is African and that she was brought to the New World in slavery, identifying her name as Yoruba, in *The Devil's Disciples: Makers of the Salem Witchcraft Trials* (Baltimore: Johns Hopkins University Press, 1996).

cally, ending his inquiry with Miller's *The Crucible* where Tituba becomes completely metamorphosed into a "Negro" woman who practices voodoo. Hansen contends that the shift in Tituba's racial identity is an expression of inverse racial prejudices, arguing that Tituba's metamorphosis is a reflection of race relations in America.[12] He shows how a major shift in Tituba's race from Indian to black took shape between the Civil War and the Second World War, a time where ethnic hatred was intense, and Miller's *The Crucible* is a telling example.

Condé's narrative complicates Tituba's racial identity in a slightly different way. Condé portrays Tituba as the daughter of an African slave who was raped by an English sailor in a slave ship.[13] Tituba recounts at the opening of her narrative: "Abena, my mother, was raped by an English sailor on the deck of Christ the King one day in the year 16** while the ship was sailing for Barbados. I was born from this act of aggression. From this act of hatred and contempt" (3) [Abena, ma mère, un marin anglais la viola sur le pont du Christ the King, un jour de 16** alors que le navire faisait voile vers la Barbade. C'est de cette agression que je suis née. De cet acte de haine et de mépris (13)]. Condé here problematizes Tituba's racial identity, first by blurring her racial boundaries as a person of mixed race, and second, by associating her coming into the world with violence and enslavement. Timothy J. Cox in *Postmodern Tales of Slavery in the Americas* argues that despite the fact that Condé does not mention the Middle Passage by name, the story "presents the middle passage as the foundation of Tituba's own life experience and as a property beyond the limits of remembrance."[14]

---

12. Hansen, "The Metamorphosis of Tituba." Rosenthal also shows in his critique how Tituba's story was given a mythical dimension, turning her into a feared black woman practicing dangerous magic. He argues that "in popular culture's unrelenting effort to shape history by elevating heroes and punishing villains, an identity was forged for Tituba, and it is not at all surprising that that identity should be racialized" ("Tituba's Story," 202).

13. Unlike Condé, Petry shows ambivalence in her construction of Tituba's racial identity. She seems to be caught between the desire to stay faithful to historical records and the desire to construct a black heroic role model for African American children. Tituba's Indian origins are mentioned only once in her narrative, when Rev. Samuel Parris baptizes Tituba and her husband, John, telling them: "You are from Barbados, and it's part of the West Indies—so—well—your last name will be Indian. John Indian and Tituba Indian" (*Tituba of Salem Village*, 7). This comment alludes only vaguely to Tituba's possible Indian origins. The illustration on the novel's front cover, though, curiously shows Tituba as having distinct African features. Petry also describes Tituba in these terms: "Her magnificent posture was due to the fact that she liked to carry baskets balanced on her head like the market women. Her hair was completely covered by a neatly wound white turban. . . . The sleeves were rolled above her elbows revealing sturdy arms, the skin a smooth dark brown" (2). This description corresponds rather well with the figure of the black slave. Still, Petry continuously avoids a direct reference to Tituba as black.

14. Timothy J. Cox, *Postmodern Tales of Slavery in the Americas: From Alejo Carpentier to Charles Johnson* (New York: Garland, 2001), 85; for more details, see chaps. 2 and 3 in Cox.

Thus, in giving Tituba this origin Condé is creating her alternative version of Tituba's story. The absence of a "legitimate" genealogy for Tituba shows that the attempt to explore origins is often problematic, because of the violence, the displacement, and the silencing of histories that characterized African diaspora identities. Condé instead creates an imaginary lineage for Tituba conveyed through the act of naming. Tituba's name was given to her by her adoptive father: "It was he who gave me my name: Tituba. TI-TU-BA. It is not an Ashanti name. Yao probably invented it to prove that I was the daughter of his will and imagination. Daughter of his love" (6) [C'est lui qui me donna mon nom: Tituba. Ti-Tu-Ba. Ce n'est pas un prénom ashanti. Sans doute, Yao en l'inventant, voulait-il prouver que j'étais fille de sa volonté et de son imagination. Fille de son amour (17)]. By asserting an imaginary parentage for Tituba, Condé addresses the impossibility of full recuperation, and locates Tituba's traumatic tale of displacement and enslavement within the larger historical context of the African diaspora.[15] Indeed, Condé insists that *I, Tituba* is not a historical novel. She says: "I really invented Tituba. I gave her a childhood, and adolescence, an old age. At the same time I wanted to turn Tituba into a sort of female hero, and epic heroine, like the legendary 'Nanny of the maroons'" (200–201). Condé here refashions Tituba by blurring both historical and fictional narratives, turning Tituba into a symbol of resistance, and destabilizing her stereotypical construction recurrent in previous narratives.

CONDÉ'S NARRATIVE develops around the meaning of witchcraft and its association with women's racial identities. Condé's text explores how Tituba's connection with magic in Puritan society is an expression of the way blackness has been associated with the concept of evil. Tituba's white mistress, for instance, regards her with suspicion because of her skin color: "Susanna Endicott had already told me she was convinced my color was

---

15. Condé's interest in diasporic histories is expressed through her life and writings, which are varied in their themes and settings. Condé, who was born in Guadeloupe and did her schooling there, left for France in 1953 to continue her studies. She lived in France until 1958, where she developed her political views; as she comments, "I really discovered that I was different. And maybe I became for the first time a Black." Condé met her ex-husband, a Guinean artist, in France and left with him for Africa. She lived in Africa for many years and wrote her first three novels about Africa. She became disillusioned with African nationalism and went back to the Caribbean; *Moi, Tituba* symbolizes this return to the Caribbean and the attempt to explore Caribbean identity. At present, Condé divides her time between Guadeloupe and the United States. For details, see Pfaff, *Conversations with Maryse Condé*, 1–77.

indicative of my close connections with Satan" (65) [Susanna Endicott m'avait déjà apprise qu'à ses yeux, ma couleur était signe de mon intimité avec le malin (104)]. Beatrice, the Reverend Parris's daughter, also accuses her of evil on the basis of her color when she tells her: "You, do good? You're a Negress, Tituba! You can only do evil. You are evil itself!" (77) [Vous, faire du bien? Vous êtes une négresse, Tituba! Vous ne pouvez faire que du mal. Vous êtes le mal! (123)]. Tituba's confessions from the Salem trial records, which Condé integrates into her text, also illustrate how the devil in colonial America was color coded as black.[16] Tituba identifies him as a black dog, and a black rat, reflecting Puritan ideas of evil and its association with black identities. Charles Long, who explores what he coins "the semiotics of racism" in white Christian discourse, argues that for the Puritans "the perseverance of the Indian in diabolical and sinful ways was to the Puritan, therefore, an infallible sign of negative predestination, and the anavoidable damning of the Indian soul."[17]

This obsession with the devil reveals the rigidity of the Puritans' beliefs, and explains their denunciation of individuals on the basis of witchcraft, in their need to blame others for their daily misfortunes. Tituba describes the Salem community as follows:

> Imagine a small community of men and women oppressed by the presence of Satan and seeking to hunt him down in all his manifestations. A cow that died, a child smitten with convulsions, a girl whose menstrual period was late in coming set off a chain of unending speculation (65) [Imaginer une étroite communauté d'hommes et de femmes, écrasès par la présence du Malin parmi eux et cherchant à le traquer dans toutes ses manifestations. Une vache qui mourait, un enfant qui avait des convulsions, une jeune fille qui tardait à connaître son flot menstruel et c'était matière a spéculations infinies (104)].

Mary Beth Norton's historical approach recalls Condé's words about the severity of Puritan society. Norton explains:

> The foundation of the witchcraft crisis lay in Puritan New Englanders' singular worldview. . . . That world view taught them that they were a

---

16. Tituba's testimonies are available in Paul Boyer and Stephen Nissenbaum, eds., *Salem Witchcraft Papers: Verbatim Transcripts of the Legal Documents*, 3 vols. (New York: Da Capo, 1977).

17. Charles H. Long, *Significations: Signs, Symbols, and Images in the Interpretation of Religion* (Philadelphia: Fortress Press, 1986), 202.

chosen people, charged with bringing God's message to a heathen land previously ruled by the devil. And in that adopted homeland God spoke to them repeatedly through his providences—that is, through the small and large events of their daily lives. Remarkable signs in the sky (comets, the aurora borealis), natural catastrophes (hurricanes, droughts), smallpox epidemics, the sudden deaths of children or spouses, unexpected good fortune: all carried messages from God to his people.[18]

Puritans who departed to North America in pursuit of a place where they could practice their religious beliefs and build a new reformed society developed a separatist attitude toward others. Their model society or "City on a Hill" was founded on the same exclusionary politics to which they were exposed in England. This intolerance or fear of the other is articulated by Reverend Parris, who tells Tituba and John Indian: "I know that the color of your skin is a sign of your damnation, but as long as you are under my roof you will behave as Christians!" (41) [Il est certain que la couleur de votre peau est le signe de votre damnation, cependant tant que vous serez sous mon toit, vous vous comportez comme des chrétiens! (68)]. Here, Parris associates blackness with evil, and views Christianity as the norm, reflecting the rigidity of the Puritans' belief and division of the world into moral absolutes, where Christianity becomes the only truth. This rejection of others is also expressed by a member of the Salem community who protests against Benjamin d'Azevedo, the Jewish merchant, settling in their community: "Did we leave England for this? To see Jews and niggers multiply in our midst?" (132) [Et est-ce pour cela que nous avons quitté l'Angleterre? Pour voir proliférer à côté de nous des Juifs et des Nègres? (206)].[19]

Condé's criticism of Puritan societies is a way to explore racial and religious intolerance in contemporary America as she conveys in her interview with Scarboro: "Writing about Tituba was an opportunity to express my feelings about present day America. I wanted to imply that in terms of narrow-mindedness, hypocrisy, and racism, little has changed since the days of the Puritans."[20] Tituba's representation in the American imagination becomes the lens through which Condé examines the contemporary religious and racial politics of the United States. Tituba was not only

---

18. Norton, *In the Devil's Snare*, 295.
19. Through her reference to Benjamin d'Azevedo and his family in the novel, Condé is creating a connection between African and Jewish diasporas.
20. Ann Armstrong Scarboro, "An Interview with Maryse Condé," forward to I, *Tituba, Black Witch of Salem*, 203

demonized by the Puritans who were projecting their inner fears on her, but she has been equally demonized in contemporary American imagination. Hansen argues that Tituba's racial misidentification and her association with evil and dark magic have not changed, but continue to carry the same weight. He gives an example from Miller's *The Crucible* (1952) where Tituba appears as a "Negro" woman, who conspires with the devil, dances wildly in the woods, sacrifices chicken, and drinks chicken blood, although there is no historical evidence that refers to Tituba following such practices. Miller here alludes to Voodoo in a very stereotypical manner. He articulates the way African diaspora religions such as Vodou are closely associated in the Western mind with "black magic" and certainly not viewed as legitimate belief systems.

Ironically, the historical records show that Tituba's alleged practices were identifiably English. The racial misidentification of Tituba and her connection with black magic fits the American stereotype of a black slave woman. The historical Tituba, who was Indian, and whose deployment of magic was European white magic under the instructions of her white mistress and neighbours, is far removed from the stereotype.

Miller also portrays Tituba as weak and characterless; she turns mad at the end of the narrative and starts mumbling about the devil: "Oh, it be no Hell in Barbados. Devil, him be pleasure-man in Barbados, him be singin' and dancin' in Barbados. It is you folks—you riles him up' round here; it be too cold' round here for that Old Boy. He freezes himself in Massachusetts, but in Barbados he just as sweet."[21] This passage reinforces the idea of the devil's association with blackness. Miller suggests that while the devil is feared in America, he is loved and embraced in Barbados! Miller's stereotyping of Tituba extends to her use of language. Miller's Tituba speaks Pidgin English expressing a sharp contrast with the language used by the actual Tituba, as recorded in seventeenth-century official documents.[22] Miller, unfortunately, is still viewed in the popular mind as the authority regarding the Salem witch trials, and his representation of Tituba has shaped to a great extent public memory and popular culture.

---

21. Arthur Miller, *The Crucible* (London: Penguin, 1968), 108.
22. Breslaw demonstrates in her project that Tituba acquired the same conversational mode as Puritan society and used the same idiomatic English used by the Parris family. To show that Tituba's speech pattern was not that of the transcribers, Breslaw compared Tituba's speech to recorded speech of other accused ethnic persons that was written down during the hearing to conclude that Tituba's speech in the recorded documents is different from that of others who spoke an obvious nonstandard English. See Breslaw, *Tituba, Reluctant Witch*, 161–63.

IN CONDÉ'S revisionary telling of Tituba's story, witchcraft also functions as a symbol of women's empowerment against an orthodox Judeo-Christian discourse. Condé uses Tituba's spiritual and magical powers to counter Puritan beliefs, and to create an alternative for women who have been absent or oppressed within the Christian discourse. Condé's choice of witchcraft is highly significant and reflects the spirit of the twentieth century where the metaphor of the witch has been revalidated by different feminist movements as a symbol of their struggle against the oppression of women.[23] Through witchcraft Condé creates a positive image for women, whom men historically attempted to repress by persecuting witches. In her exploration of Tituba's trial, Condé exposes the rigidity of the Puritans' practices and their misogynistic attitude toward women. Tituba provides a model of spirituality which defies the Christian tradition's Mariology, and celebrates the ambivalence and complexity of the feminine principle.

The novel's exploration of the witch craze of Salem refers to a long history of women's persecution which started with Christianity's rise to power. Christian law condemned witchcraft, and was responsible for the introduction of the concept of the demonic alliance between witches and the devil. This eradication of witches was carried over into the New World, and Puritans frequently used it as an excuse to punish women and blame them for their misfortunes.[24] This attitude was fed by Christian theology which perceived women as seducers and temptresses. They were seen as instruments of the devil and, therefore, responsible for human downfall. Jeffrey B. Russell explains how this misogyny was supported by the dualistic opposition of spirit/body, and good/evil in Christian discourse, with women's association with body and evil. He argues:

> Christianity affirmed the spiritual equality of men and women, but St. Paul and many of the most influential Church Fathers blurred that doctrine. Women became the temptresses of men, men who moved the

---

23. In the 1960s, modern feminist witches appeared as part of the WICCA movement. Modern witches believe in the Goddess, who represents female spirituality. Naomi R. Goldenberg writes: "Witches use their Goddess concept to give women positive self-images in all stages of life." Naomi Goldenberg, *Changing of the Gods: Feminism and the End of Traditional Religions* (Boston: Beacon Press, 1979), 97. Russell also observes that modern feminist witchcraft is mainly a spiritual movement whose main concern is not political. However, many feminist groups have taken over the metaphor of the witch and identified themselves with that image for political reasons, such as the feminist group WITCH: the Women's International Terrorist Conspiracy from Hell. See Jeffrey Russell, *A History of Witchcraft: Sorcerers, Heretics, and Pagans* (London: Thames and Hudson, 1980), 156.

24. The *Malleus Maleficarum*, a well-known fifteenth-century manual for witch-hunters, offers historical proof of the misogynistic attitude of the Church toward women.

wheels of state, or religion, and of learning, men whose souls were practically, if not theoretically, more important. In most Christian theology and tradition this misogyny was kept within bounds, but sometimes it burst out crudely.[25]

This belief in the dichotomous nature of men and women—men as spiritual and God-fearing, women as seducers and witches—dominated the Puritans' outlook and justified violence against women. The complexity of the feminine principle associated with ancient religion became suppressed within this new interpretation of Christianity. The exaggeration of the goodness and the purity of the Virgin Mary created its shadow-image of the hag. The Church exploited this duality and turned witches into ideal scapegoats.

Historically, witches also threatened the Church's hierarchy, and were viewed as a source of danger, because they provided an alternative system of knowledge. In *Beyond God the Father* Mary Daly argues:

> Those singled out as witches were frequently characterized by the fact that they had or were believed to have power arising from a particular kind of knowledge, as in the case of 'wise women' who knew the curative powers of herbs and to whom people went for counsel and help.[26]

This power that the witches possessed was threatening to the Church, as was the case in the community of Salem, where Tituba instigated both feelings of praise and fear. She was denounced for her practices, but was also needed to help. Condé captures this contradiction in views of witches in the incident where Sarah Hutchinson, a resident of Salem, pleads with Tituba to help her take revenge: "Help me, Tituba, to find the person who has done me wrong and punish them" (86) [Aide-moi, Tituba, a retrouver celui qui m'a fait du tort et punis-le! (136)]. When Tituba refuses, this latter spitefully threatens her: "You're very philosophical, my girl! You won't philosophize so much when you're swinging at the end of a rope!" (86) [Te voilà bien raisonneuse, ma négresse! Tu ne raisonnerais pas tant quand tu te balanceras au bout d'une corde (136)].

Witchcraft was also used in Salem as a justification for the shortage of scientific research. Dr. Griggs, Salem's doctor, who was aware of Tituba's curative powers—who even asks her for medicine when his son is ill—

---
25. Russell, *A History of Witchcraft*, 115.
26. Mary Daly, *Beyond God the Father: Toward a Philosophy of Women's Liberation* (London: Women's Press, 1995), 64.

denounces her in the end. Failing to cure Reverend Parris's hysteric daughter and niece, Dr. Griggs identifies their symptoms as marks of witchcraft, thus affirming the ministers' suspicion of Tituba's alliance with the devil. Paradoxically, the rise of rationalism and empirical science in the seventeenth century did not contribute to the refutation of the irrational claims about witches. At the opposite, science used witches as scapegoats for the lack of scientific explanation. The witches' possession of knowledge of plants was scientifically unexplainable, and thus became a proof against them. They were the enemies of science because they were "irrational."

Witches were especially feared, because they had knowledge about contraception and abortion, which was unacceptable to the Church. Condé mocks the methods used by doctors in Salem, and plays on their belief in rationalism and empirical science. Tituba describes how, hoping to become a professor in Harvard, a certain doctor, named Zerobabel, who was doing a study of mental illnesses, was experimenting with his potions on her when she was in jail:

> Take the milk of a woman suckling a male child. Also take a cat and cut off its ear or part of it. Let the blood flow into the milk. Get the patient to drink this mixture. Repeat three times a day (112) [Prendre le lait d'une femme qui nourrit un enfant male. Prendre aussi un chat et lui couper une oreille ou une partie de l'oreille. Laisser le sang s'écouler dans le lait. Faire boire ce mélange à la patiente. Répéter trois fois par jour (175)].

This paragraph expresses a double irony. Condé ridicules Doctor Zerobabel and his lack of scientific approach by overstating the unempirical nature of his potions. The potion described above also alludes to "black magic" or "Voodoo," which is highly significant in this context. Condé reverses the accusations against Tituba as a practitioner of Voodoo, and instead associates Voodoo with scientific experimentation, whiteness, and masculinity. Her ridiculing of Doctor Zerobabel and his study of mental illnesses also remains highly political. The novel's criticism of science evokes the argument about how psychiatric ideology in modern times replaced witch-hunting taking over from the Church, and replacing the duality of good/evil with sanity/insanity, with science deciding on what was to be deemed perverse, and what was normal.[27]

---

27. Mary Daly talks about how women were abused by the barbarities of modern psychiatry, which became a tool of social control of women's deviancy, thus replacing the witch-hunts. Daly, *Beyond God the Father*, 64–66.

Through Tituba, Condé also blurs the boundaries of good/evil, and questions the Christian division of the world into dichotomous terms: good/evil, spirit/flesh, etc. She turns witchcraft into a positive symbol for women through Tituba, who resists these dichotomies. However, Condé does not totally commit to her heroine's concept of witchcraft, and registers a poignant criticism by playing on clichéd images of witchcraft, subtly parodying Tituba and her practices. On one level, Condé's witchcraft works to expose and counter the religious, sexual, racial and political structures of Christianity. On a second level, by consciously playing on the stereotype of the witch as sexually open, in harmony with nature, and in touch with the spiritual world, Condé mockingly exhibits simplistic preconceptions to which Tituba is expected to conform.

Tituba's spirituality represents her strength in the face of the Puritans' belief in the evil of witches and their alliance with the devil. Surprised by the social injustice toward witches, Tituba questions:

> What is a witch? . . . isn't the ability to communicate with the invisible world, to keep constant links with the dead, to care for others and heal, a superior gift of nature that inspires respect, admiration, and gratitude? Consequently, shouldn't the witch (if that's what the person who has the gift is to be called) be cherished and revered rather than feared? (17) [Qu'est–ce qu'une sorcière? . . . La faculté de communiquer avec les invisibles, de garder un lien constant avec les disparus, de soigner, de guérir n'est-elle pas une grâce supérieure de nature à inspirer respect, admiration et gratitude? En conséquence, la sorcière, si on veut nommer ainsi celle qui possède cette grâce, ne devrait-elle pas être choyée et révérée au lieu d'être crainte (33)].

Tituba's model of spirituality celebrates witches as healers. She articulates her knowledge of plants and her veneration for nature—characteristic of African diaspora religions, when she describes how Mama Yaya taught her the curative powers of plants:

> Mama Yaya taught me about herbs. Those for inducing sleep. Those for healing wounds and ulcers. Those for loosening the tongues of thieves. Those that calm epileptics and plunge them into blissful rest. Those that put words of hope on the lips of the angry, the desperate, and the suicidal. Mama Yaya taught me the sea, the mountains, and the hills. She taught me that everything lives, has a soul, and breathes. That everything must be respected. That man is not the master riding

through his kingdom on horseback (9) [Man Yaya m'apprit les plantes. Celles qui donnent le sommeil. Celles qui guérissent plaies et ulcères. Celles qui font avouer les voleurs. Celles qui calment les épileptiques et les plongent dans un bienheureux repos. Celles qui mettent sur les lèvres des furieux, des désespérés et des suicidaires des paroles d'espoir. Man Yaya m'appris a écouter le vent quand il se lève et mesure ces forces au-dessus des cases qu'il se prépare à broyer. Man Yaya m'apprit la mer. Les montagnes et les mornes. Elle m'appris que tout vit, tout a une âme, un souffle. Que tout doit être respecté. Que l'homme n'est pas un maître parcourant à cheval son royaume (22)].

Condé here constructs Tituba as a healer whose worldview is ingrained in respect for the natural world, while implicitly criticising Christian theology and its negative approach to nature in the last sentence of the quote. The metaphor of man "riding through his kingdom on horseback" is a reference to the masculine attitude Christianity demonstrates toward nature as something that needs to be conquered and controlled. The importance African diaspora cosmologies give to the natural world contradicts the Judeo-Christian belief in man's superiority over nature. Naomi R. Goldenberg questions the attitude of Christianity and Judaism toward nature and their possible contribution to engendering the ecology crisis. She contends:

> Many theologians have pointed out that Judaism and Christianity consider nature as inferior to 'man'—as something to be conquered by 'him' (I put man and him in quotes because I am not pretending that the words are generic. Woman is often seen as nature in Judaism and Christianity, as an inferior being in need of taming and cultivation by 'man.') Witchcraft's view of other forms of life, as equal to the human form is certainly not shared by Judaism and mainstream Christianity, and not easily tolerated by them.[28]

Tituba's alienation from a Christian worldview is also expressed in her resistance to Christian prayers which her mistress Susanna Endicott tried to impose on her expresses her alienation from Christianity. Tituba repeats: "I believe in God the Father Almighty, maker of heaven and Earth, and in Jesus Christ, his only son, Our Lord . . . " (25) [Je crois en dieu, le père Tout-Puissant. Créateur du ciel et de la terre (46)];[29] she then com-

---

28. Goldenberg, *Changing of the Gods*, 112; see also pp. 105–6.
29. The part of the prayer that mentions Jesus Christ, "Jesus Christ, his only Son," does not exist in the French version. Interestingly, it is added by Philcox in the translation.

plains: "But these words meant nothing to me. They had nothing in common with what Mama Yaya had taught me" (25–26) [Mais ses paroles ne signifiaient rien pour moi. Cela n'avait rien de commun avec ce que Man Yaya m'avait appris (46)]. Tituba clearly feels the challenge the Christian belief system represent to her worldview. The belief in a male God as the "father" and the "creator" contradicts the organic model of spirituality she is familiar with.

After being repeatedly judged and ultimately executed for her witchcraft, Tituba is finally provided with a space in the afterlife to fully celebrate her spirituality. She continues to be useful to her people through her practices, and carries her tradition beyond the limits of time and history. In essence, she turns into a revolutionary spirit, encouraging and nourishing her people's dream of freedom and liberty. She says: "For now that I have gone over to the invisible world I continue to heal and cure. But primarily I dedicated myself to another task. . . . I am hardening men's hearts to fight. I am nourishing them with dreams of liberty. Of victory. I have been behind every revolt. Every insurrection. Every act of disobedience" (175) [Car, vivante comme morte, visible comme invisible, je continue a panser, a guérir. Mais surtout, je me suis assigné une autre tache. . . . Aguerrir le coeur des hommes. L'alimenter des rêves de liberté. De victoire. Pas une révolte que je n'aie fait naître. Pas une insurrection. Pas une désobéissance (268)]. Tituba here turns into a revolutionary figure and a positive icon for black women.

Tituba, who could not keep a child of her own in life, is also granted an adopted daughter to carry on her legacy: "I tell her the secrets I'm allowed to share, the hidden power of herbs and the language of animals. I teach her to look for the invisible shapes in the world, the crisscross of communications, and the signs and symbols" (177) [Je lui révèle les secrets permis, la force cachée des plantes et le langage des animaux. Je lui apprends à découvrir la forme invisible du monde, le réseau de communications qui le parcourt et les signes-symboles (270)]. Tituba's instructions to her daughter assert the continuity of her witchcraft as an Africanist female tradition. However, Tituba's experiencing of motherhood in the afterlife is ironic, and contains a sharp criticism of mother/daughter relationships under the institution of slavery and also perhaps a gentle satire on feminist notions of foremothers.

Nevertheless, Tituba is granted eternal existence in her island in the form of a song. She is finally granted a lasting place in the cultural memory of her people despite the earlier disdain of Christopher, the leader of the Maroon community who was dismissive of her when she expressed a desire to be remembered through a song like him. Here, Condé reclaims Caribbean history and oral tradition through an exclusively female voice undercutting a Caribbean male discourse of heroism, which often excludes Caribbean women and their achievements.

Yet, the role of the good witch given to Tituba after her death is countered by Condé's skepticism, which simultaneously undercuts Tituba, while attempting to register her as a heroic figure. This tension between the commitment to creating a powerful female figure and the desire to ridicule Tituba emanates from Condé's awareness of the politics of ethnicity often exhibited by black women writers in self-referential genres. Tituba's role as a revolutionary and a martyr in her afterlife is undermined by a self-indulgent and irresponsible Tituba, who, when alive, seemed to be more concerned with her sexual life and passion for men than with her people's cause and suffering under the institution of slavery. Most shockingly, Tituba becomes a slave out of choice, and in order to be with John Indian. She goes as far as assuming that other slaves are freer than she is, because they are not imprisoned by the same passion for men. She contends: "The slaves who flocked off the ships . . . were far freer than I was" (25) [Les esclaves qui descendaient par fournées entières des negriers . . . étaient bien plus libre que moi (45)]. When she returns to Barbados, she sees a newly arrived cargo of slaves being displayed. Tituba seems saddened by this view when she remarks: "How ugly my town was! Small. Petty. A colonial outpost of no distinction, reeking with the stench of lucre and suffering" (141) [qu'elle était laide, ma ville! Petite. Mesquine. Un poste colonial sans envergure, tout empuanti de l'odeur du lucre et de la souffrance (218–19)]. Tituba then surprises the reader by immersing herself straight into memories of bygone days of sexual passion for John Indian: "What wouldn't I have given to relive those years when I slept night after night in the arms of my John Indian, with my hand on his pleasure-dispensing object!" (141) [Que n'aurais-je pas donné pour revivre les années ou je dormais, nuit après nuit, dans les bras de mon John Indien, la main sur l'objet dispensateur de plaisir! (219)].

This almost comical representation of Tituba is elucidated by Condé who reports that she "hesitated between the irony and the desire to be serious. The result is that she [Tituba] is a mock-epic character" (201). Thus, while celebrating Tituba's spirituality, Condé is also aware of the absurdity of certain overstated stereotypes about the ethnic woman and her connection to the occult. This is apparent in the following passage where Condé mockingly parodies narratives on witches' powers. Tituba reports:

> She [Mama Yaya] taught me how to change myself into a bird on a branch, into an insect in the dry grass or a frog croaking in the mud of the river Ormond whenever I was tired of the shape I had been given at birth (10) [Elle [Man Yaya] m'apprit à me changer en oiseau sur la branche, en insecte dans l'herbe sèche, en grenouille coassant la boue de la rivière Ormonde quand je voulais me délasser de la forme que j'avais reçue à la naissance (22)].

This exaggerated representation of Tituba's sacred approach to the natural world is meant to highlight the mock-epic characteristics of witchcraft. Condé here uses Tituba's confessional voice to manipulate the reader and produce an image of Tituba that is recognisably ethnic.

The ambivalence in the representation of Tituba runs throughout the novel. While Tituba assists others with her witchcraft, she also uses it to fulfil her personal desires. For instance, she saves her mistress Elizabeth Parris and her daughter from death with her herbal recipes. She allows the desperate Benjamin Cohen d'Azevedo, her master and lover, to communicate with the spirit of his dead wife; she cures Iphigene, the son of the legendary rebel, T-Noel. Yet, Tituba also uses her art to satisfy her selfish desires. When she meets John Indian, she communicates to the spirit of Mama Yaya, asking for guidance: "I want this man to love me" (14) [Je veux que cet homme m'aime (29)]. She also becomes responsible for the death of Susanna Endicott, her white mistress: "I want her to die slowly, suffering horribly, knowing it's because of me" (29) [Je veux qu'elle meure a petit feu, dans les souffrances les plus horribles, en sachant que c'est à cause de moi (51)]; she ignores the words of the dead Mama Yaya, who advised her: "Don't let yourself be eaten up by revenge. Use your power to serve your own people and heal them" (29) [Ne te laisse pas aller a l'esprit de vengeance. Utilise ton art pour servir les tiens et les soulager (51)]. Tituba also triggers a wave of denunciations when she falsely accuses others during the Salem trial, sending them to their deaths.

Tituba's witchcraft defies the concept of good and evil as imposed by Christian doctrine, challenging both the image of the good witch, and the demonized bad witch. Russell argues that "Christianity traditionally found it difficult to accept the principle of ambivalence in the deity: the Christian God was wholly good and wholly masculine, excluding both the feminine principle and the principle of evil."[30] Thus, Condé's novel in its celebration of Tituba's witchcraft acknowledges the feminine principle, and by doing

---

30. Russell, *A History of Witchcraft*, 116–18.

so, goes beyond imposed definitions of women as good or evil. Tituba's psychic powers, and her sacred approach to nature also offer an independent knowledge system, which is different to the patriarchal view of the world.

Tituba also challenges the spirit/flesh separation and is not bashful about her sexuality. She is represented in the novel as sexually open, expressing freely her desire for men. When Elizabeth Parris complains to Tituba about being a woman, this latter replies: "What is more beautiful that a woman's body! Especially when it is glorified by man's desire!" (43) [Quoi de plus beau qu'un corps de femme! Surtout quand le désire d' un homme l'anoblit (72)]. This celebration of the female body stands in high contrast with the values of the Puritan population of Salem, who view sexuality as "a hateful act. . . . It's Satan's heritage in us" (42) [un acte odieux. . . . C'est l'héritage de Satan en nous (70)].[31] This association of Satan with sexuality and with the view of witches as responsible for lust is most apparent in the incident where the ministers of Salem pressure Tituba to confess her pact with the devil. They tie her down in the bed and abuse her with a stick, shouting at her: "Go on, take it, it's John Indian's prick" (91) [Prends, prends, c'est la bite de John Indien (144)]. The sexual nature of Tituba's torture shows how the witch-hunting becomes an outlet for the men's repressed sexual urges, but also reveals a deep fear of black women which has been fuelled by the tales of sexual deviance about witches.

To further complicate Tituba's sexuality, Condé also shows a humane side to Tituba in her relationship to the deformed Benjamin d'Azevedo. She describes her sexual intimacy with him as follows:

> I must confess that when he undressed, revealing his crooked, pasty body, I couldn't help thinking of the dark-brown muscles of John Indian. A lump would rise up in my throat and I would choke back the sobs. But that didn't last and I pitched and heaved just as well on the sea of delight with my misshapen lover. The sweetest moments, however, were those when we talked. About us. And only about us (127) [Je dois avouer qu' aù moment ou il se déshabillait et où je voyais son corps cireux et bancal, je ne pouvais m'empêcher de songer au corps musclé et sombre de John Indien. . . . Néanmoins cela ne durait pas et avec mon amant contrefait, je dérivais tout aussi bien sur la mer des délices.

---

31. Tituba's sexual openness can be seen as a statement against her invisibility, since through exploring her sexuality, she reclaims her humanity against a system that renders her invisible.

Les moments les plus doux étaient cependant ceux où nous parlions. De nous. Seulment de nous (198)].

Elizabeth Wilson writes that Condé has a "deep skepticism about doctrinaire attitudes and ideologies (whether it is Negritude, Creolization, Caribbean identity, Feminism or Black Nationalism" [une méfiance profonde de toute attitude doctrinaire ou de toute idéologie (que ce sois la négritude, la créolité, l'antillanité, le féminisme ou le nationalisme noire)].[32] Condé expresses this skepticism toward essentialist discourses in her ambiguous portrayal of Tituba who refuses to confine herself to the image of the ethnic self she is expected to resemble.

In her interview with Ann Scarboro, Condé contends: "Don't take Tituba too seriously, please" (212). Condé's statement alerts the reader to the need to treat the novel with a degree of skepticism. Tituba's historical confession is interrupted by her personal confession, directly spoken to the reader. In this respect, Tituba's account is not an attempt to recover the historical Tituba, but it is a conscious attempt to inscribe her own subjectivity denied to her by history, as she complains: "There would be mention here and there of 'a slave originating from the West Indies and probably practicing "hoodoo."'" There would be no mention of my age or my personality. I would be ignored" (110) [Mon nom ne figurait que comme celui d'une comparse sans intérêt. On mentionnerait ça et là "une esclave originaire des Antilles et pratiquant vraisemblablement le 'hoodoo.'" On ne se soucierait ni de mon age ni de ma personnalité. On m'ignorait (173)]. Condé here gives Tituba a life, a childhood, and adulthood, against her historical silencing, humanizing her and forcing a different reading of her story.

Thus, the distinction between historiography and fictional writing collapses in *I, Tituba* generating new meanings and associations. Significantly, Tituba's historical confession becomes mediated in the text by Hester Prynne, the protagonist of Nathanial Hawthorne's *The Scarlet Letter*. Hester who Tituba meets in prison, tells her: "Make them scared, Tituba! Give them their money's worth! Describe him [the devil] as a Billy goat with an eagle's beak for a nose, a body covered in long black hair with a belt of scorpion heads around his waist" (100) [Fais-leur peur, Tituba! Donne-leur-en pour leur argent! Décris-le sous la forme d'un bouc avec un nez en forme de bec d'aigle, un corps tout couvert de longs poils noirs et,

---

32. Elizabeth Wilson, "Sorcières, sorcières: '*Moi, Tituba, sorcière Noire de Salem*' révisions et interrogations," in *L'oeuvre de Maryse Condé* (Paris: Harmattan, 1996), 105; my translation.

attachée à la taille, une ceinture de têtes de scorpions (158)].[33] Here, Tituba's historical confession becomes simply a false testimony she was forced to give the judges. Tituba and Hester's encounter in Condé's novel refers to the cultural and historical inconsistencies of Tituba's confessions. Hester, the heroine of a prerevolutionary story, written in 1850 meets Tituba in prison in the seventeenth century and echoes twentieth-century feminist ideas in her conversations with Tituba. This correlation between the past and the present further questions Tituba's reliability as a narrator, as she continues to reinvent herself for the reader and for Condé, who she shares her story with, as Condé informs us in the epigraph.

Through her confession Tituba is also mocking the Puritan mode of extracting evidence, since for Puritans confession was the "most conclusive, concrete, and empirical confirmation of a guilty act and as such an important element in proving guilt."[34] According to Breslaw, "Confession lay at the base of Puritan theology, a ritual that expressed a consciousness of sin or guilt, an awareness of the deity's omniscience, and an acknowledgment of that consciousness through the spoken or written word."[35] She reports from Reverend John Hale, the only independent eyewitness of Tituba's trial that he "had found Tituba's confessions credible because of their consistency. Had she been lying, he thought, she would have contradicted herself. Moreover she seemed 'very penitent' for making a covenant with the devil, and she herself was afflicted by other witches for confessing."[36] This shows the extent to which Tituba succeeded in weaving a convincing story that fitted with the Puritan idea of a confession. Her testimony reflects her ability to comprehend Puritan culture, and manipulate the court by summoning images and stories from Puritan folklore, and that is what makes her story believable.[37] Condé's criticism of the Puritans' seemingly rational and objective methods of subtracting evidence allows her to challenge the association of monotheistic and male-centered religions with "truth" and rationality.

The confessional narrative also exposes the politics of ethnicity and the power dynamics involved in self-representation. While Tituba's account seems to suggest a production of the ethnic self, or "coercive mimeticism" to borrow Chow's words, the ambiguous space from which Tituba oper-

---

33. By showing how Tituba's confession becomes mediated in the text by Hester's Puritan imagination, Condé ironically questions the association of witchcraft with blackness.
34. Breslaw, *Tituba, Reluctant Witch*, 158.
35. Ibid., 159.
36. Norton, *In the Devil's Snare*, 29–30.
37. Ibid.

ates allows her to challenge the particular notions of identity imposed on her by the Puritans as a black woman who practices witchcraft. Unlike Tituba, John Indian represents the perfect example of how ethnicity can be exhibited and exploited to produce clichéd images that are recognisably ethnic. When Tituba objects to his incautiousness when he threw a party in the absence of his mistress, he laughs and tells her: "'And so what?' he laughed. 'They expect niggers to get drunk and dance and make merry once their masters have turned their backs. Lets play at being perfect niggers'" (32) [Et qu'importe? On s'attend à ce que les nègres se soûlent et dansent et fassent ripaille dès que leurs maîtres ont tourné le dos. Jouons à la perfection notre rôle de nègres (56)]. John Indian is aware of the stereotype to which he is expected to conform. Through him, Condé creates an example of how the ethnic self can be intentionally produced, which provides a scope for the narrative strategies used in the text. On a surface level, both Condé and Tituba ironically "play their role with perfection." Tituba exhibits her ethnicity for her audience, and so does Condé who stages for Simone Gallimard (French publisher and director of Mercure de France Press who suggested that Condé write a novel about a heroine from the Caribbean), and for her readers, a model of ethnicity they expect.

Tituba seems to be continuously faced with others who are appropriating her identity. Yet, in her desire not to conform to any preconceptions, she is persistently refusing to produce conventional views of herself. Both the whites of Salem and the slave community in Barbados seem to project on to her their own fears and insecurities. She tells how the slaves in Barbados look at her with fear: "The terror of these people seemed like an injustice to me. They should have greeted me with shouts of joy and welcome and presented me with a list of illnesses that I would have tried my utmost to cure. I was born to heal, not to frighten" (12) [Cette terreur me paraissait une injustice. Ah! C'est par des cris de joie et de bonne arrivée que l'on aurait du m'accueillir! C'est par l'exposé de maux que j'aurais de mon mieux tenté de guérir. J'étais faite pour panser e non pour effrayer (26)]. When Christopher the maroon insists she grants him power and leadership, he asks her: "'Are you a witch? Yes or no?'" (146) ["Es-tu une sorcière? Oui ou non?" (225)]. She replies: "'Everyone gives that word a different meaning. Everyone believes he can fashion a witch to his way of thinking so that she will satisfy his ambitions, dreams, and desires'" (146) ["Chacun donne à ce mot une signification différente. Chacun croit pouvoir façonner la sorcière à sa manière afin qu'elle satisfasse ses ambitions, ses rêves, ses désirs" (225)].

Tituba's witchcraft thus becomes the mirror through which Condé examines the intersection of racial, cultural, and religious discourses to articulate a particular model of Tituba's spirituality. Critics often overlook the complexity with which Condé plays on the category of witchcraft, often exhibiting clichés for her audience about black women and their spirituality as she reveals herself in her interview with Scarboro: "I don't have any knowledge of witchcraft. . . . The recipes that I give in the novel are merely recipes that I found in seventeenth-century books: how to cure people with certain plants, what kind of prayers to say in certain circumstances, and so on. I found that in books printed and published in America or in England" (206). Condé clearly manipulates her audience and ironically produces a stereotyped view of Tituba by adapting a Western seventeenth-century model of sorcery extracted from books published in America and England. Critics such as Lillian Manzor-Coats, and Leah D. Hewitt, for instance, fail to note the way the politics of ethnicity are displayed in the novel to promote Tituba's model of spirituality. They both overlook the complexity with which Condé plays on the notion of witchcraft. Hewitt argues that "belief in the supernatural, as embodied in a dialogue with spirits, in spells, in curative herbs . . . is integral to the character of Tituba, but it also represents more generally an Antillean heritage,"[38] while Manzor-Coats writes that "Condé's novel demonstrates the clash between two belief systems: the slaves' animistic and positive sorcery, one which is a product of the right hand and works for the well-being of a community; and the European belief in malevolent sorcery."[39]

Condé's forged production of the witch is exemplified by Tituba's utilisation of pseudo-scientific names for plants, which is meant to delude the reader about her supernatural skills and knowledge of the art of healing. Thus, Tituba's constant staging of her powers is a parody, highlighted by the paradox of her life suffering and her helplessness in the face of her oppressors. In this sense, Tituba's sorcery functions merely as a metaphor in the text, and by playing on the different aspects of sorcery and its association with racial and religious identities, Tituba is constantly challenging her readers by presenting the very preconceptions she is expected to resemble. Condé's use of a Western model of sorcery to manipulate her Western readers is analogous to her use of Puritan imagination in her historical confession to manipulate her Puritan audiences. Condé cleverly plays on

---

38. Leah D. Hewitt, *Autobiographical Tightropes* (Lincoln: University of Nebraska Press, 1990), 166.

39. Lillian Manzor-Coats, "Of Witches and Other Things: Maryse Condé's Challenges to Feminist Discourse," World Literature Today 67.4 (1993):, 741..

Tituba's confessional narrative in order to question the politics of ethnicity. This poses the question as to which is Tituba's "true" confession? And does she ever confess?

To further explore the politics of ethnic representation in the novel, let's examine the highly charged racial dynamics between Hester as a liberal white middle-class and Tituba as the exotic other. Hester describes Tituba when she first sees her as: "What a magnificent color she's got for her skin and what a wonderful way she has of covering up her feelings! Fear, torment, rage, disgust! I've never managed to hide my feelings and my moods have always betrayed me!" (95) [Quelle couleur magnifique a sa peau et comme elle peut sous ce couvert, dissimuler ses sentiments! Peur, angoisse, fureur, dégoût! Moi, je n'y suis jamais parvenue et les mouvements de mon sang m'ont toujours trahie! (151)]. Hester here shows a classical reaction to otherness, where Tituba is being both estranged and exoticized through her skin colour. The conversation which follows their encounter illustrates how Hester subconsciously expects Tituba to resemble an image that has nothing to do with her reality. Hester presumes that Tituba belongs to a culture that escapes gender hierarchy, and is disappointed to find out that like her, Tituba's name was given to her by her father:

"You accepted the name a man gave you?"

I was so taken aback it took me a few moments to reply. "Isn't it the same for every woman? First her father's name, then her husband's?"

"I was hoping," she said musingly, "that at least some societies were an exception to this law. Yours, for example!" (96) ["Tu portes le nom qu'un homme t'a donné?" Dans mon étonement, je fus un unstant sans répondre, puis je répliquai: "N'en est-il pas de même pour toute femme? D'abord le nom de son père, ensuite, celui de son mari?" Elle fit songeuse: "J'espérais qu'au moins certaines sociétés échappaient à cette loi. La tienne, par exemple!" (151)].

Tituba reacts with surprise to Hester's preconception of her, subtly calling attention to the way those who are labelled as ethnic are often expected to conform to certain stereotypical images.

Later on in the conversation Hester asks Tituba to tell her and her expected daughter a story about her homeland: "She wants you to tell her a story. A story about your country. Make her happy, Tituba" (98) [Que tu nous raconte une histoire! Une histoire de ton pays! Fais-lui plaisir, Tituba! (156)]. Tituba tells Hester the story of an orphan girl who deserts her life of solitude out of love for a young black man, and how that has marked the beginning of a life full of suffering. This resonates with Tituba's own life story which stands as an undeclared confession against the historical confession in the documents of her deposition. This continuous modification of Tituba's confession disrupts Tituba's narratorial voice conveying that it is impossible to tell Tituba's "true" story, and that a true representation of Tituba's life can only happen through a continuous disruption of her confessions. In this sense, Tituba's story is constantly evolving, challenging any attempt to pin down her character. After hearing Tituba's story, Hester asks her suspiciously: "What's this story you are telling me, Tituba? It's yours isn't it? Do tell me!" (99) [Qu'elle histoire me racontes-tu là, Tituba? N'est-ce pas la tienne?" (157)]. Tituba refused to answer: "But something kept me from telling her" (99) [Quelque chose me retint de me confier (157)]. Tituba's refusal to confess is key to Condé's project. Tituba produces multiple confessions communicating the impossibility of full historical recovery of diasporic histories.

Through Tituba's encounter with Hester, Condé also engages with feminism, exploring female solidarity and the possibility of cross-racial friendships. In the following dialogue between the two, Condé parodies the position of white feminists vis-à-vis black women:

> "I'd like to write a book where I'd describe a model society governed and run by women! We would give names to our children, we would raise them alone . . . "
>
> I interrupted her, poking fun: "We couldn't make them alone, even so!"
>
> "Alas, no," she said sadly. "Those abominable brutes would have to share in a fleeting moment . . . " She ended up laughing and drew me close to her.
>
> "You are too fond of love, Tituba! I'll never make a feminist out of you!"
>
> "A feminist? What's that?" (101) ["Je voudrais écrire un livre où j'exposerais le modèle d'une société gouvernée, administrée par les femmes! Nous donnerions notre nom à nos enfants, nous les élèverions seules . . . " Je l'interrompais moqueusement: "Nous ne pourrions les faire seules, tout de même!" Elle satirisait: "Hélas non! Il faudrait que ces brutes abhorrées participent l'espace d'un moment . . ." Elle finissait par rire et m'attirait contre elle: "Tu aimes trop l'amour, Tituba! Je ne ferai jamais de toi une féministe!" "Une féministe! Qu'est ce que c'est que cela?" (159–60)]

In this passage Tituba mocks Hester's feminist project, and refuses to be indoctrinated by her ideas, echoing many black women's often skeptical attitude toward white feminists' views in Condé's own time.[40] Hester's views echo white middle-class feminists' tendency to speak of women as a single entity and to analyse gender in isolation from other systems of oppression. This perspective seems to be at odds with Tituba, a poor, uneducated black woman, the same way white feminist projects have often seemed at odds with the lived experience of most black women whose main concern has been the struggle against the oppression of racism and poverty.[41] Tituba's resistance to Hester's indoctrination is just another example of Tituba's challenge to any attempt to contain her within a particular discourse or ideology.

In this dialogue Condé is also exposing the ongoing tension between feminists and modern witches. Russell talks about the difference between the feminist movement, which adopted the image of the witch as a political symbol, and the Craft, which is more concerned with female spirituality: "Most feminists regard witchcraft (and indeed spirituality in general) as a foolish diversion from political goals. Many witches on the other hand resent the politicization of the craft by feminist witches."[42] Hester is the embodiment of a radical feminist, who wants to create a female society, and who is desperately trying to politicize Tituba, while this latter expresses an open view of the world which refuses the exclusion of men from it. Tituba also reflects the witches' openness and celebration of sexuality. Here Condé uses women's voices from the past in order to explore the social, political, racial and sexual structures of the present.

Condé's adaptation of Hawthorne's novel turns Hester into a contemporary feminist figure who kills herself and her daughter rather than accept being branded with the letter A. Hester refuses to succumb to

---

40. See Manzor-Coats, who elaborates on this point in "Of Witches and Other Things," 743–45. It is possible that Condé is also reflecting on the views of African American feminists vs. their Caribbean counterparts. In her interview with Barbara Lewis, Condé points out that in Guadeloupe, women's attitude toward men is ambivalent. She reports: "We would like to see them more adult, more grown up, but we discuss with them how we would like them to change. So the crisis is not as dramatic as it is in black America, it seems to me" (Barbara Lewis, "No Silence: An Interview with Maryse Condé," *Callaloo* 18.3 [1995]: 550). Condé conveys that African American women are more radical in their approach to masculinity, unlike Caribbean women whose attitude seems to be more moderate. Perhaps in her light reaction to Hester's radical feminist views, Tituba is voicing a Caribbean approach to feminism that is less stern.

41. For more information see *Paula Giddings, When and Where I Enter: The Impact of Black Women on Race and Sex in America* (New York: Bantam Books, 1985); and bell hooks, *Ain't I a Woman: Black Women and Feminism* (London: Pluto, 1982).

42. Russell, *A History of Witchcraft*, 156.

Puritan ethics of punishment, defying a traditional Christian discourse of female heroism. Condé even suggests a homoerotic relationship between Tituba and Hester:

> That night Hester lay down beside me, as she did sometimes. I laid my head on the quiet water lily of her cheek and held her tight. Surprisingly, a feeling of pleasure slowly flooded over me. Can you feel pleasure from hugging a body similar to your own? . . . Was Hester showing me another kind of bodily pleasure? (122) [Cette nuit-là, Hester vint s'étendre a côté de moi, comme elle le faisait parfois. J'appuyai ma tête sur le nénuphar tranquille de sa joue et me serrai contre elle. Doucement le plaisir m'envahit, ce qui m'étonna. Peut-on éprouver du plaisir a se serrer contre un corps semblable au sien? . . . Hester m'indiquait-elle le chemin d'une autre jouissance? (189–190)]

Does Tituba's desire for physical intimacy with Hester symbolize a possible closeness between white and black women beyond racial and class differences? Or is this another of Condé's ironic commentaries where she is simply mocking the portrayal of female intimacy and desire in women's fiction?[43] Suggestively, however, in her afterlife existence Tituba pays homage to the dead Hester and names an orchid after her: "One day I discovered an orchid among the mossy roots of a fern and I named it Hester" (157) [Un jour, je découvris une orchidée dans la racine mousseuse d'une fougére. Je la baptisai 'Hester' (241)]. This is clearly a symbolic act of invitation to white women to share space and dialogue.

Perhaps more subversively, the relationship between Hester and Tituba, as Manzor-Coats suggests, echoes that of Condé and Mme. Gallimard, who asked Condé to write a story about a woman from the Caribbean, just as Hester asks Tituba to tell her and her expected daughter a story about her homeland.[44] Both Condé and Tituba recount their stories to white audiences. Tituba to Hester, and Condé to the French publisher and reader. The way Tituba modifies her life story for Hester and her daughter echoes the way Condé adapts the narrative for her readers by giving them a heroine who, on the surface seems to conform to the clichéd

---

43. In her interview with Pfaff, Condé talks about the element of irony in her portrayal of Tituba and Hester's relationship. She explains: "To show how much fun I was having, I imagined an encounter in jail between Tituba and Hester, the heroine of Nathaniel Hawthorne's *The Scarlet Letter*. Both talk about feminism in very modern language" (Pfaff, *Conversations with Maryse Condé*, 60).

44. Manzor-Coats, "Of Witches and Other Things," 743.

image of the ethnic witch with supernatural powers and harmony with nature.

THE NOVEL'S translation and packaging in both French and English become tangible forms through which the complexity of Condé's narrative and the way she plays on politics of otherness can be detected. Although Condé did not have any ideas about the topic initially when Mme. Gallimard solicited a story about a Caribbean woman, she decided to follow Gallimard's proposition after she came across Tituba's story.[45] The novel was commodified to suit an audience of French women, and earned Condé France's Grand Prix Littéraire de la Femme, classifying Condé as a writer of Women's fiction.[46] This classification proves ironic since a detailed reading exposes the novel as a parody of feminist writings, containing an abundance of clichés about women and their spirituality. The English translation *I, Tituba, Black Witch of Salem* came out in 1992. It was marketed as a historical narrative, and became instantly tied in with African American slave narratives. By analyzing the novel's packaging in both the French and the English versions, I will show how they target a specific gendered and racial audience through their layout, and explore the politics of ethnicity that are exploited by both versions to attract their specific targeted audiences. I will start by examining the 1986 and the 1988 French editions which were published by Mercure de France, then move on to look at the translations into English published by both Caraf Books and Ballantine Books in 1992.

The cover of the first French edition (1986) features an illustration depicting Salem village by Pierre-Marie Valat (Figure 1). Flames rise from among the buildings, forming an enormous dark cloud that casts a shadow over the village. This scene alludes to the witch trials of Salem, which grew into an uncontrollable craze threatening the village peace and casting a shadow over its people. The cover's layout establishes a direct connection between Condé and her heroine. The words "Moi, Tituba, sorcière" [I, Tituba, witch] in large white print are framed between Condé's name and the description "Noire de Salem" [black of Salem] in smaller orange print. Manzor-Coats argues that this visual layout, which connects Condé to the subtitle "Noire de Salem," anticipates the textual strategy Condé uses in the epigraph where an "intimacy" between Condé and Tituba is

---

45. Pfaff, *Conversations with Maryse Condé*, 58.
46. See Manzor-Coats, "Of Witches and Other Things," 738.

Figure 1. The front cover of the first French edition by Mercure de France (1986)

established.⁴⁷ Condé writes: "Tituba and I lived for a year on the closest of terms. During our endless conversations she told me things she had confided to nobody else" [Tituba et moi, avons vécu en étroite intimité pendant un an. C'est au cours de nos interminables conversations qu'elle m'a dit ces choses qu'elle n'avait confiée a personne]. Manzor-Coats also informs us that the cover for this edition, unlike later editions, provides the reader with the novel's genre: "Histoire romonesque" (Romantic Story/Romance) situating the novel within a feminine tradition.⁴⁸

The back cover maintains the same visual layout of the title and Condé's name, except that the colors are different. The opening sentence on the back cover quotes from the novel's first paragraph narrating Tituba's mother's rape. This reference to rape, which symbolizes women's disempowerment in a patriarchal society, signals an audience concerned with the oppression of women. This edition thus tries to cultivate sympathy for Tituba's story as a woman's story. The following paragraph is a commentary making an analogy between Condé's "black witch," [sorcière noire] and "The white witches, the ones who were hanged, and inspired Arthur Miller's *Witches of Salem*" [les sorcières blanches, celles qui furent pendues et qui inspirèrent Les sorcières de Salem, d'Arthur Miller].⁴⁹ Drawing this parallel between Condé and Miller's fictive accounts of the Salem witch trials the cover cleverly forms a link with American literature. The title's descriptive "noire de Salem" (which later editions drop) works to form this connection and to attract the reader's attention to an American theme. In her interview with Ann Scarboro—who also writes a forward to the English version of Condé's novel—Condé contends that she wanted to call the novel "simply *I, Tituba*, but the publishers said that was a bit laconic as a title and added *Black Witch of Salem*."⁵⁰ This detail sheds light on how marketing tactics work to shape the novel's packaging. The back cover's last comment significantly also makes the link between *Moi, Tituba, sorcière . . . noire de Salem* and Condé's previous work, *Ségou*, which had been favorably received in France: "From the African saga of *Ségou*, Condé moved to a more intimate chronicle, a 'romance,' which again deals with the major themes Condé has explored in her previous works, *Segou I and II*" [De la saga africaine de Ségou, Maryse Condé est allée vers une chronique plus intimiste, une "histoire romanesque" qui reprend cependant les grands thèmes traites dans ses livres précèdent:

---

47. Ibid., 737
48. Ibid., 738.
49. Translations of the front and back covers of the French editions are mine.
50. Scarboro, foreword to *I, Tituba*, 205.

Les murailles de la terre et La terre en miette (*Ségou I et II*)]. Here, the marketing strategies attract a female audience by stressing the intimacy of Condé's account, but without undermining its historical aspect. The paragraph conveys the impression that while *Moi, Tituba, sorcière . . . noire de Salem* explores the same historical topics or "grands thèmes" that *Ségou* treats, it is a "plus intimiste" [a more intimate] chronicle. Again, the intimacy of Condé's account is conveyed primarily through its autobiographical nature, where Tituba seems to be directly speaking/confessing to the reader. The novel's genre is exploited here, giving the impression that Condé's account fits within the conventional strand of autobiographical writings by women of color, where the protagonist appears to exhibit herself through clichéd images of ethnic otherness—that is, a magical exotic being organically connected to her ancestral spirits. Actually, Condé's literary project aims to parody and subvert these clichés.

The two 1988 editions published by Mercure de France in the Folio series remove the novel from its historical context (Figures 2 and 3). The subtitle "Noire de Salem" is omitted and replaced by an ellipsis. The assertion of the novel's genre "Histoire remonesque" is also dropped. Manzor-Coats argues that because Condé obtained Le Grand Prix Littéraire de la Femme for her novel in 1987, the novel was already recognized within the category of Women's Fiction by the time these subsequent editions appeared, which explains the omission of the novel's genre.[51] The illustrations on the front covers as well as the plot summary in the Folio series back covers demonstrate how these editions play on the politics of ethnicity, supporting a gendered and exoticized reading of the text, and how this process is paralleled by a de-emphasizing of the novel's historical themes.

The front cover of one edition of the Folio series depicts a beautiful and enigmatic black woman (Figure 2). Her half-frizzy hair and brown skin suggest racially mixed origins. She is standing alone in the darkness with a determined look in her eyes, completely covered in black. She holds tightly to what looks like a stick decorated with a snake. This is a clear suggestion of a traditional spiritual and medical healer. Moreover, Tituba is standing in the woods with shadows of trees behind her. In the background, the vivid orange sunset fades into darkness. The portrait of Tituba dominates. The vivid orange stands in contrast with her dark silhouette. The shadows of trees behind her enhance her enigmatic and exotic nature: the snake, the wild hair, Tituba standing alone in the forest in the

---

51. See Manzor-Coats, "Of Witches and Other Things," 738.

Figure 2. The front cover of the 1988 edition published by Mercure de France in the Folio series

Figure 3. The (alternative) front cover of the 1988 edition published by Mercure de France in the Folio series

dark—all hint at Tituba's dangerous nature, and conjure the stereotypical imagery of "Voodoo." Tituba is clearly a Voodoo priestess–which again suggests a connection to Miller's portrayal of Tituba in *The Crucible*. Text on the back cover states:

> Fille de l'esclave Abena, violée par un marin anglais a bord d'un vaisseau negrier, Tituba, née a la Barbade, est initiée aux pouvoirs surnaturels par Man Yaya ... Maryse Condé la réhabilite, l'arrache a cet oubli auquel elle avait été condamnée et, pour finir, la ramène a son pays natal, la Barbade au temps des Nègres marrons et des premières révoltes d'esclaves. [Born in Barbados, Tituba, the daughter of the slave Abena, had been raped by an English sailor on the slave ship and initiated into supernatural powers by Mama Yaya. Maryse Condé saved her from the oblivion into which she had been doomed and, eventually, brought her back to her homeland, Barbados during the time of the maroons—and the—first slave revolts.]

This portrayal of Tituba clearly fits clichéd writings about women's empowerment through spirituality and connection to the occult. Tituba's possible involvement in the slave revolt also suggests her heroism. Given its pairing of themes of female empowerment with imagery suggestive of exoticized racial otherness, this edition's packaging seems engineered to attract a specifically white female audience. It provides a sharp contrast with the plot summary in the first edition:

> So begins the novel that Maryse Condé dedicated to Tituba, daughter of a slave, who was one of the witches of Salem. How Tituba won the reputation as a witch in Barbados, how she loved and married John Indian, and how they were both sold to the Reverend Samuel Parris, who took them first to Boston and then to the village of Salem. It was in this Puritan society that collective hysteria triggered the witch-hunt and the sadly notorious 1692 trial. [Ainsi commence le roman que Maryse Condé a consacré a Tituba, fille d'esclave, qui fut l'une des sorcières de Salem. Comment Tituba acquit une réputation de sorcière a la Barbade, comment elle aima et épousa John Indien, comment ils furent tous deux vendus au pasteur Samuel Parris qui les emmena à Boston puis dans le village de Salem. C'est là, dans cette société puritaine, que l'hystérie collective provoqua la chasse aux sorcières et les procès tristement célèbre de 1692.]

Importantly, there is no mention of Tituba's supernatural powers in the first edition's plot summary, as it emphasizes more the novel's historical grounding than it appeals to racial exotica.

The other Folio edition, also published in 1988, shows an illustration on the front cover by the nineteenth-century French artist Marie-Guilhelmine Benoist, *Portrait d'une négresse* (Figure 3). The painting shows a black woman seated, half-naked, modeling for the artist. Her right breast is exposed to the viewer. Her hair is elegantly wrapped in a white headscarf. She gathers a garment, of the same color and material, around her body, just below her breasts. The white clothing creates a contrast with the blackness of her skin. The model's dark color is also enhanced by the blank background and its clear pastel color. Tituba here is domesticated, as suggested through the tamed hair, the white garment, the pastel colors of the background and her passive demeanor, which provides a contrast with the illustration on the front cover of the previous Folio edition, where Tituba looks mysterious and dangerous and the background colors are more vivid and energetic. Despite the individualization of this 1988 Folio portrait, the model remains anonymous and silenced, as indicated from the painting's title. She is merely a "négresse," without name or identity, and her passivity is highlighted by the pale color of the background. Even more, the painting establishes a parallel between Condé and the black model, who is also from Guadeloupe, and a parallel with Tituba, who is also a black woman from the Caribbean who was rendered silent and anonymous by historical records.[52]

The novel's 1986 edition seems to target a white female audience, but without a de-emphasizing of the novel's historical theme, unlike the subsequent Folio series editions which downplay the novel's historical aspect. It seems that Condé's French award for the novel put a stamp on her work as Women's Fiction, limiting her target audiences, as reflected in the marketing strategies of the Folio editions, which exploit Condé's "ethnicity" and support a gendered and a rather exoticized reading of the novel. While the first French edition cover plays on the female readers' identification with Tituba's story as a woman's story, especially with the reference to Tituba's mother's rape, the later Folio editions seem to focus more on Tituba's

---

52. In his exploration of the historical background of Benoist's painting, James Smalls comments: "It has been suggested that The *Portrait d'une négresse* was not commissioned but was painted on the artist's own initiative, and was modelled after a black slave brought back to France by Benoist's brother-in-law, a civil servant and ship's purser who had returned from the French island of Guadeloupe in 1800." James Smalls, "Slavery Is a Woman: Race, Gender, and Visuality in Marie Benoist's *Portrait d'une négresse* (1800)," *Nineteenth-Century Art Worldwide 3.1* (2004), http://www.19thc-artworldwide.org/spring_04/articles/smal.html.

exotic otherness. She is represented as either the dangerous Voodoo priestess figure, or the passive, demure "negresse."

CONTRARY TO the marketing strategies which attempt to promote the novel as a conventional self-referential genre where ethnicity is being displayed, the textual analysis shows a complex narrative strategy, where Condé is consciously producing familiar images in order to challenge racialized and exoticized perceptions of what is recognisably ethnic. Manzor-Coats tells us: "The very fact that Condé, a native of Guadeloupe is writing this story in French, and publishing it in France, signals the colonial incorporation and relation of this Caribbean island, to this day an overseas department of France."[53] But how does Condé address this relationship as a postcolonial author writing for a French audience? A reading of Condé's commentaries in her interviews show that the question of readership is a complex one. In the following extract from her interview with Barbara Lewis, Condé laments:

> When you live in a small island like Guadeloupe, nobody reads in Guadeloupe. Nobody pays attention to your work. People just know you because they see your face sometimes on TV. They don't know anything about you as a writer. They might see you on the street and they'll say, "Yes, I saw you on television, but what is your name and what are you doing?" That is the kind of discussion I have with people all the time. So, it is very frustrating to be a West Indian writer. When you go abroad, people know you and pay more attention to you. But at the same time, they are foreigners, and they don't completely understand what you wanted to put in your book.[54]

This statement articulates the issue of audiences and readership that many postcolonial and third world writers grapple with. Condé's work is more accessible to foreign audiences than to Caribbean ones, and this absence of engagement from a Caribbean readership, as Condé sees it, obscures the particularities of her work that can only be brought to the surface by a readership that fully understands the specifics of Caribbean culture. Condé also occupies the same ambivalent space as many postcolonial writers who come from economies where books are not easily accessible, and

---

53. Manzor-Coats, "Of Witches and Other Things," 739.
54. Lewis, "No Silence," 547–48.

whose use of European languages insures their accessibility to a European and international market that can also alienate them from their local and national readership.⁵⁵

However, while Condé writes from within the European canon and uses French, she creates a narrative mode which allows her to resist the linguistic and cultural domination of the Center. On a textual level, Condé uses parody which enables her to subtly challenge stereotypical nuances of ethnicity. On a linguistic level, she makes use of Creole words which are meant to signify cultural distinctiveness. Condé comments in numerous interviews on the limited notions a French readership has about Caribbean writings, noting in her interview with Pfaff: "In France I have a rather hard time counteracting the exotic fashion in which West Indian literature as a whole is perceived."⁵⁶ Hence, Condé's use of parody which dominates the narrative works to undercut and question received notions of identity. Condé deconstructs these notions mainly through the way she parodies heroic myths. Her portrayal of Tituba, Mama Yaya, Christopher the maroon, and Hawthorne's Hester, for instance, shows how she turns these characters into mock heroes.

The text accentuates Tituba's mock heroism through her communication with the dead spirits of her ancestors. Ironically, Tituba's mother and Mama Yaya from whom she constantly seeks guidance and protection hardly provide her with any. They warn her about men in a comical way: "Men do not love. They possess. They subjugate" (14) [Les hommes n'aiment pas. Ils possèdent. Ils asservissent (29)]. The symbolic voice of the ancestor, which often represents wisdom and guidance, becomes comical and ineffective in Condé's text. Condé remarks, "I know that in any female epic, some elements must be present, and I deliberately included them," continuing that the "presence of the invisible (the conversations with the mother and with Mama Yaya) is deliberately overdrawn" (212). In her interview with Pfaff she contends that her book is "a pastiche of

---

55. In the context of the postcolonial debate about the dialectic of language between the colonized and colonizer, Ngugi Wa Thiong'o comments on African literature written in European languages: "Its greatest weakness still lay where it has always been, in the audience—the petty-bourgeoisie readership automatically assumed by the very choice of language." Ngugi Wa Thiong'o, *Decolonising the Mind: The Politics of Language in African Literature* (London: Heinemann, 1986), 22. Frantz Fanon believes that "a man who has a language consequently possesses the world expressed and implied by that language," and argues that by adopting the language of the colonizer, one is accepting the world of the colonizer and its standards. Frantz Fanon, *Black Skin, White Masks* (London: Pluto, 1986), 18.

56. Pfaff, *Conversations with Maryse Condé*, 106; see also p. 101, where Condé mentions how French audiences label her work sometimes as "exotic," "savory," or "humorous."

the feminine heroic novel, a parody containing a lot of clichés about the grandmother, the sacrosanct grandmother, and about women and their relationship to the occult."[57] Condé here consciously produces banal preconceptions of what is ethnic in order to challenge simplistic notions of identity.

Christopher the maroon is another example of a mock-hero. The narrative reveals that Christopher, who forms a threat to the plantation system, is actually only interested in glorifying his image. Condé mocks him when she shows his obsession with self-image and his desire to reach immortality through a song of his own composition. Christopher almost turns into "un objet de pitié" when he seeks Tituba's help and asks her to grant him power: "Tituba, I want you to make me invincible" (146) [Tituba, je veux que tu me rendes invincible! (225)]. Tituba's reaction to his pathetic request was: "I almost burst out laughing, but refrained for fear of irritating him, and managed to reply very calmly: 'I don't know whether I am capable of that Christopher'" (146) [Je faillis éclater de rire, me retins de peur de l'irriter et parvins a répondre avec calme: "Christopher, je ne sais pas si je suis capable de cela!" (225)]. Here, the image of Christopher as the embodiment of the hyper masculine black hero is completely undermined.[58]

Condé also plays on white notions of heroism through Hester. Condé turns Hawthorne's classical heroine into a feminist who embodies twentieth-century views on feminism. In this way, Condé's anachronistic Hester is more radical and rebellious than Hawthorne's heroine. She even wants to write a book about a model society ruled by women. Condé also maps a new destiny for Hester, who kills herself and the daughter she carries, thus rewriting and recreating a controversial Hester, who challenges Christian doctrine that forbids suicide and defies white Puritan notions of morality and female heroism articulated by Hawthorne. Hester and Tituba's solidarity is based on their resistance to confession. Condé even goes

---

57. Pfaff, *Conversations with Maryse Condé*, 60.
58. This contradictory representation of Christopher the maroon in the text shows how Condé refuses to engage with narratives of black male heroism. Christopher, who represents opposition to slavery, turns out to be a conspirator with whites in the perpetuation of African slavery. He betrays Tituba and reports to the whites her involvement in the slave revolt in order to keep his own freedom. John Indian, Tituba's husband, is another example. He also betrays Tituba and abandons her to her fate when he sides with the whites during the witch craze of Salem in order to save his own skin. In these two examples, Condé also holds black men responsible for the perpetuation of the system of slavery, which shows his refusal to commit to black nationalism. Actually, this negative portrayal of black identities makes Condé quite unpopular among some critics. See Doris Kadish, "'Tituba' et sa traduction," in *L'oeuvre de Maryse Condé*, 231–47.

as far as suggesting a homoerotic relationship between Hester and Tituba, thus further destabilizing traditional notions of female heroism.

As a postcolonial writer Condé also uses specific linguistic modes in order to assert her cultural distinctiveness. She consciously chooses to import Creole words into her text in order to foreground cultural distance, and allow the reader to view difference. Words like "Akwaba," "Canari," "Grangreks," become cultural signs representing Caribbean culture against the linguistic and cultural domination of the Center. In *The Empire Writes Back,* Bill Ashcroft, Gareth Griffiths and Helen Tiffin explore similar textual strategies used by postcolonial writers to assert cultural difference, examining linguistic and semantic variations in postcolonial writing:

> Post-colonial writing abrogates the privileged centrality of "English" [in Condé's case it is French] by using language to signify difference while employing a sameness which allows it to be understood. It does this by employing language variance, the "part" of a wider cultural whole, which assists in the work of language seizure whilst being neither transmuted nor overwhelmed by its adoptive vehicle.[59]

Similarly, through these strategies Condé's text both constitutes cultural difference while simultaneously attempting to bridge it. Kathleen Gyssels in "L'intraduisibilite de Tituba Indien" establishes that from a linguistic point of view the use of the phrase "black witch" [sorcière noire] in the title is inexact since "in the Antilles, a witch is called a 'quimboiseuse,' or a 'séancière,' an 'obeah-woman' in Jamaica" [aux Antilles, une sorcière est appellée une "quimboiseuse," ou une "séancière," une "obeah-woman" a la Jamaïque].[60] Condé's use of the word "sorcière" instead of "quimboiseuse," or "séancière" provides an insight into the narrative's duplicate meaning, and expresses the way she plays on the semantic connotation of the word. Condé uses a Western term because the notion of sorcery imposed on the historical Tituba was a Western, Puritan definition. Condé's decision to bypass Caribbean terminology shows the way she appropriates white colonial definitions in order to both interrogate and undermine the notion of sorcery associated with Tituba.

There is a telling juxtaposition between the French editions of *I, Tituba* and the American ones, wherein the politics of ethnicity are displayed dif-

---

59. Bill Ashcroft, Gareth Griffiths, and Helen Tiffin, *The Empire Writes Back: Theory and Practice in Post-colonial Literatures* (London: Routledge, 1989), 50.

60. Kathleen Gyssels, "L'intraduisibilite de Tituba Indien, sujet interculrurel," *Mots pluriels* 23 (2003): 3, http://www.arts.uwa.edu.au/MotsPluriels/; my translation.

ferently. The translation to English obscures Condé's authorial motifs by heavily politicizing the novel and shaping it as a quasi neo-slave narrative. The edition by Ballantine Books (1992), for instance, includes an illustration that consumes only a quarter of the cover's space, depicting Tituba in court (Figure 4). Tituba is wearing a long plain dress, and a headscarf; she is handcuffed, with her back to an unfriendly audience. She faces two white women, and a girl who is pointing at her accusingly. A judge with an unfriendly face is standing on a pedestal on one side of the courtroom. This illustration depicts Tituba's trial and shows her as trapped in a hostile environment. Tituba, however, does not seem to be intimidated by her audience. She stands erect, and proudly defiant. The exotic looking images of Tituba in the Folio French versions stand in striking contrast to her portrayal in this illustration.

This Ballantine Books cover focuses less on the individualized portrait of Tituba, and more on the historical moment of Tituba's trial, thereby reflecting an attempt to position the novel in a slave narrative tradition, a genre which is not prominent in Caribbean literary tradition, but eminent in African American literature and well known to an American readership.[61] Furthermore, Angela Davis's name is printed on the front cover, in addition to her comment extracted from the *New York Times Book Review* just below the title. The back cover shows even more clearly the novel's particular politicization. There are extracts from the *Boston Sunday Globe,* the *Chicago Tribune,* and the last blurb is by Henry Louis Gates, Jr. These extracts from respected newspapers and a comment from a highly influential African American literary critic such as Gates surely put a stamp on Condé as a political black woman writer. The *Boston Sunday Globe* states: "Stunning . . . Maryse Condé's imaginative subversion of historical records forms a critique of contemporary American society and its ingrained racism and sexism."

Significantly, allusions to "historical records," "racism," and "sexism," do not occur on the covers of any of the French editions. The plot summary on the back cover notably highlights Tituba's journey from the Caribbean to the United States, forming the link between Caribbean and African American diasporic histories: "From the warm shores of seventeenth-century Barbados to the harsh realities of the slave trade, and the cold customs of Puritanical New England, Tituba, the only black victim of the Salem witch trial." This focus on history and the politics of racial

---

61. For more on slave narratives in Caribbean literature, see Caroline Rody, *The Daughter's Return: African-American and Caribbean Women's Fictions of History* (New York: Oxford University Press, 2001).

Figure 4. The front cover of the English-language edition by Ballantine Books (1992)

identity contrasts with the summary on the back cover of the French versions.

The book's first page contains comments about the novel from the *New York Times Book Review*, the *Boston Sunday Globe*, the *Chicago Tribune*, *Publishers Weekly*, and *Library Journal* and a blurb from another well-known neo-slave narrative author and critic, Charles Johnson. Extracts from the *Boston Sunday Globe* further emphasize this connection between the African American and Caribbean shared histories of enslavement and displacement:

> Condé restores a vital link in the spiritual and cultural chain that connects Caribbean and American descendants with their African ancestors, and helps create for them an alternative to the colonial and postcolonial traditions from which they have been excluded.

This focused publicity is intended for a readership that is not familiar with Caribbean literature. According to Caroline Rody, who examines writings by contemporary Caribbean writers such as Jean Rhys and Maryse Condé in *The Daughter's Return*, "Anglophone Caribbean literature is still foreign to U.S. English studies, and francophone literature all the more foreign, in the original or in translation,"[62] which explains to a large extent the attempt to accommodate differences and assert the novel as a quasi-historical neo-slave narrative, highlighting the characteristics that Condé's revisionary narrative ostensibly holds in common with African American narratives. The Ballantine English edition tries to portray Tituba as a noble victim of oppression, rather than as the exotic figure suggested by the French editions.

The English-language edition by Caraf Books (1992) depicts on its front cover a black woman with a dull and solemn face (Figure 5). Her African features are more pronounced than those of the exotic Tituba with mixed race features who is depicted in the covers of the French Folio series. The face is seen through what seems to be a fence, which makes it quite difficult to detect her gaze. The variations of red and orange in the background reinforce both the intense and the somber expression on the woman's face. The exotic Tituba of the French covers is replaced by an intense looking woman for a U.S. readership. In this way, the Caraf cover seems to be targeting a more political and serious audience than the one targeted by the French versions.[63] The first part of the title "I, Tituba" is

---

62. Rody, *The Daughter's Return*, 84.
63. Manzor-Coats argues that this cover targets "angry black women" ("Of Witches and Other Things," 738).

Figure 5. The front cover of the English-language edition by Caraf Books (1992)

quite prominent, and printed in big letters, as if to express Tituba's protest against her omission from history.

Both the Ballantine and Caraf English editions have a foreword by Angela Davis, and an afterword by Scarboro, in addition to a glossary, revealing further the elaborate attempt to politicize the novel. It is important to note that the French versions do not contain a foreword, or an afterword, and contain only brief translations in footnotes rather than an elaborate glossary. As Ballantine and Caraf are undoubtedly well aware, the story of Davis, who was falsely accused, judged by an all-white jury and sent to prison for sixteen months in 1970, resonates with Tituba's story. Davis writes: "Tituba looked for her story in the history of the Salem witch trials and could not find it. I have looked for my history in the story of the colonization of this continent and have found silences, omissions, distortions, and fleeting, enigmatic insinuations" (ix). The Salem trial here becomes an allegory for Davis's trial and for the trials of African Americans in the United States more broadly.

Through Davis's comments, the marketing strategies work to create an analogy between Davis's story and Condé's novel where the Salem trial is also used as an allegory to reflect on present day America. The significance of Davis's foreword in this specific context shows how texts can be manipulated in the process of translation and transfer from one culture to another. Davis's serious tone in the foreword provides a sharp contrast with the novel's satirical narrative mode, as well as with Condé's comments in the afterword. Davis views the novel as a historical construction and uses the expression "historical novel" more than once to describe Condé's project. This is countered by Condé's words in the afterword where she makes clear that she does not intend to write a historical novel: "*Tituba* is just the opposite of a historical novel. I was not interested at all in what her real life could have been. I had few precise documents. . . . I really invented Tituba" (201). Condé also states that the story is part "parody" and that Tituba is a "mock-epic" heroine (201). The reader of the translation operates in an ambivalent space, between Davis's foreword which implies the historicity of the novel, and Condé's words in the afterword which undercut the novel's historicity and insist on the fictional nature of Tituba. Davis ends her commentary by referring to the ambiguity concerning Tituba's racial origins. She comments: "there are those who dispute her African descent, countering that she was Indian, perhaps hoping to stir up enmity between black and Native American women as we seek to recreate our respective histories" (xi). Davis, unlike Condé, who complicates Tituba's lineage and racial history, is talking in terms of absolutes by giving Tituba a fixed racial identity. Davis's comment also shows disregard for historical inquiry by supposing that historians who argue for Tituba's Indianess attempt to cause hostility between African Americans and Native Americans. Davis's particular reading, however, shows how Condé's text lends itself to diverse interpretations.

To grasp fully how marketing strategies can obfuscate Condé's authorial intentions, it is also important to look at the way the original version and the translation deal with glossing. The English language translation contains a detailed glossary in the back numbering twenty-three words in total, while the original text contains a total of only six words translated in footnotes. The insertion of a glossary in the translation to English shows that an effort is being made to explain unfamiliar words to the American audience, while there is a very moderate account taken of the French reader, despite the fact that both audiences are likely to be unfamiliar with the same words. The terminology used to explain the words is also revealing. In the French version, the translations are short and concise; for example, the word "Akawaba" (15) (*Moi, Tituba,* 15) is translated as "Bienvenue," which means "Welcome," whereas the English glossary provides a more detailed translation. The same word is translated as "Ashanti greeting meaning 'welcome'" (*I, Tituba,* 185), further politicizing Condé's novel by establishing a direct connection with Africa. The definitions in the English text also make the novel easily accessible to its targeted African American readership. Put another way, the English translation is making fewer demands on the American readership by attempting to conform to its linguistic and cultural expectations. Yet, in a paradoxical way, the glossary also functions as a reminder to the reader that they are about to explore a foreign text which has a specific cultural context. Even the insertion of a glossary in the translation to English becomes problematic, given that Condé consciously uses ambiguous words in her original text as a narrative strategy. Pseudoscientific names for plants like "passionflorinde," "Populara indica," and "Prune taureau" in the French text are premeditated to keep Condé's readers under the illusion that the text provides an accurate knowledge of the science of plants. This authorial strategy, which challenges the French audiences into delving beyond a superficial reading of the text, is undermined in the translation, since the glossary points out that these words are invented by Condé.

Françoise Massardier-Kenny in "La question de la traduction plurielle ou les traducteurs de Maryse Condé" looks at Condé's *Une saison à Rihata* and *La vie scélérate* and their translations. She explores the way translations exercize their authority either through "departure culture" [la culture de départ], when "the movement is from the reader to the author rather than from the author to the reader" [le mouvement se fera du lecteur vers l'auteur plutôt que de l'auteur vers le lecteur], or the opposite, where "the movement happens from the author to the reader since the book's value is indicated by reference to the target culture" [le mouvement se fait de l'auteur au lecteur puisque la valeur du livre est indiquée par référence a la culture d'arrivée].[64] The novel's translation and transformation into English fits this second category. The cover, the comments, the glossary, the foreword, and afterword all show that the English version seeks to assimilate the novel into African American culture. In that sense it is the writer who is moving toward the reader, rather than the other way around, where the reader moves toward the author, and toward "departure culture" and its particularities. The reader of the translation thus is not challenged, since the voice of Maryse Condé becomes assimilated into the culture of the audience. This is reinforced by the example of the glossary of notes that was created for the American reader. At the level of packaging, the absence of the translator's name from both the front and back cover of the Caraf Books edition betrays an attempt to create a direct interaction between the author and her readers without the mediation of the translator, and thus further inserts her into African American culture. Yet, the question of whether one brings the text to the audience or the other way around is very much affected by the author's prestige and international reputation. Condé is less established in the United States than in France, and thus less demand seems to be placed on the American reader.

The fact that Condé uses a European language to talk about a non-European culture complicates the narrative even further and shows that there is an act of translation taking place, even before the novel reaches its French audience. Condé's attempt to turn from Caribbean terminology, as mentioned before, shows that the translation to English is a double translation, and that there is already a similar movement from "departure culture" to "target culture" taking place with the French version. Significantly, Condé and her heroine are positioned within two different linguistic codes. As a Guadeloupean, Condé is positioned within a French Caribbean cultural and linguistic code, while Tituba, who is figured as a native of Barbados, is situated in the English Caribbean. Condé becomes a translator and a mediator between the English-speaking Tituba and the

---

64. Françoise Massardier-Kenny, "La question de la traduction plurielle ou 'les traducteurs de Maryse Condé,'" in *L'oeuvre de Maryse Condé*, 250; my translation.

French reader. However, the insertion of French Creole words in the text complicates the narrative, since the reader here is dealing with a heroine from the English-speaking Caribbean, who is introduced to them through French Creole. Elizabeth Mudimbe-Boyi in "Giving a Voice to Tituba: The Death of the Author?" argues that the epigraph sets Condé outside the text, and situates Tituba within it, contending that this strategy of subversion allows Tituba to take the authority from Condé and become the narrator:

> *Tituba* unfolds a long monologic "conversation" in which the writer becomes the simple listener of a narrating subject telling her own life story. The book is thus a fictional "autobiography" from which the writer has completely disappeared, leaving Tituba to take pre-eminence and become both the narrator and the narrated.[65]

It is hard to believe that Condé completely disappears from the narrative and becomes a listener to Tituba's story. On the contrary, Condé is repeatedly interrupting Tituba's autobiographical voice. The French Creole words form a constant reminder of the author's presence in the text. It is a reminder that these words are Condé's and not Tituba's. Condé is consciously deconstructing Tituba's voice through language. She is playing on the historicity of her own project by questioning the possibility of translating/reimagining Tituba's life.

Richard Philcox, Condé's husband, and the translator of most of Condé's work, including *Moi, Tituba, sorcière . . . noire de Salem*, talks about the problematics of translating Condé in his article on *Traversée de la Mangrove*. Philcox compares Condé's writings with Virginia Woolf's and views this comparison between Condé and writers from the European canon as necessary in the process of translating Condé's work. He argues that in order to familiarize the American reader with Caribbean writings, it is important to use texts from within a canon with which the Anglophone reader is familiar:

> It is through a European linguistic system and a European literary tradition that one reaches the Antillean society. It is evident that to please a contemporary Western public, the English translation has to follow the same process and find a European literary tradition in order to commu-

---

65. Elizabeth Mudimbe-Boyi, "Giving a Voice to Tituba: The Death of the Author?" *World Literature Today* (1993): 751–756, 752.

nicate the text's Caribbeaness. [C'est par un système linguistique européen, par une tradition littéraire européenne, qu'on arrive à la société antillaise. Il était évident que pour plaire à un public occidental la traduction anglaise devait suivre le même processus et trouver une tradition littéraire européenne pour communiquer la Caribeanté du texte.][66]

Philcox's task is complicated. He has to walk a tightrope between insuring the accessibility of Condé's text to the American reader without compromising her position and her authorial strategies, which actually often call into question the supremacy of the European canon. Philcox's words suggest that the process of translation is not straightforward. When he talks about "pleasing the audience," he again raises the question of the extent to which a text can be assimilated into the target culture. It is important to note that the publication of Condé's translated work in the United States puts her books in the realm of international literature. Maria Tymoczko in "Post-colonial Writing and Literary Translation" argues: "Being marketed in the United States is often seen as an essential index of international success."[67] Yet, this international success becomes to a large extent dependent on marketing strategies which situate texts in a specific cultural and literary contexts to suit the receiving audience, as is the case of *I, Tituba*.

Condé's novel in its original version as well as in translation reaches its audience through a complex process of translation and marketing strategies. A comparison between the novel's French version, which is aimed at a French gendered audience, and the translation, whose main targeted audience is African American, shows how marketing strategies differ considerably depending on the audience. Further, it is important to note that both the French and the American versions are translations, and they reach their audiences through a complex process of transfer across both language and culture. As a result, Condé's novel generates an ambivalent narrative where the politics of ethnicity are constantly questioned, with Condé destabilizing her own project and parodying her characters, but without undermining her commitment to the task of rewriting the forgotten past of a Caribbean heroine. Condé provokingly reinserts Tituba into the pages of history, turning the stigma of the "witch" into a positive and empowering symbol of Tituba's spirituality. The cultural distance created

---

66. Richard Philcox, "Traduire 'Traversee de la Mangrove,'" in *L'oeuvre de Maryse Condé*, 230.
67. Maria Tymoczko, "Post-colonial Writing and Literary Translation," in *Post-colonial Translation: Theory and Practice*, ed. Susanna Bassnett and Harish Trivedi (London: Routledge, 1999), 15.

by Condé's status as a postcolonial author writing in the language of the Center makes it possible for her to create an elusive language which challenges the reader in its indeterminacy, and allows for a questioning and interrogation of racial, cultural and literary discourses despite the considerable constraints created by marketing and translating strategies.

5

Conclusion
The Return of Witches, Goddesses, and Angry Spirits

> I write to communicate with my ancestors.
> —Edwidge Danticat

DANTICAT, MORRISON, AND CONDÉ celebrate their female characters' legacy by granting them an afterlife. Their protagonists are in various ways crucified only to be resurrected as defiant spirits who return to provide inspiration to traumatized women. They continue to be useful to their people, carrying their traditions beyond the limits of time and history. However, Danticat's, Morrison's, and Condé's female characters return not only to inspire their people, but also to haunt and torment their oppressors. While the return of these heroines does not realistically offer solutions to the violence committed against women, their figurative death and resurrection offers an important and necessary political vision that disturbs the boundaries between the oppressed and the oppressor, and between what becomes conveniently forgotten and what needs to be remembered.

Significantly, Danticat, Morrison, and Condé assert women's liberation via strong and complex female spiritual figures who are furthest removed from traditional notions of female heroism. Their return is also indeed a critical revision of the Christian belief in the afterlife as punishment. After her death, Danticat's Martine is transformed into a malevolent and defiant manifestation of Erzulie: the Marinet, the angry spirit of the night who eats her male victims. Morrison's Convent women, Consolata, Mavis, Gigi, and Pallas, after being shot by the men of Ruby, return as goddess-like figures, accomplishing after death what they could not in their lives. In a similar vein, Condé's Tituba also returns victoriously after her execution, as a revolutionary spirit, inspiring her people's rebellion.

In *Breath, Eyes, Memory,* Sophie, who struggles with her sexuality and suffers from what her therapist calls "the Madonna complex," is liberated from these patriarchal standards of female sexuality in her mother's funeral. Sophie dresses her mother in red, which becomes the visual sign of her liberation and her refusal to conform to patriarchal notions of purity and propriety. Seeing the dress, her grandmother "looked as though she was going to fall down, in shock" (231). But this symbolic act of liberation allows Sophie to turn her mother from a helpless sexual victim to an enraged and exuberant jezebel: "I picked out the most crimson of all my mother's clothes, a bright red" (227). The symbolic meaning of the color red becomes even more meaningful when Sophie tells us that her family's name, Caco "is the name for a scarlet bird. A bird so crimson, it makes the reddest hibiscus or the brightest flame trees seem white. The Caco bird, when it dies, there is always a rush of blood that rises to its neck and the wings, they look so bright, you would think them on fire" (150). When Martine dies, we are reminded of this intense visual image, as the deceased Martine is covered from head to toe in bright red in her funeral. The association of the Caco women with red birds, flight and wings of fire clearly communicates Sophie's vision where she insists on granting agency to her mother and all the Caco women, even after death.[1] This is made even clearer as Sophie affirms: "There is a place where women are buried in clothes the color of flames, where we drop coffee on the ground for those who went ahead" (234). Sophie also rebels against oppressive Judeo-Christian images of womanhood, in favor of Africanist ones, reclaiming her family's cultural identity. She replies to the priest who believes her mother will not go to heaven on account of the way she is dressed, that "she is going to Guinea" (228), which, in Vodou cosmology, is the residing place of the loa and the ancestors, and where Vodou followers go after their death.

Similarly, the heroism of Morrison's female characters is also manifested through their transformation after death, defying traditional notions of womanhood inherent in Judeo-Christianity. Morrison's novel ends with

---

1. The association of Martine with red brings to mind another Caribbean heroine, Antoinette, Jean Rhys's protagonist in *Wide Sargasso Sea,* who before setting Thornfield Hall on fire asks for her red dress, which becomes necessary in her performance of her rite of liberation. The color red similarly inscribes Martine and Antoinette's Caribbeanness. Jean Rhys, *Wide Sargasso Sea* (New York: Buccaneer Books, 1966), 186–87.

a postscript about the Convent women who return as warriors and goddesses. Their bodies disappear miraculously after the shootings, only to be resurrected as powerful figures. Mavis and Gigi are not running from their pasts anymore. Gigi talks to her imprisoned father, and Mavis reconnects with her daughter. Pallas and Gigi return like female warriors, Pallas bearing a sword, and Gigi dressed in military gear. Consolata appears as a black goddess sitting in Piedade's lap, an image reminiscent of the "Pietà" but with the reversal of the son and mother image to daughter and mother. When the Convent women disappear after their death, Ana Fleetwood wonders meaningfully: "What would be on the other side? What on earth would it be? What on earth?" (305).

Condé's Tituba, who returns as revolutionary spirit proudly reports: "I have been behind every revolt, every insurrection, and every act of disobedience" (175) encouraging and nourishing her people's dream of freedom. Tituba also becomes one with her island's landscape: "We have become one and the same. There isn't one of its footpaths I haven't trod. There isn't one of her streams I haven't bathed in" (177). Condé celebrates Tituba's witchcraft in the Epilogue, as this latter continues to be useful to her people through her practices, carrying her tradition beyond the limits of time and history. This celebration of Tituba is a criticism of the Puritans' demonizing of witches, and a mockery of their belief in the afterlife as punishment. Far from being damned following her action, Tituba comes back as an honored witch and a celebrated heroine. Tituba, who could not keep a child, is also granted a spiritual daughter to carry her legacy. She explains: "Since I died without giving birth to a child, the spirits have allowed me to choose a descendent . . . and I finally found her, the one I needed: Samantha" (176).

However, "how might a return from the dead, from silence, be viewed as a tragic empowerment for black women?" asks Sharon Patricia Holland in *Raising the Dead,* where she meditates on the significance of Beloved's return in Toni Morrison's *Beloved*.[2] I would like to borrow Holland's question to address the political implications of death and return of black female literary heroines, whose heroic resurrection happens only after their gruesome deaths—a result of their powerlessness. Danticat's Martine, Morrison's Convent women, and Condé's Tituba are indeed tragic heroines who achieve liberation only after their death. In their lives, these heroines are often powerless in the face of patriarchal and racial oppres-

---

2. Sharon Patricia Holland, *Raising the Dead: Readings of Death and (Black) Subjectivity* (Durham, NC: Duke University Press, 2000), 7.

sion. Their liberation is attained only after grotesquely tragic deaths. Martine, who transforms into a rebellious loa after her death, is while living, a mentally unstable victim of sexual violence. Her rape at an early age by a Tonton macoute, which resulted in her pregnancy with Sophie, unsettles her and ultimately results in her drastically stabbing herself to death. Like Martine, Morrison's female heroines, who by the end of the narrative are portrayed as warriors and goddess-like figures, are paradoxically, broken and distressed women who drift away from reality because they are incapable of facing their traumatic experiences. Exiles and outsiders, they become scapegoats to the males of Ruby who raid the convent and massacre them. Similarly, Tituba, who owns supernatural powers, and who is expected to grant power to others through her witchcraft, is in fact lacking control over her life and in the face of white oppression. After leading a failed revolt in her island, Tituba is punished with public execution. She only turns into a revolutionary spirit after her death.

Thus, these works are undoubtedly ironically shaded, defying any notion of simplistic recovery of black female voices; they also articulate an Africanist vision toward life and death, where death indeed provides an occasion for return. Alfred Metraux tells us that in Vodou, after elaborate and carefully performed rituals, the dead return to be part of the world of the living: "When the appropriate ritual sequences are performed by the community, the gwo-bon-anj (soul/life force) can be reclaimed from Ginen and become an important influence in the lives of the members of the community."[3] What is clear here is that the bond between the living and the dead is essential, and their contribution to the life of the living is expected. In fact, in inhabiting the spiritual imagination of the living, the dead become a vital presence in their lives. Thus, what marks death in its finality is not the physical demise of the body, but the cessation of a connection to the dead. In the Middle Passage, those who committed suicide believed that they were going back to Africa, as opposed to those who made it to the Americas, who, estranged from their families and ancestors, were seen as "socially dead."[4] Furthermore, in *The Faces of the Gods,* Leslie G. Desmangles informs us that Vodou mythology "sees death as the cessation of the old being, but also as the birth of a new being," as "its ethereal nature transcends the struggles and limitations of profane existence."[5] Death thus signifies renewal, rebirth, and liberation.

---

3. Alfred Metraux, *Voodoo in Haiti* (New York: Schocken Books, 1972), 69.

4. See Orlando Patterson, *Slavery and Social Death: A Comparative Study* (Cambridge, MA: Harvard University Press, 1982).

5. Leslie G. Desmangles, *The Faces of the Gods: Vodou and Roman Catholicism in Haiti* (Chapel Hill: University of North Carolina Press, 1992), 61–66.

Clearly, Danticat, Morrison, and Condé express this Africanist vision of the relationship between the dead and the living in their works. In doing so, they create narratives of continuity between the past and the present, challenging what Joseph Roach calls the politics of forgetting.[6] The return of Martine, the convent women, and Tituba constitutes a constant reminder to their loved ones as well as their oppressors of what should not be lost or silenced. Roach, who looks at the historical relationship between the dead and the living in order to inquire into the unrecorded genocidal histories of the African Americas, considers the modern invention of cemeteries that led to the segregation of the dead from the living, a project of modernity. He explains: "As the place of burial was removed from local churchyard to distant park, the dead were more likely to be remembered (and forgotten) by monuments than by continued observances in which their spirits were invoked."[7] Roach considers the separation between the dead and the living a tactic of whiteness that was meant to suppress the horrific and violent histories of the New World, as he pointedly asks: "If the dead are forever segregated, how are the living supposed to remember who they are?"[8]

The dead, however, according to an Africanist worldview, are never forgotten, but, rather, they are seen as active participants in the temporal world of the living. In fact, the dead are so powerful that, if they have not been shown enough respect, they return to terrorize the living. Alfred Metraux explains that if not honored properly, the dead come back as evil spirits to torment and haunt: "Near cemeteries and in lonely places there is risk of meeting *zombi* (which should not be confused with flesh-and-blood *zombi*): these are the wandering souls of people who perished as a result of an accident and who are condemned to roam the earth for as long as God meant them to live."[9] Danticat's Sophie feels the presence of the wandering spirits: "our dead relatives who we had such a kinship to, as though they were our restless spirits, shadows wandering in the darkness" (205). The violent deaths of Danticat's, Morrison's, and Condé's protagonists have indeed turned them into restless spirits who were not honored properly. Quite the opposite, they were unjustly scapegoated and subjected to extreme forms of violence. They come back to torment their oppressors—something they could not do while alive—destabilizing the power dynamics between the dead and the living.

---

6. Joseph Roach, *Cities of the Dead: Circum-Atlantic Performance* (New York: Columbia University Press, 1996), 6–7.
7. Ibid., 50.
8. Ibid., 55.
9. Metraux, *Voodoo in Haiti*, 258.

Thus, while Danticat, Morrison, and Condé do not suggest realistic solutions to violence committed against African Diaspora women, they provide the necessary vision that insures the return of the oppressed to protest their erasure from history. In her meditation on Vodou spirits and the significance of their return in colonial Haiti in *Haiti, History and the Gods,* Joan Dayan tells us that the spirits of those who were mistreated and tortured return in different shapes and forms to claim their place in history: "In this regenerative, reinterpreted, and vengeful history, dislocated bodies return to find their place. What whites called 'superstition' and 'fetishism' turned out to be something more akin to the journeys of bodies that relocalize themselves as spirits."[10] As these heroines continue to haunt and terrorize the imagination of the living, Danticat, Morrison and Condé too haunt the literary canon of the Americas in their daring rendition of black female spirituality. In *Paradise* Billie Delia wonders about the menacing return of the Convent women: "When will they return? When will they reappear, with blazing eyes, war paint and huge hands to rip up and stomp down this prison calling itself a town?" (308).

---

10. Joan Dayan, *Haiti, History, and the Gods* (Berkeley: University of California Press, 1998), 258.

Bibliography

Alvarez, A. *The Savage God: A Study of Suicide.* London: Weidenfeld and Nicolson, 1972.
Anderson, Linda. "The Re-Imagining of History in Contemporary Women's Fiction." In *Plotting Change: Contemporary Women's Fiction,* ed. Linda Anderson, 128–41. London: Edward Arnold, 1990.
Antoine, Régis. *La littérature franco-antillaise: Haïti, Guadeloupe et Martinique.* Paris: Karthala, 1980.
Araujo, Nara. "The Contribution of Women's Writing to the Literature and Intellectual Achievements of the Caribbean: *Moi, Tituba sorcière* and *Amour, colère et folie.*" *Journal of Black Studies* 25 (1994): 217–30.
Asante, Molefi Kete. "African Elements in African-American English." In *Africanisms in American Culture,* ed. Joseph E. Holloway, 19–33. Bloomington: Indiana University Press, 1990.
Ashcroft, Bill, Gareth Griffiths, and Helen Tiffin. *The Empire Writes Back: Theory and Practice in Post-colonial Literatures.* London: Routledge, 1989.
Ashcroft, Bill, Gareth Griffiths, and Helen Tiffin. *The Post-colonial Studies Reader.* London: Routledge, 1995.
Bailey, Randall C., ed. *Yet with a Steady Beat: Contemporary U.S Afrocentric Biblical Interpretation.* Atlanta: Society of Biblical Literature, 2003.
Balutansky, Kathleen M., and Marie-Agnès Sourieu, eds. *Caribbean Creolization: Reflections on the Cultural Dynamics of Language, Literature, and Identity.* Gainesville: University of Florida Press, 1998.
Bassnett, Susan. *Translation Studies.* London: Methuen, 1980.
Bassnett, Susan, and André Lefèvere. *Constructing Culture: Essays on Literary Translation.* Clevedon: Multilingual Matters, 1998.
Begg, Ean. *The Cult of the Black Virgin.* London: Arkana, 1985.
Bellegarde-Smith, Patrick. *Fragments of Bone: Neo-African Religions in a New World.* Urbana: University of Illinois Press, 2005.
Berlinerblau, Jacques. *Heresy in the University: The Black Athena and the Responsibilities of American Intellectuals.* New Brunswick, NJ: Rutgers University Press, 1999.

Bermann, Sandra, and Michael Wood. *Nation, Language, and the Ethics of Translation.* Princeton, NJ: Princeton University Press, 2005.
Bery, Ashok. *Cultural Translation and Postcolonial Poetry.* New York: Palgrave Macmillan, 2007.
Best, Wallace. "The Spirit of the Holy Ghost Is a Male Spirit: African American Preaching Women and the Paradox of Gender." *Women and Religion in the African Diaspora: Knowledge, Power, and Performance,* ed. Griffith, R. Marie, and Barbara Dianne Savage, 101-127. Baltimore: Johns Hopkins University Press, 2006.
Boyer, Paul and Stephen Nissenbaum, eds., *Salem Witchcraft Papers: Verbatim Transcripts of the Legal Documents,* 3 vols. New York: Da Capo, 1977.
Breslaw, Elaine. *Tituba, Reluctant Witch of Salem: Devilish Indians and Puritan Fantasies.* New York: New York University Press, 1996.
Brown, Karen McCarthy. *Mama Lola: A Vodou Priestess in Brooklyn.* Berkeley: University of California Press, 1991.
Brumana, Fernando Giobellina, and Elda Gonzales Martinez. *Spirits from the Margin: Umbanda in Sao Paulo.* Uppsala: Uppsala University, 1989.
Chancy, Miriam. *Framing Silence: Revolutionary Novels by Haitian Women.* New Brunswick, NJ: Rutgers University Press, 1997.
Chow, Rey. *The Protestant Ethnic and the Spirit of Capitalism.* New York: Columbia University Press, 2002.
Collins, Patricia Hill. *Black Feminist Thought: Knowledge, Consciousness, and the Politics of Empowerment.* London: Harper Collins Academic, 1990.
Condé, Maryse. "Civilisation noire de la diaspora." *Présence africaine* 94.2 (1975): 184–94.
———. *I, Tituba, Black Witch of Salem.* Trans. Richard Philcox. Charlottesville: Caraf Books, 1992.
———. *I, Tituba, Black Witch of Salem.* Trans. Richard Philcox. New York: Ballantine Books, 1992
———. *Moi, Tituba, sorcière . . . noire de Salem.* Paris: Mercure de France, 1986.
———. *Moi, Tituba, sorcière . . .* Paris: Mercure de France/Folio Series, 1988.
———. *Moi, Tituba, sorcière . . .* Paris: Mercure de France/Folio Series, 1988. (alternative cover)
———. *Ségou: La terre en miettes.* Paris: Seghers, 1998.
———. *Ségou: Les murailles de terre.* Paris: Lafont, 1984.
———. *Traversée de la mangrove.* New York: Distribooks, 1989.
Condé, Maryse, and Madeleine Cottenet-Hage. *Penser la créolité.* Paris: Karthala, 1995.
Cox, Timothy J. *Postmodern Tales of Slavery in the Americas: From Alejo Carpentier to Charles Johnson.* New York: Garland, 2001.
Daly, Mary. *Beyond God the Father: Toward a Philosophy of Women's Liberation.* London: Women's Press, 1995.
———. *The Church and the Second Sex.* New York: Harper Colophon Books, 1975.
Daniel, Yvonne. *Dancing Wisdom: Embodied Knowledge in Haitian Vodou, Cuban Yoruba, and Bahian Candomblé.* Urbana: University of Illinois Press, 2005.
Danticat, Edwidge. *After the Dance: A Walk through Carnival in Jacmel, Haiti.* New York: Crown, 2002.
———. *Breath, Eyes, Memory.* New York: Soho, 1994.
———. *Brother, I'm Dying.* New York: Knopf, 2007.
———. *The Butterfly's Way: Voices from the Haitian Dyaspora in the United States.* New York: Soho, 2001.
———. *The Dew Breaker.* New York: Vintage, 2005.

———. *The Farming of Bones*. New York: Soho, 1998.
———. *Le cri de l'oiseau rouge*. Paris: Livre de poche, 1995.
———. *Le cri de l'oiseau rouge*. Trans. Nicole Tisserand. Paris: Pygmalion, 1995.
———. *Krik? Krak!* New York: Soho, 1991.
Dash, J. Michael. *Haiti and the United States: National Stereotypes and the Literary Imagination*. New York: Macmillan, 1988.
Davis, Wade. *The Serpent and the Rainbow*. New York: Simon and Schuster, 1985.
Dayan, Joan. "Caribbean Cannibals and Whores." *Raritan* 9.2 (1989): 45–67.
———. "Erzulie: A Women's History of Haiti." *Research in African Literatures* 25.2 (1994): 5–31.
———. *Haiti, History, and the Gods*. Berkeley: University of California Press, 1998.
Depestre, René. *A Rainbow for the Christian West*. Trans. and intro. Joan Dayan. Amherst: University of Massachusetts Press, 1977.
Deren, Maya. *Divine Horsemen: The Living Gods of Haiti*. New York: McPherson, 1970.
Desmangles, Leslie G. *The Faces of the Gods: Vodou and Roman Catholicism in Haiti*. Chapel Hill: University of North Carolina Press, 1992.
De Weever, Jacqueline. *Mythmaking and Metaphor in Black Women's Fiction*. New York: St. Martin's Press, 1992.
Dick, Bruce and Amritjit Singh. *Conversations with Ishmael Reed*. Literary Conversations Series. Jackson: University Press of Mississippi, 1995.
Donovan, Josephine. *Gnosticism in Modern Literature: A Study of the Selected Works of Camus, Sartre, Hesse, and Kafka*. London: Garland, 1990.
Du Bois, W. E. B. *The Souls of Black Folk*. New York: Penguin. 1996.
Duinn, Sean. *The Rites of Brigid: Goddess and Saint*. Dublin: Columbia Press, 2005.
Dunne, John S. *The City of the Gods: A Study in Myth and Mortality*. New York: Collier-Macmillan, 1965.
Durrant, Sam. *Postcolonial Narrative and the Work of Mourning: J. M. Coetzee, Wilson Harris, and Toni Morrison*. New York: State University of New York Press, 2004.
Dyer, Richard. *White*. London: Routledge, 1999.
Ellison, Ralph. *Going to the Territory*. New York: Vintage Books, 1987.
———. *Shadow and Act*. New York: Random House, 1964.
Faiq, Said. *Trans-Lated: Translation and Cultural Manipulation*. Lanham: University Press of America, 2007.
Fanon, Frantz. *Black Skin, White Masks*. London: Pluto, 1986.
Farmer, Paul. *The Uses of Haiti*. Monroe, ME: Common Courage Press, 2003.
Fernandez, Ronald. *America's Banquet of Cultures: Harnessing Ethnicity, Race, and Immigration in the Twenty-First Century*. London: Praeger, 2000.
Fernández Olmos, Margarite, and Lizabeth Paravisini-Gebert. *Creole Religions of the Caribbean*. New York: New York University Press, 2003.
———, eds. *Sacred Possessions: Vodou, Santeria, Obeah, and the Caribbean*. New Brunswick, NJ: Rutgers University Press, 1997.
Fitzgerald, Frances. *Cities on a Hill*. London: Picador, 1987.
Foley, Barbara. "History, Fiction, and the Ground Between: The Uses of the Documentary Mode in Black Literature." *PMLA* 95 (1980): 389–403.
Foley, Helene P. "A Question of Origins: Goddess Cult Greek and Modern." *Women, Gender, Religion: A Reader*, ed. Elizabeth A. Castelli and Rosamond C. Rodman. New York: Palgrave, 2001.
Forbes, Thomas Rogers. *The Midwife and the Witch*. New Haven, CT: Yale University Press, 1966.

Frazier, Franklin. *The Negro Church in America*. New York: Schocken, 1974.
Freud, Sigmund. *Moses and Monotheism*. Trans. Katherine Jones. London: Hogarth Press, 1939.
Gates, Henry Louis. *The Signifying Monkey: A Theory of African-American Literary Criticism*. Oxford: Oxford University Press, 1988.
Gervais, Karen Grandstand. *Redefining Death*. New Haven, CT: Yale University Press, 1986.
Giddings, Paula. *When and Where I Enter: The Impact of Black Women on Race and Sex in America*. New York: Bantam Books, 1988.
Gilroy, Paul. *The Black Atlantic: Modernity and Double Consciousness*. Cambridge, MA: Harvard University Press, 1993.
Glaude, Eddie S, Jr. *Exodus!: Religion, Race, and Nation in Early Nineteenth-Century Black America*. Chicago: University of Chicago Press, 2000.
Glissant, Edward. *Poétique de la relation*. Paris: Gallimard, 1990.
Goldenberg, Naomi R. *Changing of the Gods: Feminism and the End of Traditional Religions*. Boston: Beacon Press, 1979.
Gomez, Michael, ed. *Diasporic Africa: A Reader*. New York: New York University Press, 2006.
Griffith, R. Marie, and Barbara Dianne Savage, eds. *Women and Religion in the African Diaspora: Knowledge, Power, and Performance*. Baltimore: Johns Hopkins University Press, 2006.
Hansen, Chadwick. "The Metamorphosis of Tituba, or Why American Intellectuals Can't Tell an Indian Witch from a Negro." *New England Quarterly* 47 (1974): 3–12.
Harding, Rachel E. *A Refuge in Thunder: Candomblé and Alternative Spaces of Blackness*. Bloomington: Indiana University Press, 2000.
Harris, Joseph E., ed. *Global Dimensions of the African Diaspora*. Washington, DC: Howard University Press, 1982.
Hartman, Saidiya V. *Scenes of Subjection: Terror, Slavery, and Self-Making in Nineteenth-Century America*. Oxford: Oxford University Press, 1997.
Hawthorne, Nathaniel. *The Scarlet Letter*. London: Penguin, 1986.
Hedrick, Charles W. and Robert Hodgson eds. *Nag Hammadi, Gnosticism, and Early Christianity*. Peabody, MA: Hendrickson, 1986.
Herskovitz, Melville J. *The Myth of the Negro Past*. Boston: Beacon Press, 1958.
Hess, David J. *Samba in the Night: Spiritism in Brazil*. New York: Columbia University Press, 1994.
Hewitt, Leah D. *Autobiographical Tightropes: Simone de Beauvoir. Nathalie Sarraute, Marguerite Duras, Monique Wittig, and Maryse Condé*. Lincoln: University of Nebraska Press, 1990.
Higgins, Therese. *Religiosity, Cosmology, and Folklore: The African Influence in the Novels of Toni Morrison*. New York: Routledge, 2002.
Hill, Francis. *A Delusion of Satan: The Full Story of the Salem Witch Trials*. New York: Doubleday, 2002.
Hoffer, Peter Charles. *The Devil's Disciples: Makers of the Salem Witchcraft Trials*. Baltimore: Johns Hopkins University Press, 1996.
Holland, Sharon Patricia. *Raising the Dead: Readings of Death and (Black) Subjectivity*. Durham, NC: Duke University Press, 2000.
Holloway, Joseph E, ed. *Africanism in American Culture*. Bloomington: Indiana University Press, 1991.
Holloway, Karla F. C. *Moorings and Metaphors: Figures of Culture and Gender in Black Women's Literature*. New Brunswick, NJ: Rutgers University Press, 1992.

hooks, bell. *Ain't I a Woman: Black Women and Feminism.* London: Pluto, 1982.
Hopkins, Dwight N., and George C. L. Cummings, eds. *Cut Loose Your Stammering Tongue: Black Theology in the Slave Narratives.* New York: Orbis Books, 1991.
Hopkins, Pauline. *The Magazine Novels of Pauline Hopkins.* Oxford: Oxford University Press, 1988.
Howe, Stephen. *Afrocentrism: Mythical Pasts and Imagined Homes.* London: Verso, 1998.
Hughes, Langston. *I Wonder as I Wander.* New York: Rinehart, 1956.
Hunt, Kristin. "Paradise Lost: The Destructive Forces of Double Consciousness and Boundaries in Toni Morrison's *Paradise.*" *Reading under the Sign of Nature: New Essays in Ecocriticism,* ed. John Tallmadge and Henry Harrington, 117–27. Salt Lake City: University of Utah Press, 2000.
Hurston, Zora Neale. *Moses: Man of the Mountain.* Urbana: University of Illinois Press, 1985.
———. *Tell My Horse: Voodoo and Life in Haiti and Jamaica.* New York: Harper and Row, 1990 [1938].
Idowu, E. Bolaji. *African Traditional Religion: A Definition.* London: SCM Press, 1973.
———. *Olodumare: God in Yoruba Belief.* London: Longmans, 1962.
Iser, Wolfgang. *Prospecting: From Reader Response to Literary Anthropology.* Baltimore: Johns Hopkins University Press, 1989.
Jackson, Tommie Lee. *An Invincible Summer: Female Diasporean Authors.* Trenton, NJ: Africa World Press, 2001.
James, C. L. R. *The Black Jacobins: Toussaint L'Ouverture and the San Domingo Revolution.* New York: Vintage Books, 1989.
Japtok, Martin. *Postcolonial Perspectives on Women Writers from Africa, the Caribbean, and the US.* Trenton, NJ: Africa World Press, 2003.
Jennings, La Vinia Delois. *Middle Passage.* Edinburgh: Payback Press, 1999.
———. *Toni Morrison and the Idea of Africa.* New York: Columbia University Press, 2009.
Johnson, James Weldon. "Self-Determining Haiti: The American Occupation." *The Nation* 111.2878 (August 28, 1920): 237.
Johnson, Paul Christopher. *Secrets, Gossip, and Gods: The Transformation of Brazilian Candomblé.* Oxford: Oxford University Press, 2002.
Jones, Gayle. "Re-Imagining the African-American Novel: An Essay on Third World Aesthetics." *Callalloo* 17.2 (1994): 507–18.
Katz, William Loren. *The Black West: A Documentary and Pictorial History of the African American Role in the Westward Expansion of the United States.* New York: Touchstone, 1996.
King, Karen L., ed. *Images of the Feminine in Gnosticism.* Philadelphia: Fortress Press, 1988.
Kligueh, Basile Goudabla. *Le Vodu à travers son encyclopédie, la géomancie Afa.* Porto-Novo, Bénin: Éditions Afridic, 2001.
Landes, Ruth. *The City of Women.* Albuquerque: University of New Mexico Press, 1994.
Layton, Bentley. "The Riddle of the Thunder (NHC VI, 2): The Function of Paradox in a Gnostic Text from Nag Hammadi." In *Nag Hammadi, Gnosticism, and Early Christianity,* ed. Charles W. Hedrick and Robert Hodgson, 37–54. Peabody, MA: Hendrickson, 1986.
Lewis, Barbara, "No Silence: An Interview with Maryse Condé," *Callaloo* 18.3 (1995): 543–50.
Lionnet, Françoise. *Autobiographical Voices: Race, Gender, Self-Portraiture.* Ithaca, NY: Cornell University Press, 1989.

Lipsitz, George. *Time Passages: Collective Memory and American Popular Culture.* Minneapolis: University of Minnesota Press, 1990.
Logan, Alastair H. B. *Gnostic Truth and Christian Heresy: A Study in the History of Gnosticism.* Edinburgh: T & T Clark, 1996.
Long, Charles H. *Significations: Signs, Symbols, and Images in the Interpretation of Religion.* Philadelphia: Fortress Press, 1986.
Manzor-Coats, Lillian. "Of Witches and Other Things: Maryse Condé's Challenges to Feminist Discourse." *World Literature Today* 67.4 (1993): 737–44.
Mardorssian, Carine M. "From Literature of Exile to Migrant Literature." *Modern Language Studies* 32.2 (2002): 15-33.
Matthews, Caitlin. *Sophia, Goddess of Wisdom: The Divine Feminine from Black Goddess to World Soul.* London: Mandala, 1991.
Metraux, Alfred. *Voodoo in Haiti.* New York: Schocken Books, 1972.
Michelet, Jules. *Satanism and Witchcraft: A Study in Medieval Superstition.* Trans. A. R. Allinson. London: Arco Publications, 1958.
Miller, Arthur. *The Crucible.* London: Penguin, 1968.
Miller, Joseph, ed. *The African Past Speaks: Essays on Oral Tradition and History.* Folkstone, Kent: Dowson, 1980.
Mitchem, Stephanie Y. *African American Folk Healing.* New York: New York University Press, 2007.
Morrison, Toni. *Beloved.* London: Vintage, 1997.
———. *The Bluest Eye.* 1970. London: Vintage, 1999.
———. "Introduction: Friday on the Potomac." In *Race-ing Justice, En-gendering Power: Essays on Anita Hill, Clarence Thomas, and the Construction of Social Reality,* ed. Toni Morrison, vii–xxx. New York: Pantheon, 1992.
———. *Love.* New York: Vintage, 2005.
———. *A Mercy.* New York: Vintage, 2009.
———. *Paradise.* London: Chatto & Windus, 1998.
———. *Playing in the Dark: Whiteness and the Literary Imagination.* London: Picador, 1993.
———. "Recitatif." In *Ancestral House: The Black Short Story in the Americas and Europe,* ed. Charles H. Rowell, 422–36. Boulder, CO: Westview, 1995.
———. "Rootedness: The Ancestor as Foundation." In *Black Women Writers 1950–1980: A Critical Education,* ed. Mari Evans, 339–45. New York: Anchor, 1983.
———. *Song of Solomon.* New York: Signet, 1978.
———. *Sula.* London: Picador, 1991.
Mortley, Raoul. *Womanhood: The Feminine in Ancient Hellenism, Gnosticism, Christianity, and Islam.* Sydney: Delacroix, 1981.
Moses, Wilson Jeremiah. *Afrotopia: The Roots of African American Popular History.* Cambridge: Cambridge University Press, 1998.
Mudimbe–Boyi, Elizabeth. "Giving a Voice to Tituba: The Death of the Author?" *World Literature Today* (1993): 751–56
Mudimbe, V. Y. *The Invention of Africa: Gnosis, Philosophy, and the Order of Knowledge.* Bloomington: Indiana University Press, 1988.
Munro, Martin, and Elizabeth Walcott-Hackshaw. *Echoes of the Haitian Revolution: 1804–2004.* Kingston, Jamaica: University of the West Indies Press, 2008.
Murphy, Joseph. *Working the Spirit: Ceremonies of the African Diaspora.* Boston: Beacon Press, 1995.
Murray, Margaret Alice. *The Witch-Cult in Western Europe.* Oxford: Clarendon Press, 1962.

Ngugi Wa Thiong'o. *Decolonising the Mind: The Politics of Language in African Literature.* London: Heinemann, 1986.
Norton, Mary Beth. *In the Devil's Snare: The Salem Witch Crisis of 1692.* New York: Knopf, 2002.
N'Zengou-Tayo, Marie-Jose. "Rewriting Folklore: Traditional Beliefs and Popular Culture in Edwidge Danticat's *Breath, Eyes, Memory,* and *Krik? Krak!.*" *MaComère* 3 (2000): 123–40.
Marie-José N'Zengou Tayo and Elizabeth Wilson, "Translators on a Tight Rope: The Challenges of Translating Edwidge Danticat's *Breath, Eyes, Memory* and Patrick Chamoiseau's *Texaco.*" *Traduction, terminologie, rédaction* 13.2 (2000): 75–105.
O'Donnell, Patrick, and Robert Con Davis, eds. *Intertextuality and Contemporary American Fiction.* Baltimore: Johns Hopkins University Press, 1989.
Ojo-Ade, Femi. *Of Dreams Deferred, Dead or Alive: African Perspectives on African-American Writers.* Westport, CT: Greenwood Press, 1996.
Pagels, Elaine. *The Gnostic Gospels.* 1979. London: Penguin, 1990.
Painter, Nell Irvin. *Exodusters: Black Migration to Kansas after Reconstruction, the First Major Migration to the North of Ex-Slaves.* New York: W. W. Norton, 1992.
Patell, Cyrus R. K. *Negative Liberties: Morrison, Pynchon, and the Problem of Liberal Ideology.* Durham, NC: Duke University Press, 2001.
Patterson, Orlando. *Slavery and Social Death: A Comparative Study.* Cambridge, MA: Harvard University Press, 1982.
Pearson, Birger A. *Gnosticism, Judaism, and Egyptian Christianity.* Minneapolis: Fortress Press, 1990.
Pearson, Joanne. *Wicca and the Christian Heritage: Ritual, Sex, and Magic.* New York: Routledge, 2007.
Perkins, Pheme. *Resurrection: New Testament Witness and Contemporary Reflection.* London: Geoffrey Chapman, 1985.
Peterson, Nancy J. *Against Amnesia: Contemporary Women Writers and the Crisis of Historical Memory.* Philadelphia: University of Pennsylvania Press, 2001.
Petry, Ann. *Tituba of Salem Village.* 1964. New York: Harper Trophy, 1991.
Pfaff, Françoise. *Conversations with Maryse Condé.* Lincoln: University of Nebraska Press, 1991.
Pieterse, Jan Nederveen. *White on Black: Images of Africa and Blacks in Western Popular Culture.* New Haven, CT: Yale University Press, 1992.
Raboteau, Albert J. "African-Americans, Exodus, and the American Israel." In *African-American Christianity: Essays in History,* ed. Paul E. Johnson, 1–17. Berkeley: University of California Press, 1994.
———. *Slave Religion: The "Invisible Institution" in the Antebellum South.* Oxford: Oxford University Press, 1978.
Reed, Ishmael. *Mumbo Jumbo.* New York: Atheneum Macmillan, 1972.
Renda, Mary A. *Taking Haiti: Military Occupation and the Culture of U.S. Imperialism, 1915–1940.* Chapel Hill: University of North Carolina Press, 2001.
Rhodes, Jewell Parker. *Voodoo Dreams: A Novel of Marie Laveau.* New York: Picador USA, 1993.
Rhys, Jean. *Wide Sargasso Sea.* New York: Buccaneer Books, 1966.
Rigaud, Milo. *Secrets of Voodoo.* San Francisco: City Lights Books, 1985.
Roach, Joseph. *Cities of the Dead: Circum-Atlantic Performance.* New York: Columbia University Press, 1996.
Robinson, James M., ed. *The Nag Hammadi Library in English: The Definitive New Translation of the Gnostic Scriptures.* 4th rev. ed. Leiden: E. J. Brill, 1996.

Rody, Caroline. *The Daughter's Return: African-American and Caribbean Women's Fictions of History.* New York: Oxford University Press, 2001.

Rosenthal, Bernard. "Tituba's Story." *New England Quarterly* 71 (1998): 190–203

Rushdy, Ashraf H. A. "Daughters Signifyin(g) History: The Example of Toni Morrison's *Beloved.*" In *Toni Morrison,* ed. Linden Peach, 140–53. New York: St. Martin's, 1997.

———. *Remembering Generations: Race and Family in Contemporary African American Fiction.* Chapel Hill: University of North Carolina Press, 2001.

Russell, Jeffrey B. *A History of Witchcraft: Sorcerers, Heretics, and Pagans.* London: Thames and Hudson, 1980.

Satinover, Jeffrey. *The Empty Self: Gnostic and Jungian Foundations of Modern Identity.* Nottingham, UK: Grove Books, 1995.

Smalls, James. "Slavery Is a Woman: 'Race,' Gender, and Visuality in Marie Benoist's *Portrait d'une négresse* (1800)." *Nineteenth-Century Art Worldwide* 3.1 (2004). http://www.19thc-artworldwide.org/spring_04/articles/smal.html

Smith, Barbara, ed. *Home Girls: A Black Feminist Anthology.* New York: Women of Color Press, 1983.

Smith, Theophus H. *Conjuring Culture: Biblical Formations of Black America.* Oxford: Oxford University Press, 1994.

Storace, Patricia. "The Scripture of Utopia." *The New York Review* 14 (1998): 64–69.

Thompson, Robert Farris, and Joseph Cornet. *Flash of the Spirit: African and Afro-American Art and Philosophy.* New York: Vintage Books, 1984.

———. *The Four Moments of the Sun: Kongo Art in Two Worlds.* Washington, DC: National Gallery of Art, 1981.

"The Thunder: Perfect Mind." Trans. Anne McGuire. In *Diotima: Material for the Study of Women and Gender in the Ancient World.* http://www.stoa.org/diotima/anthology/thunder.shtml (accessed September 10, 2007).

Tompkins, Jane P., ed. *Reader Response Criticism: From Formalism to Post-Structuralism.* Baltimore: Johns Hopkins University Press, 1994.

Tymoczko, Maria. "Post-colonial Writing and Literary Translation." *Post-colonial Translation: Theory and Practice,* ed. Susanna Bassnett and Harish Trivedi. London: Routledge, 1999.

Voeks, Robert A. *Sacred Leaves of Candomblé: African Magic, Medicine, and Religion in Brazil.* Austin: University of Texas Press, 1997.

Wafer, Jim. *The Taste of Blood: Spirit Possession in Brazilian Candomblé.* Philadelphia: University of Pennsylvania Press, 1991.

Warrior, Robert Allen, "Canaanites, Cowboys and Indians," in *Christianity and Crisis,* (September 11, 1989): 261–65.

White, Hayden. *Metahistory: The Historical Imagination in Nineteenth-Century Europe.* Baltimore: Johns Hopkins University Press, 1974.

———. *The Content of the Form: Narrative Discourse and Historical Representation.* Baltimore: Johns Hopkins University Press, 1987.

Williams, Michael Allen. *Rethinking "Gnosticism": An Argument for Dismantling a Dubious Category.* Princeton, NJ: Princeton University Press, 1996.

Wilson, Elizabeth. "Sorcières, sorcières: '*Moi, Tituba, sorcière noire de Salem*' révisions et interrogations." in *L'oeuvre de Maryse Condé.* Paris: Harmattan, 1996.

Zéphir, Flore. *The Haitian Americans.* London: Greenwood Press, 2004.

Index

acculturation, 6, 20, 101, 107
Africa: as axis of black female spirituality, 26; colonizing structure in, 31; cultural continuity with, 98; deconstruction of stereotypes of, 25; migration to, 99; romanticization of, 27; significance of in construction of African American consciousness, 26; simplification and exoticization of traditional beliefs of, 31
African American consciousness, 26, 99
African American diasporic history, 143, 145
African American heritage, 27
African American identity, 27
African American men, 26
African American psychological and spiritual transformation, 25
African Americas: genocidal histories of, 157
African diaspora consciousness, 4–7, 25, 26, 46, 49, 55
African diaspora cultures, interconnectedness of, 14, 24, 26
African diaspora religions, 3, 4–7, 9, 17, 24–25, 30, 34, 53, 64, 98–99, 105, 113, 117; colonial construction of, 9; cosmologies of, 17–18, 118; criminalization of, 12; as mechanism of female transformation, 11; music and dance of, 17–18; ritual practices of, 17–18; as sites of memory, 17; as sites of recovery, 25; superficial and romanticized vision of, 30; tension between Christianity and, 12; and traditions of healing, 44, 64
African diaspora women, 9, 10, 35, 36, 158
Africanism, simplistic discourse of, 27
Afrocentrism, 30–31
afterlife, 14, 36, 119, 120, 130, 153–58; as punishment, 153, 155
agency: self-affirming, 5; spiritual, 8; women's, constraints on, 34
Alvarez, Julia: Yo!, 65
American dream, 63
androgyny, 94–95
Angelou, Maya, 34
anti-religious rituals, 101
Apocryphal texts, 21, 50, 52
Ashcroft, Bill, 20, 33, 142
assimilation vs. resistance, 5, 6
Ati-Bon Legba, 47
audience: manipulation of, 104, 107, 126, 127; readership and, 139–40; targeted, 131, 134, 137–39, 145, 151
autobiography, 106, 134

167

Baker, Josephine, 27
Barbados, slave community in, 125
Benoist, Marie-Guilhelmine: *Portrait d'une négresse*, 138
Best, Wallace, 11; "The Spirit of the Holy Ghost is a Male Spirit," 32
biblical literature, 21–22, 50, 52, 53, 91. *See also* Exodus narrative
black consciousness movement, 55, 61n49
black cultural aesthetics, 26
black female body: negative perceptions of, 11; as site of contention, 10; vilification of, 10
black female heroism, 46, 155
black female spirituality, 2–3, 7, 8–14, 26–28, 32, 105, 158; Africa as axis of, 26; celebration of, 8–14; diasporic vision of, 18; resistance to romanticization of, 32; and sexuality, 32
black magic (dark magic), 13, 44, 49, 56, 75, 96, 98, 113, 116
Black Nationalism, 83, 141n58
blackness: devil and, 111, 113; diasporic notion of, 7; and evil, 9, 110, 112; as positive symbol in Haiti, 60; pride in, 88; and witchcraft, 14, 138n33
Black Power movement, 73, 83, 98
black women: autobiographical writings of, 120, 134; clichés of, 126; closeness between white women and, 130; fear of, 122; fiction of, 23, 34; as morally corrupt and sexually deviant, 10; reclamation of place in history, 15; restrictions on, 11; skepticism of toward white feminism, 128–29
body/spirit duality. *See* spirit/body opposition
Boston Sunday Globe, 143, 145
Breath, Eyes, Memory (Danticat), 1, 2, 7, 12–14, 28, 35, 37–70, 154, 158; as act of translation, 67, 69; afterlife in, 153; biblical literature in, 22; bleeding woman story in, 21–22, 37–38, 46, 53; blood and milk in, 47; Caco, name of in, 38–39, 54–55, 58, 154; as celebration of working-class women, 55–59; "chagrin" in, 40; as challenge to linear narratives of history, 33; and changes to masculinist discourse, 46; class divisions in, 43–44, 46, 57, 59–60; creolization in, 20–21; criticism of, 65–66; cultural identity in, 154; dedication of, 38, 40; Erzulie in, 38, 40–46, 50, 64, 153; female sexuality in, 51–52, 154; female subjectivity in, 15–16; female victimization in, 47; gender dynamics in, 50; genre of, 65; Guinea in, 18, 49, 154; Haitian folk stories in, 50, 53–54; and Haitian literary movement, 55; Haitian women's struggle in, 42; heterosexuality vs. homosexuality in, 47–48; historical trauma in, 40, 42; as intellectually challenging, 27; intertextuality in, 53; language as liberating force in, 48; language play in, 67–68; literacy in, 48, 56; living vs. dead in, 157; Madonna complex in, 12, 45, 154; Marinet in, 45–46, 153; motherhood in, 43; naming in, 15, 46–51, 54–55, 60; and new reality for Haitian women, 46; oral vs. written history in, 48–49, 60; patriarchy in, 38, 39, 41, 46, 47–48, 51, 55, 154; peasant women in, 48, 56–59, 70; power dynamics in, 157; quest for wholeness in, 42; rape in, 43, 44, 54, 60; reception of, 51–52; relationships with Africa in, 25, 26; revisionist strategies in, 23–24, 46–51, 53–54; scapegoating in, 157; self-violence in, 38, 54; sexual abuse in, 38, 45, 51; sexual purity in, 44, 46; sexual violence in, 43; and simplistic notions of place, 61; as site of political contestation, 29; symbolic meaning of red in, 12, 42, 45, 68, 154; testing in, 38–40, 42, 49, 51, 52, 54; therapy sessions in, 44–45, 64; translation of into French, 68–69; and transnationalism, 65, 66–67, 69; victimhood in, 40; violence and rape in, 39; virginity in, 44, 52; Vodou in, 4, 12, 14, 18, 21–22, 37–70, 154; womanhood in, 41–44, 51, 61, 154; women's place, interrogation of, 50

Breslaw, Elaine G., 103n2, 107, 108n11, 113n22, 124
Brigitte (Brigit; Brijit), 51
Brown, Karen McCarthy, 41–42, 43–44
Brumana, Fernando Giobellina, 96

Candomblé, 1, 4–5, 6, 9, 12, 13, 27, 30, 34, 72, 75, 81n14, 96–98, 100–102; as alternative space for female spirituality, 98; as creolized religion, 101; dynamics between Catholicism and, 96; as female-centered religion, 97–98; juxtaposition of European and African cultures in, 100; as model of racial and cultural hybridity, 100; police harassment of, 96; symbiosis between Africanist and Christian symbols in, 14, 101; syncretism in, 100–101
cannibals/cannibalism, 32, 56–57
Caribbean: approach to feminism, 129; cultural and literary phenomena of, 19, 139, 142–43, 145, 149; experience of, 69; history of, 120, 143, 145
Caribbeanness, 21, 69, 154n1
Catholic Church: and suppression of African diasporic religions, 12; triumph of, 6
Catholic imagery, African cosmology and, 14
Catholicism, 41–42, 60, 92, 96, 101; dynamics between Candomblé and, 96
cemeteries, modern invention of, 157
Chancy, Miriam, 61n49
chastity, 39, 47
Chicago Tribune, 143, 145
Chow, Rey: *The Protestant Ethnic and the Spirit of Capitalism*, 106–7, 124
Christianity, 72, 115; absence of feminine principles from, 91; acculturation into, 6, 101; ambivalent feminine principle of, 75; challenges to, 33, 86; criticism of, 118; denunciation of female powers by, 92; duality of, 93; forced appropriation of, 5; idealization of, 100; moral values of, 73; new interpretation of, 115; as norm,

112; as only form of "Truth," 31; resistance to norms of, 30; rise to power of, 10, 114; sinning flesh and immaculate soul in, 94; symbiosis between Vodou and, 22, 53; symbolism of feminine element in, 94; tension between African diasporic religions and, 12; validation against, 28; vs. paganism, 31; witchcraft and, 117. *See also* Judeo-Christianity
class: in Haiti, 43–44, 46, 57, 59–60
coercive mimeticism, 107, 124
collective consciousness, mythologization of, 88
collective memory: American, 77; Haitian, 40, 77
colonial America: devil in, 111; history of, 76
colonial discourse, 23
colonialism: American, 80; white, 76
colonial power relations, 30
color-consciousness, 84, 88
color symbolism, 10
Condé, Maryse, 1–2, 4, 7, 9, 12–14, 15, 16–17, 19, 26–28, 30, 35; and Black Nationalism, 141n58; connection of to subtitle "Noire de Salem," 131; "Créolité without the Creole Language?," 19; and diasporic histories, 110n15; Grand Prix Littéraire de la Femme, 131, 134, 138; intimacy of with Tituba, 131–33; *La vie scélérate*, 148; as less established in the U.S. than France, 149; obscuring of authorial motifs of, 143, 148; as postcolonial writer, 142; problematics of translation of, 150–51; resistance to linguistic and cultural domination by, 140; *Segou I and II*, 28, 133–34; *Traversée de la Mangrove*, 150–51; *Une saison à Rihata*, 148; use of French by, 140, 149–50; as writer of women's fiction, 131. See also *I, Tituba, Black Witch of Salem*
conquest, 79, 81, 93
continuity: cultural, 98; narratives of, 14, 157; between past and present, 18; and transformation, 25, 30; vs.

rupture, 5, 6; of witchcraft as Africanist feminist tradition, 119
cosmology: African, 14; African diaspora religious, 17, 118; Vodou, 18, 30, 35, 49, 57, 154
countercultural narratives, 6, 29
Cox, Timothy J.: *Postmodern Tales of Slavery in the Americas*, 109
Craft, the, 129
Creole. *See* French Creole
creolization, 3, 5, 6, 19–24, 29, 36; linguistic and cultural, 33–34; religious, 13, 14, 101
cross-ethnic representation, politics and complexity of, 106–7
cross-racial friendship, 22, 128
cross-racial representation, 85
cultural codes, subversion of, 29
cultural continuity, 98
cultural discontinuities and survivals, 18
cultural discourse, 2, 10, 24, 50, 55, 98, 126, 152
cultural distance, 21, 142, 151
cultural distinctiveness, 140, 142
cultural dynamism, 6, 8
cultural/ethnic politics, productionism in, 106
cultural fusion, 19, 61
cultural hegemony, 30, 34
cultural heritage, 21, 55
cultural hybridity, 5, 6, 7, 100, 101
cultural identity, 1, 49, 61n49, 86, 154
cultural inequities, 36
cultural memory, 14–15, 119
cultural narratives, 17, 46
cultural nationalism, 20, 29
cultural othering, 63
cultural politics, 105–6
cultural resistance, 55
cultural retention, 48, 100
cultural syncretism, 100
cultural traditions, 28, 55
cultural translation, 33, 67, 69
cultural trauma, 69

Daly, Mary: *Beyond God the Father*, 33, 115, 116n27

dancing, 95, 97–99; as barbaric, 10
Daniel, Yvonne: *Dancing Wisdom*, 34
Danticat, Edwidge, 1–2, 4, 7, 12–14, 15–16, 26–28, 30, 35, 153; *After the Dance*, 55–56, 62; "Nineteen Thirty-Seven," 50n18; as real "tale master," 50; as transmitter of Haitian culture, 52. *See also* Breath, Eyes, Memory
dark magic. *See* black magic
Dash, Julie, 34
Dash, Michael: *Haiti and the United States*, 66
Davis, Angela, 143, 147–48
Davis, Robert Con, 21
Dayan, Joan, 52, 55; "Caribbean Cannibals and Whores," 32, 46n13; *Haiti, History, and the Gods*, 30, 34, 40–41, 45–46, 50n18, 158
death: life and, 4, 14, 49, 156–58; political implications of, 155; as signifying renewal, 156
demonology, 14, 30
Depestre, René, 55, 59
Deren, Maya, 53
Desmangles, Leslie G.: *The Faces of the Gods*, 156
Dessalines, Jean-Jacques, 59, 60
devil: as black, 111, 113; demonic alliance with witches, 10, 114, 117; and sexuality, 122
diaspora: as condition and process, 30; as discourse of difference and discontinuity, 4. *See also under* African diaspora
diasporic consciousness: and literary expression, 24–28
discrimination, 62, 87
disempowerment, women's, 93, 133
displacement, 18, 36, 110, 145
divine power, masculine vs. feminine, 90–93, 101–2
divinity, men and, 32, 91–92, 101, 119
djablesse, 52
documentary history, 17
Dominican Republic, relationship of with Haiti, 64–65
Donovan, Josephine: *Gnosticism in Modern Literature*, 95n35

drumming, as barbaric, 10

ecology crisis, 118
The Empire Writes Back (Ashcroft, Griffiths, and Tiffin), 33, 142
empirical science, rise of, 116
empowerment: and exoticized racial otherness, 137; of female protagonists, 1; narrative of female, 35, 68; politics of female, 32–33; witch as symbol of women's, 3, 114; of women, 5, 6, 38, 137
English language: translation into as double translation, 149; use of, 20, 67
enlightenment, European discourse of, 9
enslavement, 5, 109, 110, 145
errancy, 66–67
Erzulie, 12, 13, 14, 21, 27, 35, 37, 38, 40–46, 50, 53, 64, 153; Erzulie Danto, 40, 41, 44; Erzulie Freda, 40, 41–45; Erzulie Jewouj, 40, 42, 45–46; as Virgin Mary, 41
essentialism, 30, 35, 83
Ethiopia, reconstruction of civilization of, 25–26
ethnicity: politics of, 124, 126–27, 134, 138–39; production of, 105, 125; resistance to performance of, 106–7; stereotypical nuances of, 140
ethnic minorities, self-referentiality and, 106
ethnic otherness, 23, 107, 134
ethnic purity, 20, 29
ethnic self, 123; as form of production, 106, 108, 124, 125
ethnic witch, clichéd image of, 130–31
ethnic women: occult and, 120–21; preconceptions of, 36, 105
Eve, 91, 94, 101
evil: blackness and, 9; and good, 11, 75, 114, 116–17, 121, 122; Puritan ideas of, 111
exclusion: of Caribbean women, 120; politics of, 16, 72
Existentialism, 95n35
Exodus narrative, 22, 77–83, 93; as resistance to oppression, 80

exoticization, 138–39; of Africa's history, 31; of Haiti, 56–57, 63; of Haitian immigrants to U.S., 40; through skin color, 127

factuality, illusion of, 16
Fanon, Frantz, 140n55
fantasy, 2, 33
female body: celebration of, 122; control over, 39; vilification of, 10
female solidarity, 128
feminine principle: absence of, 91; ambivalence of, 75, 114; celebration of, 89, 121; complexity of, 33, 50, 114; power of, 13, 100; suppression of, 115
feminine wisdom and knowledge, 87
feminism, 124, 128–29, 141; metaphor of witch in, 114; notion of foremothers, 119
Fernandez, Ronald, 61n50
Fernández Olmos, Margarite, 5, 6; *Creole Religions of the Caribbean*, 30
fictional narrative: historiography vs., 123; literature as, 33
Fitzgerald, Frances: *Cities on a Hill*, 81–82
Foley, Barbara: "History, Fiction, and the Ground Between," 17
Foley, Helene P.: "A Question of Origins," 33
folklore, 2, 33; Haitian, 21, 30, 50, 53–54
foremothers, feminist notion of, 119
fragmentation, 36
France, colonial, 56, 58
French Creole, use of, 21, 67, 140, 142, 150
French language, use of, 20–21, 67, 140, 149–50

Gallimard, Simone, 125, 130, 131
Gates, Henry Louis, Jr., 143
gender dynamics, 6, 50, 72, 73, 95, 97
gender hierarchy, 127
genocide, 18, 33, 157

Gilroy, Paul: *The Black Atlantic*, 20, 29–30
Glissant, Edward: concept of "errance," 66; *Poétique de la relation*, 19–20, 29–30, 33–34
glossing, 148–49
gnosis, 95
Gnosticism, 13, 21, 34, 50, 71–102; Egyptian, 27; idealized construction of, 100
Goddess Cult, 33
goddesses: ancient, 16, 18, 36, 50, 51, 91–93, 100, 102; archetypal female, 11, 75, 90–93, 100, 101; Candomblé, 102; Vodou, 64
Goldenberg, Naomi R.: *Changing of the Gods*, 33, 114n23, 118
good/evil opposition, 11, 75, 114, 117, 121, 122
Grande Brigitte, 51
Gray, Paul, 84
Greco-Roman traditions, 26
Griffith, Marie, 8, 32
Griffiths, Gareth, 20, 33, 142
Guinea, 18, 49, 154
Gullah traditions, 26
Gyssels, Kathleen: "L'intraduisabilité de Tituba Indien," 142

Haiti: and AIDS stigma, 61–62; blackness as positive symbol in, 60; Caco resistance in, 15–16, 39, 57–58; class in, 43–44, 46, 57, 59–60; and colonial France, 56, 58–59; contestation of values of, 61; cultural heritage in, 55; dominant narratives of history in, 46; Duvalier regimes in, 39, 59, 61; and exoticization, 56–57; as first independent black republic in West, 58; folk stories, 21, 30, 50, 69; history of struggle and resistance in, 39, 60, 61, 69; history of torture in, 50n18; immigrants to U.S. from, 40, 43, 56, 61–62, 64; independence movement, 56; Indigenist movement in, 40, 55, 60, 61; literary identity in, 55; literary movement of 1920s in, 55; Macoutes in, 39, 59–60; nationalistic discourse, 66; nationalist movement, 60; negative accounts of, 61; neo-colonialism in, 58; oppressiveness of, 61; peasantry in, 56–59, 70; primitivism in, 57, 63; racial equality in, 60; reclamation of history in, 38; relationship with Dominican Republic, 64–65; relationship with U.S., 61; revolution in, 58; romanticization of, 61; rural, culture of, 55; slavery and oppression in, 56; U.S. invasion of, 15–16, 40, 55–59; women in, 38, 42–51, 60. See also *Breath, Eyes, Memory*; Vodou
Hale, Rev. John, 124
Hansen, Chadwick: "The Metamorphosis of Tituba," 108–9, 113
Harding, Rachel, 9; *A Refuge in Thunder*, 30, 34, 96
Harlem Renaissance, 26
Hawthorne, Nathaniel: *The Scarlet Letter*, 22–23, 123, 141
healing, 4, 8, 23, 27, 44, 53, 64, 92, 105, 118; celebration of, 22; psychological, 75; witches and, 117, 126
hegemony: cultural, 30, 34; linguistic, 34; resistance to, 6, 9; Western, 13
heritage, African, 25, 26
heroism, 137; black female, 46, 155; Caribbean male discourse of, 120; female, 130, 141–42, 153–55; mock, 140, 141, 147; and resistance in Haiti, 61; tragic, 155; U.S. narrative of national, 58; vs. defeat, 14; white notions of, 141
Hess, David J.: *Samba in the Night*, 96
Hewitt, Leah B., 126
Higgins, Therese: *Religiosity, Cosmology, and Folklore*, 34
historical consciousness, 28, 58
historical discourse, 2, 24, 50, 55, 105; as truth, 33
historical identities, 1, 49, 99
historical narratives, 2, 46, 110, 131, 147; objectivity of, 33; rewriting, 46
historical recovery, 15–19, 22
historical revision, 15–19, 23
history, 2; alienation from, 76; American, 16, 72, 76, 83, 84; control of, 86;

rigid attitude toward, 87; silenced, 33; and storytelling, 21; tension between oral and written, 48–49; women's places in, 5
Hoffer, Peter, 108n11
Holland, Sharon Patricia: *Raising the Dead*, 155
homoeroticism, 130, 142
Hopkins, Pauline: *Of One Blood*, 24, 25–26
Howe, Stephen: *Afrocentrism*, 83
Hughes, Langston, 56–57
Hunt, Kristin, 76
Hurston, Zora Neale, 15, 56; exoticization and, 57; political conservatism of, 57; *Tell My Horse*, 15, 57–58
hybridity, 30; cultural, 5, 6, 7, 100, 101; racial, 100; religious, 101
hypermasculinity, 141

identity: African American, 27; African diaspora female, 4; appropriation of, 125; as black woman, 125; challenges to simplistic notions of, 141; cultural, 1, 49, 61n49, 86, 154; diasporic African, 64, 110; fluid, 66; historical, 1, 49, 99; men's, 87–88; refashioning of personal, cultural, and historical, 1; racial, 108–9, 110, 148; religion and, 34; skepticism toward essentialisms of, 1; stereotyped notions of, 105; subversion of, 8; transnational, 19–24
Idowu, E. Bolaji, 31
Ile-Ife, 48
Indigenism, 40, 55, 60, 61
intertextuality, 19–24, 53; as "boundary-crossing," 21
irony, 2
Isis, 11–12, 13, 18, 27, 50, 91, 94, 101
I, Tituba, Black Witch of Salem (Condé), 1, 2, 19, 20, 28, 36, 103–52, 153–58; aesthetic of narration in, 107; afterlife in, 119, 120, 130, 153–54; appropriation of identity in, 125; assimilation of into African American culture, 149; authenticity in, 7; as autobiography, 105, 134; Ballantine Books edition of, 131, 143–45, 147–49; blurring of historical and fictional narratives in, 110, 123–24; Caraf Books edition of, 131, 145–49; Caribbean history, reclamation of, 120; as celebration of witchcraft, 121; challenges to identity in, 141; as challenge to linear narratives of history, 33; Christianity in, 118–19; clichés of black women in, 126, 131; closeness between black and white women in, 130; complexity of witchcraft in, 126; confession/confessional voice in, 16–17, 36, 103–8, 121, 123, 134; creolization in, 20–21; deconstruction of Tituba's voice in, 150; de-emphasis of historical themes of, 134; devil in, 107, 111; duplicate meaning of, 142; estrangement and exoticization in, 127; ethnicity in, 105, 108, 124–27, 130–31, 134, 138–39, 140, 142; female audience for, 134; female heroism in, 130; female subjectivity in, 15, 16–17; feminine principle in, 121; feminism in, 124, 128–29, 131, 141; Folio French editions of, 134–39, 143, 145; gendered and racial audience for, 131; gendered and exoticized reading of, 134, 138; gender hierarchy in, 127; genre of, 134; glossing in, 148–49; good vs. evil in, 117, 122; healing in, 105, 126; Hester episode in, 22–23, 123–24, 127–30, 141–42; as historical construction, 147, 150; historic Tituba in, 103–5, 107–10, 111, 123–24; homoeroticism in, 130, 142; illusion of factuality in, 16; as intellectually challenging, 27; juxtaposition of editions of, 142–52; link with American literature, 133; living vs. dead in, 157; magical powers in, 105, 113; Mercure de France edition of, 131–39, 145; mock heroism in, 140, 141, 147; motherhood in, 119; narrator and narrated in, 105; narrative reliability in, 124; as not a historical novel, 110, 147; omission

of "Noire de Salem" subtitle from, 134; oral tradition in, 120; otherness in, 107, 127, 131; packaging of, 131–52; parody in, 7, 120–21, 131, 134, 140, 147; patriarchy in, 122; politicization of, 143, 148; politics of race, class and gender in, 104; positioning within linguistic codes, 149–50; power dynamics of self-representation in, 107, 124; Puritanism in, 107, 112–15, 122, 124–25, 141, 142, 155; as quasi neo-slave narrative, 143, 145; racial dynamics in, 127–28; racial identity in, 108–9, 110, 113, 148; and racial and religious intolerance, 112; rape in, 133, 138; relationships with Africa in, 25, 26; religiosity in, 105; religious, racial, and historical discourses in, 105, 108, 117, 126; resistance to performing ethnicity in, 106–7; reviews and blurbs for, 143; revisionist strategies in, 23–24, 114; as satire, 147; scapegoating in, 104, 115–16, 157; sexuality in, 122–23; as site of political contestation, 29; situation of within feminine tradition, 133; skepticism in, 120, 123; and slave narrative tradition, 143; stereotyped notions of identity in, 105, 108, 125; strategy of subversion in, 150; subversion of clichés in, 134; supernatural powers in, 138; translation of, 131–52; use of language in, 107; use of ambiguous words as narrative strategy in, 148; use of word "sorcière," 142; Vodou in, 1, 4, 12, 14, 16, 137; witchcraft in, 4, 103–52, 155; women's disempowerment in, 133; women's empowerment in, 114, 137

Jennings, La Vinia Delois: *Toni Morrison and the Idea of Africa*, 34
Jezebel, 11–13: Erzulie and, 42, 45, 46
Johnson, Charles, 145
Johnson, James Weldon, 56, 58; "Self-Determining Haiti," 56–57
Johnson, Paul Christopher, 6
Jones, Gayle: "Re-Imagining the African-American Novel," 29
Judeo-Christianity: challenges to, 33, 75, 118; cultural and intellectual domination of, 27; exclusion of women from discourse of, 2; images of womanhood, 154; mainstream, 13; male-centered discourse, 9; as monotheistic, 93; orthodox, criticism of, 89; paradise as male-centered discourse in, 72; standards of women's propriety and purity, 11; traditions of, 26

Katz, William Loren, 77, 99

Laferrière, Dany, 66
language: appreciation for, 54; dialectic of between colonized and colonizer, 140n55; elusive, 107, 152; estrangement through, 20; as liberating force, 48; manipulative, 84; play on, 67; power of, 47; to signify difference, 33; transfer across, 151
Layton, Bentley, 91
"Le cri de l'oiseau rouge." See *Breath, Eyes, Memory*
Lewis, Barbara, 129n40, 139
liberation: African diaspora religions as sites of, 4, 6–7; and deliverance, 79; Haiti as site of, 61, 65; narrative of, 81; oppression vs., 14, 78; personal and cultural, 155–56; U.S. as site of, 61, 65; women's struggle for, 38, 153
life and death, 4, 14, 49, 156–58; Africanist vision of, 156–57
linguistic boundaries, 24
linguistic codes, 149
linguistic domination, 140, 142
linguistic fusion, 19
linguistic standards, colonial, 21
linguistic strategies, 19–20, 68–69
literary expression, diaspora consciousness and, 24–28
literature, as form of cultural resistance, 55

living and dead, 4, 14
Long, Charles: *Significations*, 10, 31, 111
loup-garou (lougawou), 50

Madonna complex, 12, 45, 154
magic, 9, 35, 90, 92, 104–5, 108, 110, 114; Africanist tradition of, 28; dangerous, 109n12; white European, 105, 113. *See also* black magic
male consciousness, 26
male heroic discourse, 38
male god, supremacy of, 13, 75, 91, 92, 101, 119
male Judeo-Christian discourse, 2, 9, 72
male literary discourse, 61
Malleus Maleficarum, 114n24
Manzor-Coats, Lynn, 126, 129n40, 130, 131, 133, 134, 139, 145n63
Marassa, 53–54
Mardorssian, Carine M.: "From Literature of Exile to Migrant Literature," 65–66
Marinet Bwa-chech, 45–46, 153
Mariology, 11, 52, 114
Marshall, Paule, 24; *Praisesong for the Widow*, 27, 28
Martinez, Elda Gonzales, 96
masculinist discourse, 46; Haitian, 60, 69; interrogation of, 94
masculinity: Christianity and, 118; Vodou and, 116
Massardier-Kenny, Françoise, 148–49
memoirs, 106
memory: American collective, 77; cultural, 14–15, 119; diasporic, 8, 15; Haitian collective, 40, 60; public, 36, 60, 83, 113; silenced, 15; sites of, 17, 18, 33
men: connection with spirit and divinity, 32, 115, 119; desire of to control the feminine, 86; dichotomous nature of women and, 115; identity of, 87–88; rigid attitude toward history, 87; witch-hunting, 122
menstruation, 38
Metraux, Alfred: *Voodoo in Haiti*, 52–54, 156, 157

Miller, Arthur: *The Crucible*, 17, 20, 109, 113, 137; *Witches of Salem*, 133
miscegenation, 87
misogyny, 114
mock-heroism, 140, 141, 147
modernity, African diaspora at heart of, 29
Moi, Tituba, sorcière . . . noire de Salem, 1n1. See also *I Tituba, Black Witch of Salem*
monotheism, 93, 124
morality, 141
Morrison, Toni, 1–2, 4, 7, 9, 11–14, 15–16, 18, 26–28, 30, 34, 35; *Beloved*, 71, 155; *Jazz*, 71, 90n25; *Playing in the Dark*, 83–84; racial representations of, 84–85; "Recitatif," 84–85; and religious narratives, 90n25; *Song of Solomon*, 26; *Tar Baby*, 90n25. See also *Paradise*
Moses, Wilson, 7; *Afrotopia*, 30–31
motherhood: experience of, 119; ideal of, 42–43
Mudimbe, V. Y., 31
Mudimbe-Boyi, Elizabeth: "Giving a Voice to Tituba," 150
Murphy, Joseph, 4–5; *Working the Spirit*, 34, 98
myth, 2, 33; American foundation, 86; ancestral, 28; creation, 90; heroic, 140; of Wild West, 77
mythologization, 32, 61, 82, 85, 88
mythology, 31; Egyptian, 26; Vodou, 48, 156

Nag Hammadi, 89
naming: power of, 15; technique of, 46–51, 54–55
narrative: black fictional, 23; of continuity, 14, 157; countercultural, 6, 29; cultural, 17, 46; of female empowerment, 35, 68; historical, 2, 33, 46, 110, 131, 147; male, 85; of oppression, 80; of power, 120–21; racial, 17; of revision, 2; slave, 143, 145; transcultural, 2; transnational, 2
narrators: historical, 33; unreliability of, 23, 124

Index

nationalist discourse: American, 78, 81, 84–85; Euro-American, 86
Native Americans, 73, 76–77, 80–81; Christianizing of, 80; hostility between African Americans and, 148; traditions of, 96
Naylor, Gloria, 24; *Mama Day*, 27, 28
Negro spirituals, 64
neo-colonialism, 58
New York Times Book Review, 143, 145
Norton, Mary Beth, 111–12
N'Zengou-Tayo, Marie-Jose, 54–55, 68

Obeah, 12
occult: ethnic women and, 120–21; spirituality and, 137
O'Donnell, Patrick, 21
Oklahoma, migration to, 73, 76, 99
oppressed/oppressor distinction, 22, 78, 80, 83, 84, 153
oppression: Catholicism and, 28; colonial France and, 56; cycle of, 39; gender-based, 25; in Haiti, 56, 61; of racism and poverty, 129; resistance to, 3, 22, 80, 104, 114; vs. liberation, 14, 78; narrative of, 80; racial, 137–38, 156; sexual, 61; white, 156; of women, 49, 114, 133
oral histories, 2, 48–49, 60, 120
otherness, 105–6, 107, 127; ethnic, 23, 107, 134; exoticized racial, 137; politics of, 131; witchcraft and, 107

paganism, 6, 12; vs. Christianity, 31
Pagels, Elaine: *Gnostic Gospels*, 33, 92–93, 95n35
Palcy, Euzhan, 34
Paradise (Morrison), 1, 2, 7, 8–9, 12–14, 28, 35–36, 71–102, 154–55, 158; African Americans in, 77; African diasporic traditions in, 98–100; afterlife in, 153–54; American history in, 16, 72, 76, 83, 84; androgyny in, 94–95; Black history in, 83; black vs. white in, 84; Candomblé in, 4–5, 13, 27, 72, 75, 81n14, 95–98, 100–102; as challenge to Christian discourse, 91; as challenge to linear narratives of history, 33; Christian moral values in, 73; construction of religiosity in, 72; Convent as coven in, 89; Convent massacre in, 74–75, 79, 82, 156; creolization in, 20–21; as critique of essentialist discourses in U.S., 83; "Disallowing," 73, 88; discrimination in, 87; Eve in, 91, 94, 101; exclusionary politics in, 72; Exodus narrative in, 22, 77–83, 93; female subjectivity in, 15–16; female victimization in, 16; gender in, 72, 97; Gnosticism in, 71–102; and heroic version of past in, 86; heroism in, 154–55; history and storytelling in, 21; as intellectually challenging, 27; interrogation of masculinist discourses in, 94; inward vs. outward in, 93, 95; Isis in, 11–12, 13, 18, 27, 91, 101, 102; Judeo-Christianity, challenges to male god of, 75; liberation vs. destruction in, 95; living vs. dead in, 157; male- vs. female-centered religions in, 93; marginalization of whiteness in, 84–85; men's mythologizing of history in, 85; Native Americans in, 73, 76–77, 80–81; old vs. new generations in, 82, 86–87; oppressed vs. oppressor in, 84; the Oven in, 86–87; paradoxes of American national discourses in, 78, 81, 84–85; patriarchy in, 73, 74, 85, 86, 88–89; Piedade in 102; power dynamics, 97, 157; race in, 72, 75, 84–85; racial purity in, 73, 77, 87–88; relationships with Africa in, 25, 26; revisionist strategies in, 23–24, 83; rules against miscegenation in, 87; scapegoating in, 74, 156–57; as site of political contestation, 29; syncretism in, 100–102; and "Thunder: Perfect Mind," 12, 90, 94–95; tolerance in, 87; utopias in, 16, 71–102; violence in, 71, 75, 76; wilderness in, 76; Wild West myth in, 77; womanhood in, 94; women's spirituality in, 89–90

Paravisini-Gebert, Lizabeth, 5, 6; *Creole Religions of the Caribbean*, 30
Parker Rhodes, Jewell, 24; *Voodoo Dreams*, 27, 28
parody, 2, 7, 22, 77; in *I, Tituba*, 108, 117, 120–21, 126, 131, 134, 140–41, 147, 151
paternalism, 56, 57
patriarchy, 8, 11: in *Breath, Eyes, Memory*, 38, 39, 41, 46, 47–48, 51, 55; in *I, Tituba*, 122, 133, 154, 155–56; in *Paradise*, 73, 74, 85, 86, 88–89
Peralte, Charlemagne, 15, 58
performances, as sites of memory, 18, 33
persecution, female, 2, 3, 10, 114
Petry, Ann: *Tituba of Salem Village*, 104, 109n13
Pfaff, Françoise, 7, 104, 130n43, 140
Philcox, Richard, 150–51
pidgin, 20, 113
Piedade (piety), 18, 101, 102, 155
plants, knowledge of, 4, 9, 23, 116, 117, 126
platonade, 50
poisoning, fear of, 9, 12
politics of forgetting, 157
postcolonialism, 29, 33, 69, 139, 142, 152; linguistic and semantic variations in, 142
postcolonial translation, 67
The Post-colonial Studies Reader (Ashcroft, Griffiths, and Tiffin), 20
power dynamics, 20, 97, 107–8, 124, 157
powerlessness, 155
productionism, 106
pseudo-history, 31
psychiatric ideology, 116
puberty, 38
Publishers Weekly, 145
Puritanism, 9–10, 17, 111–15, 122, 124–25, 141, 142, 155; acculturation to, 107; misogynistic attitudes of, 114

Raboteau, Albert J.: "African-Americans, Exodus, and the American Israel," 78
race, 7, 25, 72, 105; assumptions of, 85; and female spirituality, 31; and gendered body politics, 32; irrelevance of, 84; politics of, 104
race relations, 109
racial awakening, 25
racial boundaries, 84–85, 87, 109
racial discourses, 105, 108, 126, 152
racial dynamics, 84, 127
racial equality, 60
racial hybridity, 100
racial identity, 108–9, 110, 143, 148
racial injustice, 73, 75
racial intolerance, 112
racial misidentification, 113
racial mixing, 77
racial narratives, 17
racial oppression, 156
racial politics, 85, 104, 112
racial prejudice, inverse, 109
racial purity, 73, 77, 87–88
racial superiority, 32
racism, 9, 63; oppression of, 129; semiotics of, 10, 111
rape, 39, 43, 44, 54, 60, 133, 138
rationalism, rise of, 116
recovery: historical, 15–19, 22; and loss, 25
Reed, Ishmael, 24, 25; *Mumbo Jumbo*, 24n33, 26–27
regeneration, 100
Reis, João Jose, 10
religion: ancient, 75, 90–93, 115; creolized, 101; female-centered, 97–98; institutionalized, 75, 97; interrogation of discourses of, 105; of masses, 46, 55, 60; monotheistic and male-centered, 124. *See also* African diaspora religion
religiosity, 34, 38, 105; construction of, 72
religious creolization, 13–14
religious discourse, 2, 3, 10, 35, 36, 72, 90, 98, 100, 105, 108, 126
religious orthodoxy, 101
religious syncretism, 12, 102
religious traditions, 4, 5, 12–13, 22, 28, 35, 53, 92, 102
Renda, Mary A., 58–59
representation, ethics of, 106
"return of the witch," 36

revision: historical, 15–19; narratives of, 2; strategies of, 23, 46–51, 53–54, 83, 114
Rhys, Jean, 145; *Wide Sargasso Sea*, 154n1
Roach, Joseph: *Cities of the Dead*, 18, 33, 157
Rody, Caroline: *The Daughter's Return*, 145
Rosenthal, Bernard, 109n12
Roumain, Jacques, 21n30
Roumer, Emilie: "Marabout de mon Coeur," 68n58
rupture, 18
Russell, Jeffrey B.: *A History of Witchcraft*, 32, 33, 79n12, 94, 114–15, 114n23, 129
Ryan, Judylyn: *Spirituality as Ideology*, 34–35

Salem, 115–16, 125; witch craze, 10, 114; witch trials, 103–4, 107, 111, 131, 147
sanity/insanity duality, 116
Santeria, 44, 64
Savage, Barbara Dianne, 8, 32
scapegoating, 74, 104, 115–16, 156–57
Scarboro, Ann Armstrong, 112, 123, 126, 133, 147
scientific experimentation, Vodou and, 116
scientific explanation, witches as scapegoats for lack of, 115–16
self-referential genres, 105–6, 120, 139; ethnic minorities and, 106; as liberatory, 106
self-representation, power dynamics of, 107, 124
sexual abuse, 38, 45, 51, 52, 74
sexual deviancy, 13, 75, 122
sexuality: aggressive, 61; and black female spirituality, 32; bleeding of women as symbol of, 38; control over, 48, 51, 60; empowering image of, 12; female, fear of, 10; and female spirituality, 31; and mythologizing of women, 61; negative perceptions of, 11, 44; preconceived notions of, 10; and reception of *Breath, Eyes, Memory*, 51; Satan and, 122; suppression of, 93–94; women's, 60, 75, 88–89, 154
sexual oppression, 61
sexual purity, 39, 44
sexual violence, 43, 61, 156
Shange, Ntozake, 34
slave revolts, 137; fear of, 9, 12
slavery, 119; in Haiti, 56; history of, 10
Smalls, James, 138n52
Smith, Bessie, 27
Song of Eve, 91
Sophia, 50
sorcery: condemnation of, 10; interrogation and undermining of notion of, 142; as metaphor, 126
spirit, men and, 32
spirit/body opposition, 11, 75, 94, 114, 117, 122
spirituality: ambiguous model of, 75, 105; appropriation of, 2; black female, 2–3, 7, 8–14, 26–28, 32, 105, 158; as epistemology, 35; female, 13, 129; feminine principle in, 100; gender-inclusive, 95; as "life force," 35; and occult, 137; organic model of, 119; and race, 31; and sexuality, 31–32; witchcraft and, 126; women's places in history as powerful models of, 5; women's, 25, 34–35, 36, 49, 72, 75, 89, 90, 98, 137
Storace, Patricia: "The Scripture of Utopia," 84
storytelling, history and, 21, 49
subjectivity, female, 15–17
subversion, 29, 150
supernatural powers, 91–92
survivals, 30
syncretism, 5–6, 12, 18, 100–102; cultural, 100

testing. See under *Breath, Eyes, Memory*
theologies opaques, 31
theoretical perspectives, 29–36
Thinog'o, Ngugi Wa, 140n55
"Thunder: Perfect Mind," 12, 90, 94–95

Tiffin, Helen, 20, 33, 142
Tisserand, Nicole, 68
tolerance, 6, 13, 87, 101
traditional vs. modern, 31
transcultural narratives, 2
transformation, 18, 30; after death, 154; desire for, 38; female, 11, 38, 50, 69; inner growth and, 92; psychological and spiritual, 25, 89
translation, 68–69, 131–52; acts of, 67, 149; authority and manipulation of, 148–49; cultural, 33, 67, 69; double, 68, 149; postcolonial, 67
transnational experience, 61, 62
transnational identities, 19–24, 33, 63
transnationalism, 65, 66–67, 69
transnational narratives, 2
transnational reality, 40
trauma, historical, 25, 40, 42, 69
Tymoczko, Maria: "Post-colonial Writing and Literary Translation," 151

United States: African Americans in, 147; attitude toward minorities in, 16, 63–64, 81, 85; contemporary religious and racial politics in, 112; contestation of values of, 61; critique of essentialist discourses in, 83; foundation myth of, 86; immigrants from Haiti to, 40, 43, 56, 61–62, 64; isolationist policies of, 61, 64–65; occupation of Haiti, 15–16, 40, 55–59; paradoxes of national discourses of, 78, 81, 84–85; as place of divine intervention, 65; racial and historical politics in, 17; relationship with Haiti, 61; as site of liberation, 61, 63, 66, 81; visionary ideals of, 81
universalism, 31
utopias, 16, 71–102

Valat, Pierre-Marie, 131
vernacular, use of, 21
victimization: female, 16, 47, 68; of Haitians, 63
violence, 18, 36, 71, 76, 93, 109; embedded in diasporic histories, 30; perpetuation of, 75; against women, 2, 3, 8, 39, 43, 61, 115, 153, 156, 158
virgin/hag duality, 75, 93, 100
virginity, 39, 42, 44, 52
Virgin Mary, 12, 41, 52, 101, 102, 115
virgin/whore duality, 8, 10, 32, 46
Vodou, Haitian, 1, 4, 12, 14, 16, 18, 21–22, 26–27, 30, 37–70, 113, 116, 154, 156–57, 158; as alternative space for examination of black womanhood, 41; association of with scientific experiment, whiteness, and masculinity, 116; and empowerment, 49; and oral history, 49; as organic religion of the masses, 55; revision of symbols of, 42; stereotypical imagery of, 137; symbiosis between Christianity and, 22, 53
Voeks, Robert, 5, 6, 98n41; *Sacred Leaves of Candomblé*, 34, 101

Warrior, Robert Allen: "Canaanites, Cowboys and Indians," 93; "A Native American Perspective," 80–81
werewolves, 50n18
White, Hayden: *The Content of the Form*, 33
white feminism, 128, 129
white magic, 105, 113
whiteness: marginalization of, 84–85; tactic of, 157; and Vodou, 116
white settlers, 22, 76, 78
Wicca movement, 114n23
Wild West, myth of, 77
Williams, Michael Allen: *Rethinking "Gnosticism,"* 33, 100
Wilson, Elizabeth, 68, 123
Winthrop, John, 81
WITCH (Women's International Terrorist Conspiracy from Hell), 114n32
witch(es): as angry spirit, 11; as archetypal goddess, 11; bad, demonized, 121; black vs. white, 133; as cannibal, 32; condemnation and persecution as, 92; craze of in Salem, 10; and devil, 10, 114, 117; eradication of, 114; ethnic, clichéd image of, 130–31; fear of, 116; as female war-

rior, 11; good, image of, 121; as hag, 32; as healer, 32, 117; as Jezebel, 11; and knowledge of contraception and abortion, 116; liberatory potential of, 33; metaphor of, 3, 114; parody of narratives of power of, 120–21; as prophetess, 32; Puritan demonizing of, 155; as scapegoats, 115–16; sexual deviance of, 122; as sexually open, 117; social injustice toward, 117; symbol of, 2, 3; as symbol of women's empowerment, 3; as temptress, 32; as threat to Church's hierarchy, 115

witchcraft, 1, 3, 4, 13–14; as Africanist female tradition, 119; blackness and, 14; clichéd images of, 117; complexity of, 126; as counter to Christianity, 117; as justification for shortage of scientific research, 115–16; meaning of, 103–52; as mirror for intersection of racial, cultural, and religious discourses, 126; mock-epic characteristics of, 120–21; and otherness, 107; as positive symbol, 117; as women's empowerment, 114

witch hunts, 13, 75, 116; as outlet for men's repressed sexual urges, 122

womanhood: celebration of, 1, 3, 41; division of, 94; Haitian, reimagining of, 37–70; idealization and de-idealization of, 32; non-realistic standards of, 8; passive and desexualized image of, 12–13, 42, 44; romanticization of, 61; struggle with, 38; suppression of complexity of, 41; unattainable image of, 43; witch as symbol of, 3

women: African diaspora, 9, 10, 35, 36, 158; authority of, 8; bleeding of, 21–22, 37–38; Caribbean, mythologizing of, 32; connection with body and carnality, 32; control of body and sexuality by, 48; "deviant," 3; dichotomous nature of men and, 115; disempowerment of, 133; empowerment of, 5, 6, 137; ethnic, occult and, 120–21; exclusion of, 2, 120; exclusion of from priesthood, 11; leadership of, 8; liberation of, 38, 153; oppression of, 114, 133; persecution of, 10, 114; place of in history, 5; power of, 8; propriety and purity of, 11, 41, 46, 61, 89; racial identity of, 110; rape of, 39; religious experiences of, 32; search for wholeness by, 36; as seducers or temptresses, 10–11, 114, 115; sensuality of, 45; sexuality of, 75, 88–89; silenced histories of, 36, 69; silenced voices of, 16, 87; social injustices against, 7; spirituality of, 25, 34–35, 36, 49, 72, 75, 89, 90, 98, 137; as spiritually inferior, 16; strength of, 45; struggle of in Haiti, 38, 42, 60; suffering of, 64; and supernatural powers, 91–92; suppression of power of, 89; traditional roles of, 88; transformation of, 50; violence against, 2, 3, 8, 39, 115, 153, 158; as virgins or whores, 8, 10, 46; as virgins or witches, 10; witch as symbol of empowerment of, 3; working-class, 55–59. *See also* black female; black women

Women and Religion in the African Diaspora (Griffith and Savage), 32

Woolf, Virginia, 150

Yemanja, 27, 102

Zéphir, Flore, 62
zombi, 157

www.ingramcontent.com/pod-product-compliance
Lightning Source LLC
Chambersburg PA
CBHW020800160426
43192CB00006B/398